IDENTITY POLITICS

IDENTITY POLITICS
Where Did It All Go Wrong?

David Pilgrim

PHOENIX
PUBLISHING HOUSE
firing the mind

First published in 2022 by
Phoenix Publishing House Ltd
62 Bucknell Road
Bicester
Oxfordshire OX26 2DS

Copyright © 2022 by David Pilgrim

The right of David Pilgrim to be identified as the author of this work has been asserted in accordance with §§ 77 and 78 of the Copyright Design and Patents Act 1988.

All rights reserved. No part of this publication may be reproduced, stored in a retrieval system, or transmitted, in any form or by any means, electronic, mechanical, photocopying, recording, or otherwise, without the prior written permission of the publisher.

British Library Cataloguing in Publication Data

A C.I.P. for this book is available from the British Library

ISBN-13: 978-1-80013-100-2

Typeset by Medlar Publishing Solutions Pvt Ltd, India

www.firingthemind.com

Contents

Acknowledgements vii
About the author ix
Introduction xi

CHAPTER ONE
The reality of identity politics 1

CHAPTER TWO
Identity politics and freedom of expression 21

CHAPTER THREE
Sex and gender 47

CHAPTER FOUR
Antisocial sexual identities 67

CHAPTER FIVE
Racial politics 91

CHAPTER SIX
Mental health politics 123

CHAPTER SEVEN
Religious identities 149

CHAPTER EIGHT
Class war, blood and soil 165

CHAPTER NINE
Six lessons about identity politics 191

Glossary of terms 213
References 223
Index 239

Acknowledgements

A number of people have helped me by commenting on draft material and during exploratory conversations about our widespread current angst about identity politics. Their thoughts have been invaluable. Thanks go to David Bell, Heather Brunskell-Evans, Beatrix Campbell, Natasha Chart, Kirsty Entwistle, Alison Faulkner, Mary Garner, Alec Grant, Joe Guinan, Pat Harvey, Nagore Calvo Mendizabal, Nimisha Patel, Jack Pilgrim, Anne Rogers, Glory Rigueros Saavedra, Valentina Stilo, and Charlie Winstanley.

About the author

David Pilgrim, PhD, is Honorary Professor of Health and Social Policy at the University of Liverpool and Visiting Professor of Clinical Psychology at the University of Southampton. Now semi-retired, he trained and worked in the NHS as a clinical psychologist before completing a PhD in psychology and then a Master's in sociology. With this mixed background, his career was split then between clinical work, teaching and mental health policy research. He remains active in the Division of Clinical Psychology and the History and Philosophy Section of the British Psychological Society, and was Chair of the latter between 2015 and 2018.

His publications include *Understanding Mental Health: A Critical Realist Exploration* (Routledge, 2015) and *Key Concepts in Mental Health* (5th edition, Sage, 2019). Others include *A Sociology of Mental Health and Illness* (Open University Press, 2005—winner of the 2006 BMA Medical Book of the Year Award), *Mental Health Policy in Britain* (Palgrave, 2002) and *Mental Health and Inequality* (Palgrave, 2003) (all with Anne Rogers). His recent books are *Child Sexual Abuse: Moral Panic or State of Denial?* (Routledge, 2018) and *Critical Realism for Psychologists* (Routledge, 2020).

Introduction

I set the scene here for themes expanded in later pages. My overall intention is to avoid replicating the flawed binary logic of identity politics (good or bad, woke or not woke, racist or not racist, transphobic or trans-affirmative, etc.). Instead, I assume that the world is nuanced and contradictory and that our awareness of it is highly partial. With their tendency towards absolutism and premature certainties, identity politics are an inadequate response to that complexity and mystery of life. I concede though that sometimes they offer us fully legitimate starting points of reflection, about both social inequality and the constraints upon the citizenship of some individuals. A problem, though, is that these fair enough places of departure all too often have led us into a cul-de-sac. As a consequence, identity politics quite quickly fail to deliver on their rhetorical goal of human betterment and instead we find irritability and self-righteousness. We have more heat than light.

The field day on the right and the wrong turn on the left

Identity politics is a curate's egg: good and bad in parts. However, the bad parts have proved to be extremely time consuming and divisive in "progressive" discussions in recent years. Indeed, this has led at times to political paralysis and factionalism amongst those who are, on paper at least, on the same side. Political parties have been divided, and even new ones formed, as a result of the indignation and dogmatism generated.

For their part, the right has had a field day. Their laments about "political correctness gone mad" used to have a hollow ring and were condemned for being a veiled excuse for bigotry (because often they were). More subtly in the broadsheet conservative press, commentators note the capture of the polity of Western representative democracies by the "woke" agenda of critical social justice warriors. Here, for example, in the *Daily Telegraph* 15 April 2021 we find this from Allister Heath:

> Biden's first blunder has been to give free rein to the woke revolutionaries. Their ideology is a fusion of post-modernism, Marxism, Freudianism, critical race theory, gender studies, intersectionality and much else besides, and the brew is toxic, explosive and *potentially fatal to Western democracy and capitalism*. It detests rationality, the rule of law and even the presumption of innocence. It is obsessed with race and gender, assumes extreme amounts of never-ending exploitation, posits that progress is impossible and rejects the liberal, meritocratic, colour-blind approach that has done so much to improve society and combat racism since the Fifties. It claims to believe in "social justice" but rejects the very concept of a functioning polity and the possibility of objective, enlightenment-style justice. It considers free speech to be a form of violence and assumes that anybody who disagrees is guilty of false consciousness and, as such, deserves to be cancelled as a dangerous heretic. (Emphasis added)

Heath continued with this theme in another *Daily Telegraph* piece (2 August 2021) entitled "Biden's woke, Left-wing America is no longer a model for the world". The conservative logic of Heath scorns both Biden and the recently failed Corbyn project; it is an amalgam dismissal of all things to his personal left (and that of his employing newspaper).

Freedom for the right refers to the market, whereas for the left it is about fighting oppression. This reminds us that the word is readily adored but not always fully explored. Heath repeats the refrain of capitalism being humanity's only hope. However, beneath his standard anti-leftism we find in his text a problem conceded about "the land of the free", which he has idealised since his student days. His lament includes a list of how US capitalism has actually *failed* working class people by impoverishing them and depriving them of needed education. He goes further:

> The Right, for its part, has also gone mad: too many Republicans have ditched their old principles—be it free market, limited government or social conservatism—and instead embraced a dumbed-down populist demagoguery.

That demagoguery has required its own version of identity politics. From Trumpism and its desire to Make America Great Again, to the role of nostalgic Little Englander politics in Brexit, we can spot that the virtue signalling "wokery" of the left is not the only version to ponder. I return specifically to this question of ethnocentric nationalisms and *their* attendant fetishised identities in Chapter Eight and theocratic reliance on ingroup exceptionalism in Chapter Seven.

Thus, Heath makes two main errors in his argument. First, he conflates identity politics with what used to be called in Britain, for a while, the "loony left". In fact, the assumed benefits and virtues of identity politics can now be found *across* the political spectrum, including the problematic dumbed-down populist demagoguery that understandably concerns him. Second, Heath is concerned with the threat that identity politics is allegedly posing to capitalism, the system he loves so much. However, an argument made in this book is the reverse of this: **neoliberalism** and identity politics fit very comfortably, hand in glove.

Freedom of expression

Some on the left are discovering that the hurtful and gloating prejudices from the right, which were often rationalised by freedom of expression, might actually have some merit, at least in their consequences. Moreover, the right could make the claim that they are not oppressive ogres but instead the tolerant defenders of a fundamental civil liberty. They were also permitting themselves the right to humour, casting the left as dour and humourless.

With the exception of online journalism such as *Savage Minds*, with its strong left-wing slant, other libertarian outlets such as *The Spectator* and *The Critic* are funded by the rich and reflect right-wing tropes about Brexit, anti-lockdown indignation, and the absurdities of decolonising the curriculum. As with my note about Heath above, some of these regular columnists and right-wing thinkers, like David Starkey in *The Critic*, are afforded validation for their snooty contempt for all things progressive. Without the authoritarianism and illiberalism that typically characterises identity politics, the opportunity for this validation would be missing.

Voices from the left certainly creep in at times in the libertarian response (especially from gender-critical writers) but they are in the minority. *Sp!ked*, which I return to later, arguably has the reverse balance of *The Critic*, though it has had funding from the fossil-fuel billionaire Koch brothers, and so its provenance is also open to quite legitimate query. Nonetheless, the funding of these outlets can be taken into account, without assuming commercial reductionism as an *explanation* for the legitimacy of the arguments in their pages.

Arguments can be examined for their validity with reference to logic and evidence, despite the varied range of ideological motives for raising them. Indeed, as I will argue as a critical realist later, this is a both/and, not an either/or, exercise in the serious appraisal of the complexities of identity politics. To argue that only the right benefit from a defence of freedom of expression is like arguing that the confidence trick of selling bottled water means that water itself is not a fundamental human need. Water and free speech are desirable and fundamental, whichever political regime prevails for us at a moment in time and space.

However we might appraise the ideological character of these "woke-sceptical" outlets, what is not in doubt is that they all champion freedom of expression and celebrate satire to good effect. Here, for example, is the satirist "Titania McGrath" in *The Critic* (March, 2021: 45) calling for "a bonfire of Dr Seuss":

> just because Dr Seuss was born in 1904, that doesn't mean that he shouldn't have a firm grasp of the values of twenty-first century intersectional feminists. Besides the anti-lesbian subtext of *The Cat in the Hat* is unmistakable. In addition, Amazon has started

to remove books that it classifies as "hate speech" ... As left wing activists, it is imperative that we encourage multi-billion dollar corporations to monitor what we are able to read. So let us go forth and burn books, rename streets and erase the past and re-educate the masses so they have the correct opinions. It's the only way to defeat fascism.

"Titania McGrath" is a parody account on Twitter, penned by the comedian Andrew Doyle, a regular columnist for *Sp!ked*. Doyle depicts this alter-ego as a "militant vegan who thinks she is a better poet than William Shakespeare". This humour is not always appreciated in liberal outlets like *The Observer*, where woke defenders such as Alex Clark call Doyle's writing a "cheap shot" (10 March 2019). Whilst seriousness is important for all of us in life, humour can also be used to expose ideological cant and self-serving rhetoric.

For Doyle to speak and for Clark to disagree requires a shared and inviolable premise, guaranteed for and from both protagonists: freedom of expression. If only determined libertarians (right, left, or centre) are now defending free speech, and the rest of us have naively, and with good intentions, drunk the "Kool-Aid" of identity politics, then culturally we are in a very precarious state. Authoritarianism from below is just as restrictive of human freedom as that imposed by the state.

Doyle describes himself clearly as someone from the traditional left of the political spectrum, rendering our traditional understanding of what "left" and "right" mean now as problematic. Maybe the political struggle today is between libertarianism and authoritarianism, with the latter coming from both above (for example in theocratic and Leninist regimes) and below (in Western liberal democracies). If this is the case, then defending freedom of expression on behalf of humanity as a whole is a vital starting point, as those like Suzanne Nossel in her book *Dare to Speak* have counselled (Nossel, 2020).

Thus, whilst the benefits for right-wing libertarians of attacking "wokery" and defending freedom of expression are obvious, those on the left have been ambivalent. This has been for a range of reasons noted and explored further in the coming chapters. Nonetheless, there have been clearly articulated objections. For example, Mark Fisher in his pithy essay from 2013 ("Exiting the Vampires' Castle") offers a critique of the divisive and hyper-moralistic character of identity politics. He notes that:

> The Vampires' Castle specialises in propagating guilt. *It is driven by a priest's desire to excommunicate and condemn, an academic-pedant's desire to be the first to be seen to spot a mistake, and a hipster's desire to be one of the in-crowd.* The danger in attacking the Vampires' Castle is that it can look as if—and it will do everything it can to reinforce this thought—that one is also attacking the struggles against racism, sexism, heterosexism. But, far from being the only legitimate expression of such struggles, the Vampires' Castle is best understood as a bourgeois-liberal perversion and appropriation of the energy of these movements. (Fisher, 2013, emphasis added)

These points about the divisive and diversionary logic of identity politics were made clear previously by the grand old man of the intellectual left in Britain in the 1990s, Eric Hobsbawm, using some terminology which might arouse sensitivities today, with our new norms of language policing:

> The political project of the Left is universalist: it is for all human beings. However we interpret the words, it isn't liberty for shareholders or blacks, but for everybody. It isn't equality for all members of the Garrick Club or the handicapped, but for everybody. It is not fraternity only for old Etonians or gays, but for everybody. *And identity politics is essentially not for everybody but for the members of a specific group only.* (Hobsbawm, 1996, emphasis added)

In a similar vein, and from the same period, we find this from Ambalavaner Sivanandan:

> The touchstone of any issue-based or identity-based politics has to be the lowest common denominators in our society. A women's movement that does not derive its politics from the needs, freedoms, rights of the most disadvantaged among them is by that very token reformist and elitist. Conversely, a politics that is based on women qua women is inward-looking and narrow and

nationalist and, above all, failing of its own experience. So, too, the blacks or gays or whoever. So, too, are the green and peace movements Eurocentric and elitist that do not derive their politics from the most ecologically devastated and war-ravaged parts of the world. Class cannot just be a matter for identity, it has to be the focus of commitment. (Sivanandan, 1990)

More recently the retiring founder of the Southall Black Sisters, Pragna Patel, made a similar point:

> Identity politics is a considerable challenge for us, not just in feminist circles but actually within all social justice movements. Identity politics has taken root in a way that I feel is profoundly regressive. It is a focus on individual experiences of victimhood. It is a focus on difference rather than unity ... It is an analysis of the politics that arise from individual experiences rather than a political analysis of structural discrimination and oppression ... I fear that all social movements are now tainted by a narrow form of identity politics ... it has fragmented our struggles ... It is leading us down a political blind alley. I am reminded of June Jordan's very wise words that identity politics is *'very important to get things started but it is nowhere near to getting anything finished'*. (Interview on *Woman's Hour*, 5 January 2022, emphasis added)

We can see in these sentiments from intellectuals on the left, with their disquiet about identity politics, that their agenda is somewhat different from the haughty and self-satisfied reactionaries to be found in the *Daily Telegraph* or *The Critic* noted above. What they all agree on, though, is that the suppression of debate is not a route to either democracy or human progress, a cue for the next section.

The centrality of freedom of expression and the inanities of cancel culture

Free speech was used by the right to celebrate current power relationships, inherited from the past and defended conservatively in the present (for example about sex and race). The response of the left was then to assume that to tolerate the existence of these views was the same as endorsing them, or encouraging them to flourish in the public imagination. The solution was to damn ("call out") and suppress them instead ("cancel", "no platform", or "no debate").

This response was understandable, but it was, in my view, fundamentally mistaken. Suppressing prejudicial speech does not eliminate prejudice; the path to the latter is long and hard, with few short cuts. Prejudicial speech is wrongheaded, hurtful, and at its margins will explicitly motivate violence. All that is true, but its blanket suppression creates problems, not just solutions. We need to reflect on an alternative path, but to invite that alternative path for the left is not to be naive.

It is clear that those with power disproportionately use it to control information in their own interests. Clear examples are the control of our political discourse by the Murdoch empire and, in the UK context, there has been the control freakery of New Labour ideologues (depicted satirically in the TV show *The Thick of It*). For New Labour this entailed the manipulation of information to pave the way for an illegal war in Iraq and then to punish those trying to expose that mystification. A more recent example is the purging of the left in the British Labour Party, post-Corbyn. Those with wealth use legal means to control the exposure of their wrongdoing, which is not an option for the poor. Whistleblowing employees are gagged or paid off with non-disclosure agreements. The list of the use of information suppression from the forces of reaction is a long one but two wrongs do not make a right.

Power and knowledge are intimately linked within all political regimes at the governmental level, as well as in organisations in the public, private, and third sectors in civil society. Thus, freedom of expression is unevenly available, with forces of suppression being evident on both the right and left. Freedom of expression is a necessary but not a sufficient condition for social progress and human flourishing. Nonetheless, it must be our starting point to defend. Both freedom of expression and whistleblowing favour the public interest and are both defended, quite properly, in Article 10 of the European Convention on Human Rights. When it was drafted in 1950, "the century of blood" was still absorbing the shock of both Stalinism and Nazism. It seems today as if identity politics, of all political hues, are discounting this needed reckoning about democracy.

The right certainly has a stake in arguing for freedom of expression, but so does the left. If the left attack freedom of expression because it is depicted as *merely* a right-wing ideological strategy, then this is a serious error of judgement. We know from the recent past that once that authoritarian strategy became the dominant, and sometimes singular, political strategy aimed at producing social progress, then it gave a green light to the authoritarian right (both secular and theocratic). *Their* traditional desire to use repressive dogma and force to defeat their opponents was then legitimised. Accordingly, it was simply a matter of who was in power, contingently, to censor those who were a threat to their interests.

Authoritarianism from the left has encouraged libertarians on the right to defend credibly the post-Enlightenment liberal principle of freedom of expression. This plausibility can be found, for example, in writings in *The Spectator*, *Daily Mail*, or *Daily Telegraph* I cited above. This in turn has rendered the left unsure and so it has mainly resorted to simplistic name-calling in response. "Calling out" and assertion of notions of "privilege" and the glib and vacuous use of the suffix "phobic" have often become knee-jerk substitutes for serious analysis.

That name-calling and lack of seriousness have provided a wide-open goal for the libertarian right and so its writers have, quite understandably and intelligently, relished the opportunity offered. Their ranks have been joined by a residual Trotskyist culture from the 1970s, the tiny Revolutionary Communist Party. This group on its fragmentation maintained a network of writers who promoted libertarianism on the left, first in *Living Marxism* and more recently the *Academy of Ideas* and the online journal *Sp!ked*. However, its association with right-wing libertarian funders noted earlier now leave its political allegiances difficult to discern.

Speculations about CIA funding at this point are quite legitimate (though difficult to prove), in light of the eventual political careers of those like Claire Fox, from the *Academy of Ideas*. She joined the Brexit Party and then entered the House of Lords for services rendered to the Conservative government. The ex-Trotskyist appears routinely on British media as a brash controversialist, expressing views most readers of the *Daily Telegraph* would probably fulsomely endorse.

These combined forces, of seemingly unlikely bedfellows, are now gunning for identity politics and they have a large target to hit, even if they came historically from different political stables. My interest then is unpicking this contradictory scenario in a considered and academic manner. The book is not intended as a mere polemic against identity politics. However, it does take that brand of politics, favoured by so many now on the left (especially in the young), to task for its palpable shortcomings and failures. Where credit is due, I will make sure that it is given. However, the hole that the left has dug for itself has to be honestly explored and alternatives examined.

The need for cautious definitions

There has been a nihilistic tendency from postmodernism of rejecting definitions as futile, favouring instead unending "situated perspectives". However, identity politics *exist* and so we can broadly describe them and critically appraise their recurring premises.

The basis for being in a social group that claims an oppressed status, or the assumption that one has to experience that oppression in order to report its character authentically, reflect our material history as a species. This has contained demonstrable forms of exploitation and power play between groups and between humans and nature. These are examples of the master–slave relationships explored by Hegel and Marx.

I do concede, though, that what sort of emphasis we place on our working understanding of the character of identity politics will shape whether we are "on the same page", or whether we are talking at cross purposes. For example, some protagonists seem to conflate anti-Zionism with anti-Semitism but others do not. Those with these competing viewpoints will tend to "talk past each other" when debating or in political conflict.

Notwithstanding these sources of potential misunderstanding, wilful or unintended, we can be confident that (say) the slave trade and colonialism definitely existed, as did the Nazi holocaust and its consequences. We can also be confident that (say) patriarchal power has, on average, definitely limited the life chances of girls compared to boys in the past and the present. We can say with confidence people with brown skins experience a range of aggressive acts large and small, intended and not intended, from white people in daily life. Thus, when dealing with reports of oppression, these are not *merely* "narratives", because they reflect real historical events, current social processes, and individual actors, as oppressors and victims. In practice, in the complex open systems of societies, we all at different times find ourselves in either or both roles.

My working definition has already mentioned two points: particular reported experiences of oppression and particular forms of group membership. The first feature is typified in the political currency of "lived experience" or even "epistemological privilege" and the second implies a natal or acquired social status. More will be said about both of these in the pages to come. I could also add a meaningful distinction between identity politics and **new social movements (NSMs)**, whilst recognising that they are often entwined.

For example, being a woman provides a strong natal basis for joining the ranks of a version of feminism as a social movement. However, women are not obliged to be feminists, while men may at times may provide critiques of patriarchy. Another overlap to note is that some NSMs have not been about humans but other species (animal rights activism) and some about the precarious future of our species as a whole, not the rights of one particular subgroup of people (climate change activism and nuclear disarmament). This book will not be dealing with these linked phenomena but will limit its remit to illustrative social groups and even then, for reasons of space, will not deal with all NSMs.

A final qualifier, when we are considering definitions, and which is the most important for the purpose of this book, is that we cannot assume that either identity politics or NSMs *inevitably* reflect persuasive struggles against oppression. Nor do they *necessarily* offer a generic advantage to human flourishing. As will be clear in these chapters, sometimes identity politics clearly undermine these assumed advantages and sometimes NSMs work to oppress others, while advancing the interests of in-group members. The ultra-right nationalist and the paedophile draw on the logic of identity politics with glee.

From group solidarity to personalised spite

The **emergence** of identity politics at the turn of this century, like older forms of politics, at first focused strongly on practical group solidarity and on the notion of **intersectionality** to point to the multiple material causes of oppression. Both of these promising starting points soon degenerated into individualism and personalistic forms of reasoning. Now political worthiness has often degenerated into armchair "virtue signalling", with little requirement needed other than an angry emoji on Facebook or a spiteful quip on Twitter. There is little need for personal responsibility or considered debate in draughty rooms in winter evenings to address a complex world with this new political form. Now the alias, once only the favoured deception of the career criminal, has become normal and acceptable on social media. Anonymity is now boasted and normal and it has lost its traditional connotations of shame, deviousness, and cowardice.

Auden may have counselled us to "love your crooked neighbour/ With your crooked heart" but instead we have created a sanctimonious world, in which the imperfections of others are contrasted with our own asserted political purity. Along with those who agree with me, I am a good person, but you and those agreeing with you are evil and deserve to be scorned or worse. Some "identities" then have become a convenient cover for bullying at a distance and without consequences for the bully ("trolling"). If there is any genuine solidarity remaining in this exercise, it seems to be directed at gaining and retaining "friends" in cyberspace and it permits a casual contempt for those victimised at a distance, with moral accountability going absent without leave.

The use and abuse of freedom of expression then has become a necessary focus when we examine identity politics. Freedom of expression is then both suppressed and used aggressively in order to achieve that goal. This contradiction in and of itself bears examination. This scenario of highly personalised politics reflects our neoliberal times and its rewarded forms of strong individualism. Today in "progressive" circles, expressed virtue (in the slang of today being "woke") is a badge of *personal* pride, honour, and warranted *personal* indignation. This leaves out-group individuals lacking that virtue to be *personally* vilified justifiably and their viewpoints closed down. They have become fair game for vindictiveness and occasionally violence. In this process the experiential character of oppression becomes confused and confusing; rather like aiming for peace by killing people. If capital punishment involves taking a life as a punitive response to a life having been taken, then in this case, personal offence is allegedly solved by creating more personal offence.

Having said all of this, without identity politics, historical injustices, for example in relation to sex discrimination or racial prejudice, exploitation, and slavery, may not be revealed to public consciousness. Moreover, governments today might be unconcerned about their daily relevance for public policy. In other words, power and its exploitation between social groups, past and present, are real sources of oppression and that oppression *really is* experienced at the individual level.

Thus, a focus on personal experience is a completely legitimate *starting point* to understand oppression. However, does that exhaust our understanding of political forces in their complexity and dynamic flux? Does it exhaust our way of "doing" politics? Does it bring costs as well as benefits, especially when self-righteous indignation is used to bully and belittle others? Does the legitimate starting point simply become a reified end in itself, with nothing else really required from any of us anymore? Does anxiously watching our "Ps and Qs" imply that politics might now have been reduced to the life-long discipline of self-censorship? These are the hares set running by identity politics and are questions worth exploring, together or apart, in personal reflections in or out of political or academic settings.

The courtroom of daily life and new technology

Norbert Elias' work on the character of civilisation was misread by some as a celebration of ongoing progress in Western societies since the Enlightenment. More modestly he was trying to highlight the need to reflect on the costs and benefits of increasing personal restraint and moral probity, when risking offending others (etiquette and civility). As both Stalinism and Nazism demonstrated in the twentieth century, these habits can characterise daily life for many, even in the most barbaric of regimes. The norms of restraint and civility by no means ensure civilisation.

In a similar vein, Sigmund Freud was concerned to demonstrate that the superego (our ideal imagined self and our conscience) can have contradictory consequences. They may ensure the preservation of the status quo and have a cost to the mental health of individuals. Some psychoanalysts went as far as arguing that the superego was an "internal saboteur". We punish ourselves for "getting it wrong" and often direct that censure outwards, when coming across the misdeeds of speech and action of others. The process of "projection" is one amongst many safety mechanisms to discharge anxiety and aggression. I will be exploring these and other psychodynamic processes in relation to the practice of identity politics episodically in the following pages.

Given that identity politics places moralisation centre stage, and then personalises that obligation, a range of eventualities can accrue, when the superego is in overdrive. The wrongdoer may be properly identified but what sanction should be imposed and on whose authority? What if they are wrongly identified or the rationale for condemning them is debateable? What if the self-righteous judgements of one social group are diametrically opposed to those of another?

Daily life then becomes a diffuse and often confusing courtroom for us all to be judged and to judge others. Now we are all the judge and jury and we are not always clear of the rules and the regime of punishment we are party to. This is a precarious state of affairs, whether we consider it in relation to rationality, evidence confirmation, or natural justice. It is not at all clear how it will enhance human flourishing. It may achieve little except making people feel bad about themselves and suspicious of anyone not in their contingently defined peer group. It divides people against one another. As it does not create solidarity amongst ordinary people, those divisions can be exploited by the rich and the powerful.

How has this messy modish trend of identity politics arisen? Possibly their ideological proximity to, or enmeshment with, postmodern social science and its constituent elements of idealism and "perspectivism" have sometimes culminated in the abandonment of the gains of the Enlightenment. A respect for reason, the judicious weighing up of evidence, the assurance of tolerant debates between competing ethical or political viewpoints and the rejection of *ad hominem* reasoning have been cast aside casually at times in the practice of identity politics. This has undermined the absolutist claim of critical social justice warriors to be an unalloyed progressive force.

At times, these eventualities have been amplified by the emotive and reckless norms of social media, where "the only way is down" for intelligent respectful exchanges. Social media have become a lawless playground in which those who shout loudest, or are following the comfortable norms of the cyber-mob, can threaten the well-being of others in a range of ways. When this happens, a social trend (which might be judged as being good, bad, or indifferent with the benefit of later hindsight) becomes a self-satisfied ersatz "social revolution".

Social media as a rapid-fire form of communication held the promise of increasing public participation but, in practice, all too often, the opposite has occurred. The aspirations in the late twentieth century of those like Hannah Arendt to create a daily context of deliberative democracy have been dashed by the false promise of new technology. For example, the rational use of Twitter to enhance quick and easy access to new research for academics is soon drowned out by the noise of bile and contempt for others. When there is little or no respect for the distinction between fact and fiction and when all perspectives make an equal claim to authority or wisdom then democracy is undermined, not strengthened.

In this contemporary technological context, the *seeming* libertarianism of postmodernism and its expression on social media have culminated in authoritarianism and the closing down of debate. The surface defence and celebration of "diversity" have disguised a barely veiled undertow of intolerance. A diversity of viewpoints are not genuinely defended but shut down casually. When that occurs, the traditional defence of freedom of expression in life in general, but in academic life in particular, is threatened. Amongst other things then, identity politics has tested the willingness and ability of intellectuals to protect, rather than subvert, freedom of expression. The response has been divided and ambivalent, reflecting a period since the 1960s in which, for a variety of sound and sometimes unsound reasons, our traditional confidence in scientific evidence and truth claims has been queried.

A broad separation in US culture was identified by J. D. Hunter in his book *Culture Wars: The Struggle to Define America* (Hunter, 1991). A cleavage then began to emerge, according to him, between progressives in American politics and those defending cultural orthodoxy. Hot topics such as homosexuality and abortion would then flush out those taking sides in this divide.

I would suggest some cautions about these (understandable) broad sociological brush strokes. First, this was a comment on US culture and so we might be wary to explore the strengths and weaknesses of identity politics globally by the norms of US society at a particular historical moment. Second, that broad description did not take into account contradictions. For example (as I will be exploring in Chapter Three in relation to sex-based rights), a civil rights yardstick for social justice can lead to one group's rights being pitched against another. American individualism found its expression on the American left with these contradictions but, for example, the reconciliation of identity politics with both social democracy and Marxism in Europe is today being played out in a "non-American" way at times.

Ambiguities and contradictions

These ambiguities and contradictions then are explored in the coming chapters, using critical realism as a philosophical resource. I will say more about this in the first chapter and will offer a glossary of relevant terms at the end of the book for those wishing to extend their understanding of this approach, which treads a middle way between old-fashioned positivism and postmodernism. I will place glossary terms in bold in the chapters, when they first appear, to cue the reader.

A basic starting point for critical realists is to begin with an empirical description of X and then pose and answer a question about its emergence. In this case, where X is identity politics, what must have the world been like for them to emerge and then gain legitimacy in today's society? That tracing of relevant antecedents allows us to make sense of why identities have emerged during human history, which at the turn of this century began to constitute a different form of politics from the past, though some of the topics explored in the book suggest a far longer tradition of claims to an oppressed status (for example, the struggles against anti-Semitism and colonialism). Also, insights about divisions of social classes and their forms of consciousness and special pleading were described by Adam Smith, not just Marx.

A final caveat, by way of introduction, is that the topics chosen and listed are commonly known but they do not exhaust each and every group that might have been discussed under the rubric of "identity politics". I have deliberately selected some to highlight their usefulness and worthiness (for example, in debates about sex, gender, and race) but also some that legitimise reactionary goals (antisocial sexual identities and theocratic special pleading); a curate's egg indeed.

CHAPTER ONE

The reality of identity politics

Introduction

This opening chapter introduces critical realism and outlines a broad empirical picture of identity politics in recent times, as a starting point for consideration. Critical realism begins with a description of a topic or event and then works backwards to trace the range of mechanisms that might account for what we agree we are witnessing. I have supplied further information about the philosophy in the glossary that will be signalled in bold, where it is relevant. Having outlined critical realism, I move then to consider the character and origins of identity politics, using it as a framework of understanding.

For those new to critical realism, it treads a middle way between the older claimed certainties of positivism and the newer ultra-relativism of postmodernism. It accepts some of the claims of each but then seeks to reject their errors. Positivism was a form of realism but it was naive. It emphasised a fixed world awaiting discovery, with laws incrementally discovered that were assumed to occur in all times and places (**empirical invariance**).[1] Moreover, truth claims for positivism, as the name suggests, could only be about what was positively present. Critical realism instead argues for impermanence or flux, with trends and tendencies existing but not fixed laws independent of their context. Metaphysically, this has much in common with some Eastern ways, especially Buddhism and Taoism, for example, "Let reality be reality. Let things flow naturally forward in whatever way they like" (Lao Tzu). In ancient Greece we find a similar proposal from Heraclitus: "a man cannot step into the same river twice, for fresh waters ever emerge around him".

Critical realism is in the Heraclitan philosophical tradition of seeing reality as flowing not fixed (Bhaskar, 2016). This does not make it an illusion or totally incomprehensible, but it is challenging to study in a fair and accurate way; hence why we need to approach it sceptically or critically as realists. A tolerance of uncertainty faced with fluxing complexity is thus required in a cautious stance of **epistemic humility**. Moreover, most of reality is absent but may be influential about what is present.

For example, a drought (the absence of water) causes crops and animals to die. Positivism emphasises events occurring together to explain a causing b (constant conjunctions), whereas critical realism considers that we need to consider underlying **generative mechanisms**, not the events themselves or correlations between them, which though evident must always be treated sceptically. Those mechanisms are there whether or not they are actualised and made manifest in empirical events and whether or not they are ever witnessed directly.

We can then draw a distinction between **the empirical**, **the actual**, and **the real**. The first is what we experience or witness via our senses alone or in consensus with others (hence empiricism as a limited philosophy). The second refers to events that actually occur (whether or not we witness them). The third refers to all the complex interactions of generative mechanisms in the world across time and space: everything that is present and absent, been and gone, as well as prospective.

All realists, naive or critical, agree that the world does exist, but critical realists emphasise that it is deep and complex. It goes beyond the surface of empirical presence favoured by positivism. The existence of

---

[1] This expectation of fixity is derived from the pre-Socratic arguments of Parmenides which are at odds with those of Heraclitus that underpin critical realism today.

the world (including our inner worlds) does not require our knowledge of it. We are ignorant of ourselves (the unconscious or bad faith) and our embedding context, which even the best education only manages to dent by our knowledge. The world beyond our species simply exists and will continue to do so when we become extinct, at the end of the Anthropocene. The generative mechanisms in the world will continue to operate in our absence in the remaining natural world.

Beyond positivism and idealism

Critical realism is not only different from positivism but also from the modern representative of philosophical idealism, particularly since the "postmodern turn" during the 1980s in social science. This tradition has placed ideas at the centre of understanding human activity. Generally, idealists do not reject material reality but they do see it as of secondary importance and may allude to it opportunistically to make their case without seeking to understand it fully. Idealists use material reality because they have to: when we have an experience and recall or report it, it has to be *about* something and that something is referring to reality outside or inside us. For idealists this obvious basic connection between material reality and our contingent understanding of it is readily ignored or underplayed methodologically. For them knowledge, stories, talk, writings, and texts are the central matter for consideration. It is the meanings that arise from these that are considered to be what constitutes human reality. The latter is deemed to be socially produced or constructed.

The focus on deconstruction or discourse analysis that then flows from this position is not far removed from ideological critique or the analysis of rhetoric, myths, and mystifications favoured by Marx. However, the latter located such critiques in an ontological context of real extra-discursive powers in nature and in human practice. The risk of breaking that link between material reality and ideas is that everything becomes a linguistic game, which might have dire political consequences.

As George Orwell, who I return to later, noted in his book *1984*, "Who controls the past controls the future; who controls the present, controls the past." Today trans activists argue that being male or female was merely a value judgement *assigned* at birth by the adults present.

4 IDENTITY POLITICS

By contrast, realists say that sex is *determined* at fertilisation and then *described* at birth or on a prenatal scan. The first makes it all about ideas, whereas the second recognises material reality and our empirical descriptions are then responding to it (more or less adequately). Ideas unanchored from material reality can be farcical, but more worryingly they can be dangerous.

Early proponents of idealism expressed in social constructivism, such as Berger and Luckmann (1967) in their book *The Social Construction of Reality* were careful not to reject the contributions of realists like Marx and Durkheim, even if they backgrounded our reliance on material reality. However, later more radical constructivists, largely under the sway of French poststructuralist philosophers like Foucault and Derrida, became more anti-realist, developing a preoccupation with words and words about words (Lemert, 1980). Not only has social science paid the price by painting only half a picture of society and its deep ontology, but a generation socialised in its ways has been encouraged to reduce politics to words of praise or punishment.

Critical realists accept that human thought and talk is important, because ideas can have causal powers and these can be substantial. For example, people might "die on a hill" for their beliefs. However, as the Marxist cultural theorist Raymond Williams noted:

> We become ill, we become old, we die … To die for a cause, and be honoured for it, is one thing. To attempt to override the physical realities, which persist in and through and beyond all historical causes is quite another. (Williams, 1980: 114)

Thus of course ideas, knowledge, and ideologies are important but they are not *all important* when considering the totality of ourselves and the world. Accordingly, the "everything is socially constructed" trope in modern social science simply does not do justice to our task. For critical realists, the emphasis is not on reality being *constructed* but it being *construed*. Within human science the latter emphasis was made by George Kelly in his *The Psychology of Personal Constructs* (Kelly, 1955). We do indeed construe the world and ourselves, and over time we can reconstrue them in a variety of ways. But this is a weak, not strong, version of constructivism, which according to some critical realists characterises their shared philosophy, though some reject it as being fundamentally misleading or diversionary in its focus (Sayer, 2000; Elder-Vass, 2012).

Much of social science has been characterised by phases of social constructivism, first of symbolic interactionism and personal construct theory. This gave way to the stronger postmodern version in social theory. Social constructivism creates risks, according to critical realists, both in terms of misleading us about reality, by alluding to it at will but then scorning it, but also creating rather than exposing injustices. Here, for example, leading critical realists attack social constructionism (the alternative term often used for social constructivism), considering it to be:

> morally irresponsible and outrageous. This is because there are serious problems that affect humanity and these problems need to be understood in an interdisciplinary way. It is vital to be able to describe them, to theorize them and to critique them. Yet strong social constructionism disallows this critique. (Bhaskar, Danermark, & Price, 2018: 81)

This disallowance comes from ultra-relativism, perspectivism, the "undecidability of propositions", and the unending exercise of discourses about discourses. This reflects idealism's narrow emphasis on epistemology. By contrast, critical realists consider that this needs to be understood in relation to ontology. Knowledge arises from the material reality of our enlarged brains bequeathed to us as a species by evolution. It is not sufficient therefore to look at knowledge independent of its ontological roots. By understanding the relationships between **ontological realism** and **epistemological relativism** we can decide what we consider to be true in a particular context (**judgemental rationality**). If we settle narrowly on epistemology (as the strong social constructivists do) then we end up with judgemental relativism instead.

In this book both positivism and idealism will be points of reference at different times. For critical realism, reality is the focus both in its presence and its absence. Our ways of understanding reality are *part* of reality but they are not the whole picture by any means. For this reason, social scientists who argue that "everything is socially constructed" are wrong. They reduce reality to our socially negotiated meanings, narratives, or discourses alone. Social constructivists are methodologically preoccupied by discourse analysis or deconstruction or personal account analysis. They deny the presence and force of extra-discursive reality, which warrant additional research methodologies.

For critical realism, this is a narrow and misleading focus as it relativises reality to such a degree that we lose sight of the world *as it is in its material complexity*. This requires methodological pluralism, depending on the research question being posed. We can provisionally and in a state of **epistemic humility** (because our knowledge is partial and fallible) take our best shot at agreeing on what is true. Truth is not a dirty word for critical realists and does not require the speech marks placed around it in a state of tired irony by postmodernists. It is always approached cautiously but never with disdain.

Tracing the antecedents of identity politics

When offering a critical realist account of any topic, we have to start somewhere and a good place to start is what we might agree on is before us. We can then ask what the world must have been like for us to witness what we agree on today. This then is the overall logic of critical realist analysis—how do we trace the antecedent generative mechanisms that might account for what we see before us? This weighing up of possible antecedents is retrodiction, which might lead to us specifying particular mechanisms to explain the picture before us (**retroduction**). This research logic rejects the naive deductions of positivism (going from the general to the particular) and notes the limitations of induction (going from the particular to the general) favoured by idealists, though the latter specific descriptions are valid aspects of reality to understand and might be a good starting point for deeper critical explorations.

With this goal of tracing antecedents in mind, we start empirically with a broad current agreement of what identity politics *is*, whether or not we are or for or against its ambitions. I noted in the introduction that identity politics have been described, as both a new form of politics (since the 1970s) and yet elements of it are discernible to older political struggles, especially about sex-based rights and anti-slavery. Thus, a prefigurative feature of today's identity politics relative still to its working definition relates to the matter of *civil rights* (Schlesinger, 1991).

With the **emergence** of **new social movements (NSMs)** in the 1960s and 1970s we already saw two directions of travel for what we now call "identity politics". One direction entailed special pleading for *particular* groups with a shared experience, who considered themselves oppressed and marginalised in Western democracies. For example, women or black people or homosexual people organised to defend and extend their rights, with group membership being defined by a single characteristic of identity. In that tendency there was a veering away from traditional coalition politics of elected political parties of left, right, or centre to represent their interests in legislation and policy formation more generally.

Moreover, a distinction could now be discerned between the old labour movement, which was largely male and employment based, and the NSMs. These marked a departure from both the ballot box and the traditional labour movement, with their new focus on civil society and rights for individuals, who were disproportionately oppressed within it. Citizenship within existing socio-economic arrangements was being emphasised by the right to live like any other (less oppressed) person. This did not *necessarily* require that those structural arrangements were scrutinised or attacked. Diversity now joined equality as a mark of social progress and, some were to argue, the former began to displace the latter at a price.

The second tendency was for overlapping campaigning *within* identity politics, rather than single identity rights-based claims. For example, gender non-conforming individuals who were gay, lesbian, or bisexual might ally with transsexuals and transvestites, as was clear in the early days of Gay Liberation. However, this was to sow the seeds of later tensions and splits, not just offer the potential for the solidarity of greater numbers. From the outset gay men and lesbians did not always cooperate comfortably and today the role of trans activism remains highly contentious. For example, in Britain the umbrella organisation Stonewall witnessed a major split on the matter in 2019, when a new LGB Alliance was formed, alongside the "Get the L Out" movement. The same ambivalence about trust could be found in anti-racism, which contained many white activists, who were not necessarily trusted by black activists, with the result that some of the latter moved towards separatism.

The prospect of intra-group alliances (and problems pregnant within it) emerged in the late 1970s, with what many now identify as a key moment in defining what we today call "identity politics". This was the recognition by a group of black socialist lesbians (the Combahee River Collective) that white activists could not do justice to their struggle as black women (Crenshaw, Gotanda, Peller, & Thomas, 1995). For them their concomitant identities of being women, black, and attracted to the same sex offered particular insights borne of experience about the daily oppression of patriarchy under capitalism. The collective emphasised (erotic and non-erotic) love between black sisters and that their unique *experience* should be privileged in the goals, strategies, and tactics of political struggles they, *not others*, defined.

We can see in these important defining features of the 1970s the grounds for new forms of solidarity in politics but also there were the seeds of fragmentation. The latter reflected ontological differences (being a woman, not a man or being black, not white) and epistemological differences (how factions or splinter groups might see and represent the world within their developing rhetorics of justification and ideologies).

In the introduction to the book, I noted concerns from leftist writers (Hobsbawm, Sivanandan, Fisher, and Patel) that this special pleading about group membership was diversionary and mystifying. Once some groups make a claim to epistemological privilege then equality is displaced by a contested hierarchy of diversity. The mandate for defining the goals of politics, or the criteria for what might constitute power discrepancies and forms of oppression, becomes differentiated and divisive. Those without a version of asserted "lived experience" are afforded no right to a view or their view is deemed to be a vehicle for oppression of the in-group.

Identity politics amongst other things altered the way we had traditionally thought about legitimate critique and leadership. For example, in the past the international labour movement looked to the authority of two white men, one a struggling intellectual, Karl Marx, and the other an ambivalent rich industrialist, Friedrich Engels, to pronounce authoritatively on both working-class oppression and patriarchy. By today's criteria of identity politics, Marx and Engels, to say the least, would struggle to have "skin in the game".

This now raises questions that will be explored in the coming pages. By the criteria of identity politics, can we only understand oppression if we are oppressed in a particular way personally? If so, what if groups and subgroups of oppressed people make competing and even incommensurable claims? Can oppression be still investigated from the outside looking in or are the testimonies of the oppressed the *necessary and sufficient* basis for politics?

An argument could be made that *all* forms of politics have personal impacts (there are winners and losers in power struggles, both acutely and chronically) and they implicate personal motives and personal thoughts and feelings. This is a truism but for analytical reasons it might also divert us from examining the *particular* aspect of the **social ontology** of identity politics we have been discussing at the turn of this century. When we address that social ontology, the defining features of experienced oppression and social group membership attend what we, for now, call "identity politics". It is also tempting to include a third feature: outrage in its new technological context. The emergence of the internet has been a major factor in the salience of identity politics, as it is typically discussed today. In Box 1.1. I expand on this point as it helps to ground us in the contradictions of identity politics I will be considering throughout the book.

Box 1.1 Outrage in its technological context

The volume (in both senses) of noise created by outrage on social media is explored pithily and very wittily by Ashley "Dotty" Charles in her book *Outraged: Why Everyone Is Shouting and No One is Talking*. The author certainly ticks enough of the intersectional boxes to be in a justifiable state of constant self-righteous indignation. She is a young black lesbian "living with her wife and son". However, in an adept and thoughtful contrarian move, she adopts the role of sceptical critic, not fervent participant, and so can make many valid critical points about the paradox of identity politics. For Charles (2020) they might start with radical intentions, but energy is diverted immediately into a state of frenetic passivity that simply confirms the neoliberal status quo and its complicit and obsessive individualism. To get to this conclusion she explores some celebrity case studies. Her insights come from these unlikely villains (not heroes) of "wokery": the faux black woman Rachel Dolezal, the smug ex-public schoolboy and Murdoch editor Piers Morgan, and the racist misanthrope Katie Hopkins. Her personal engagement with these figures, when writing the book, generated key learning points for Charles. First, these well-known targets of vilification have enjoyed celebrity status for psychological and/or financial reasons. In their own way they "play" their outraged audiences for narcissistic gain. In a world of conspicuous individual success, it is better to be notorious than inoffensive and ordinary, and notoriety can be generated by simply offering "clickbait". In the case of Morgan, Charles admits falling into this very trap herself, when she attacked him on social media. Second, the internet was a game changer. Today with barely an interruption in our mundane routines we can click our way, on a daily basis and in just a few minutes, into virtuous groups in the world who are angry about its range of injustices. What matters is not whether we are *really* outraged but that we *signal* to that the world we are, cueing the next point. Third, "calling out" wrongdoers consolidates the moral worthiness of the group on the attack. After some reticence to admit it, Charles considered that Dolezal was probably correct in her conclusion that it was black women who gained the most from deriding her pretence. Fourth, although outrage has always been an emotional driver for political action, today it has become a mere goal in itself. There is no requirement for online petitioners, cancellers, and those "calling out" lesser mortals to actually develop any strategy to deal pragmatically and in a sustained manner (i.e., in a state of genuine struggle) with the complexities of structural oppression in the world, if all that is required is to signal disapproval. I would add here there is also no need for them to deal with the higher order moral hazard of negating freedom of expression in society (a point I return to beyond this box). That question did arise in the encounter Charles had with Richard Wilson, the leader of the Stop Funding Hate campaign directed at shaming advertisers about the links with hateful journalism (*The Sun's* Richard Littlejohn's hostile comments on same-sex parenting started the ball rolling). Charles concedes this more considered strategic approach might work, compared to the outraged clicking of atomised individuals on their screens. But in a state of forlorn "outrage fatigue" she then noted that advertisers apologise, move on, and still make their profits. Such was her despondency by the end of writing the book, Charles stopped using social media and even paid for the online service "Tweet Delete" to erase her old posts from the internet.

I mentioned that outrage might be a third working criterion for defining and discussing identity politics today. However, the critical reflections offered by Charles start with outrage but then bring it into question, noting fairly that the emotion itself may be missing. What matters instead is the *performative signal* of outrage, in order to enhance the clicker's ego and ensure their group membership.

This process of online virtue signalling has been described as "grandstanding" by Tosi and Warmke (2020) in their discussion of "the use and abuse of moral talk". Platforms such as Twitter encourage short simplistic statements, which lack nuance or qualification. Indeed, if complexity and cautious caveats were introduced, then the personal venom and its acquired moral high ground would lack narcissistic traction for clicktivists. Not only are we encouraged to join a digital lynch mob,[2] we are also encouraged to play top dog in our indignation. This whole process reflects an online norm of adults behaving like toddlers, which also resonates with "cancel culture". (I return to the poor compatibility of identity politics and mature reasoning in the final chapter.)

Some of us, some of the time, are genuinely outraged and for good reason. However, that authentic state is not actually required in order to participate in identity politics; virtue-signalling and grandstanding will suffice. But worse, that hive of performance online might be based on ignorance and traps. We might be drawn into futile clickbait responses that merely massage the egos of provocateurs (Morgan and Hopkins) or give attention to the sad troubled state of those like Dolezal. In relation to ignorance, Charles cites the Danish study of a false announcement about the intention of local government to remove a much-loved fountain in Copenhagen. Though this was a completely bogus claim invented by the researchers, within days there were thousands who were signing an e-petition in protest.

A troubling aspect of this study is not only that our generic desire to be seen online as virtuous people means that we might be readily duped but also the *rapidity* of our clicks confirms an absence of our critical reflection. Do we bother to research the history and character of a topic of injustice presented to us? Indeed, do we *need to bother* doing this if those posting the invitation for us to agree have already done the "working out", leaving us merely as signatories to a cause that might have never even crossed our minds? The implications of this scenario of duped

---

[2] This term was used in a discussion of dysfunctional online vilification in an episode of *The Digital Human* (BBC Radio 4, 28 June 2021).

ignorance for the prospect of sophisticated deliberative democracy are serious in three senses.

First, sober study, reflection, and research, which used to be the stock in trade of older forms of politics, is now redundant. This then leads to a dereliction of our democratic duty. Identity politics might then simply become an exercise in mass stupidity. As Charles noted in the vernacular, "clictivism, it wants to be activism but it can't be arsed" (2020: 75).

Second, the ideologues of identity politics, who *are* prepared to do their version of "working out", might then have an open goal in their efforts to capture the political process about their aims. I return to this process, when discussing institutional capture by trans activists in Chapter 3. They *actively avoid* open democratic discussion, favouring instead surreptitious tactics to influence policymakers.

Third, as Charles noted when checking on the well-intentioned collective action of the Stop Funding Hate campaign, short-term successes to shame some businesses have no substantive impact on wider structural inequalities and the exploitation of labour. Not only does capitalism, as a whole system, survive intact, the diversion diverts us from seeing it for what it is.

Charles cites a couple of famous examples to illustrate this last point. Frothing indignation about a black child model wearing a H&M T-shirt with the word "monkey" on it, or the celebrity chef Jamie Oliver committing the sin of "cultural appropriation", by promoting his "jerk rice", have little real impact on their targets. But, more importantly, less personalised and "sexy" injustices about the lack of unionisation, zero hours contracts, and health and safety protection for young people on their Deliveroo or Eat Me bikes in busy urban traffic can be left off the agenda. Who cares about the working-class kid with no hope of employment risking life and limb on their push bike, when we can all feel good about shaming a TV chef? I return to an **omissive critique** of identity politics and various points in the coming chapters.

The point about picking one's battles in politics is not just about personal choices, cost-effectiveness, wisdom, or mental health self-protection, though these are important. Those battles reflect a suprapersonal ontology (part biological and part socio-economic) which is differentiated, deep, and complex. If we limit our politics to demanding diversity at all costs and assume that all self-identifying groups and their claims have a logical and moral equivalence, then we will be mistaken. Supporting a diversity of identities, without reference to different version of ethical warranting, cannot produce social justice.

The rights of the white supremacist cannot be deemed to be equivalent to those of those with black skin. The rights of a transwoman, with immutable XY chromosomes, cannot be deemed to have the same existential mandate and trajectory afforded by material reality as a person with their immutable XX chromosomes raised under patriarchy. The rights of adult homosexuals cannot be judged by the same criteria as the demands of those wanting to enjoy sex with animals, corpses, or children, even though they are all versions of "sexual orientation" and all might claim a particular group identity. This "diversity at all costs" approach to politics is deeply flawed, because each case needs to be appreciated in its own ethical context and those contexts are different, as I hope to show in the coming chapters.

Identity as an emergent aspect of human experience

Critical realism emphasises emergence in fluxing open systems. The emergence of an enlarging cerebrum in mammals during evolution ensured that they developed an increasingly sophisticated capacity for reasoning and problem-solving. Our species is characterised by an addition to this trend: the use of symbolic representations, via the use of language. The latter ensures that we make statements and statements about statements (and so becomes the fetishised methodological focus of social constructivism). We can conceptualise time (to and fro) and construe and re-construe its meaning to us. We can record our thoughts in versions of writing. All animals communicate with one another but we do it with elaborated style. This also means that we can deceive ourselves and one another in ways not evident in other mammals; one understandable reason at times why some of us prefer to relate to pets, not our fellow humans.

There is little wonder that in the past religious authorities considered that only people, not other animals, had souls. We do not need to invent God to make this deduction, as it comes from an emergent aspect of evolution. Our elaborated capacity to use language affords us the unique option to go beyond the instinctive reactions to threat common in all fauna. Words allow us to identify ourselves as unique beings who are not someone else. They allow us to predict the certainty of our individual death and to make choices about how we live our lives with that certainty in mind. We can identity who we can trust, who is the same boat as us, and, if they are in a different boat, whether they are out to sink us.

If we have unique biographies and within our particular journey from the cradle to the grave, we form bonds of trust with others based upon commonalities of interests and experiences, then that is one basis for "doing" politics. It is not the *only* prospect but it is one. It reflects a complex set of elaborations of primate conduct in general which, according to ecological conditions might lead to all monkeys and apes co-operating with those of their own kind but also warding off competing groups *within their own species, not just others*. However, we are different because the elaborations of language mean that our identification with our own, and our suspicion of out-group members, are then overlain by a range of symbolic considerations.

If we can codify being a man or woman, black or white, old or young, or sane or insane, etc., then in-group identification and out-group threat can be abstracted from their immediate material conditions (the daily concern of other species). They can now be posed and reflected upon at a distance of time and place. Our group solidarity might start, for example, with the general primate-based considerations about competition for food, sex, and territory. However, in the minds of humans these can be extended to both general abstracted principles of justice and, in practice, to those we deem to be allies or enemies *who we have never met*. Moreover, our capacity to record our histories, both personally and collectively, leads to new eventualities compared to our primate cousins.

All four, not just two, planes of our social being

It is here that as a critical realist I can spot the seductive attraction of social constructivism. We can indeed go on and on about our meanings and those we exchange with others. Our narratives and discourses are genuinely fascinating and legitimate material for any human scientist. However, this discursive focus limits itself to the interpersonal and the personal, leaving two of the four planes in our **four planar social being** under-scrutinised or even simply ignored. The extra-discursive aspects of our lives (the impersonal or supra-personal mechanisms operating or *in potentia* within the planes of the natural world and in socio-economic structures) are equally important to consider. The uniquely personal and relationality are important but they do not exhaust our task of understanding for critical realism.

Given that identity politics have emerged in part because of these conditions of possibility of evolution, we need to invoke forms of analysis and critique that go beyond seeing ourselves as just another primate species (though we are that as well). If the word "identity" is used so freely now about modern politics, then the emergent psychological dimension to being human requires special attention. We are not the only species with inner lives, nor are we uniquely strategic tool users. However, our capacities in these regards are more elaborate and with this comes new emergent features about our lives, compared to other animals. In particular, our sense of self becomes important (and depending on our degree of narcissism it might be all-important). Our experience of ourselves brings with it opportunities to turn our attention both outwards and inwards.

Given that Janus-faced prospect for identity politics, at best it might ensure social outsight or what the grand old man of academic Marxism, C.W. Mills, called "the sociological imagination". It also might be the basis for new forms practical action in solidarity, which was the offer being rehearsed by the Combahee River Collective noted earlier. At worst it becomes the narcissistic "poor me" indulgence of the person seeking unending victimhood or the person seeking group belonging by their mindless "clictivism". It also might obscure deep ontology. It will validate the paedophile and the incel, using the same logic as anti-racism or gay liberation. Basically, identity politics might invite us all into a highly mystifying flight of fancy: we become so open-minded that our brains fall out.

The psychological (personal and interpersonal) aspects of our four planar social being deserve attention. However, we must be mindful of the risk of **reductionism**, when and if we ignore the other two plains of our four planar social being. With this caution in mind, we can note these clarifying points:

1. Our experience is part of the ontology of being human; it is not merely an epistemological matter. Our experience, like the grass and the rain, simply exists. It is there and we can reflect on it as well; both are true.
2. Our personhood comes from our **concrete singularity** embedded in unique biographical conditions. We do not need to invoke the notion of "soul", but that is an option.
3. As reflective beings, we make choices (we have agency) but we do so under conditions that we cannot always control nor be fully aware of.
4. Our personhood may or may not lead to a sense of identity, though for most of us much of the time it does. For example, someone in the advanced stages of dementia is still a person but they may have lost their sense of who they are and others may have also lost that sense remembered from a shared life with them.
5. We can make a distinction between our conscious sense of self and aspects which are unknown to us. Since Freud, this distinction has been made between the ego (the conscious part of us), the id (our unconscious instincts driving us without our knowledge), and the superego (part conscious and part unconscious aspect of the mind related to our conscience and ideal self). All of these might be illuminative in relation to identity politics. Also, we cannot access our social world by *simply* asking ourselves and others about it (the methodological preference of many social scientists). We are in a state of constant ignorance about the deep ontology of both our inner lives *and* the world we are embedded within.
6. In different times and places the experience of who we are and how to discuss that general tendency might change. We construe and reconstrue who we are as time passes, while usually retaining some sense of continuity as well; this is a both/and, not an either/or, matter. If our sense of self is an illusion (which arguably as an abstraction it is), then it is a coherent and consistent illusion, so is an aspect of ontology we may as well take seriously on pragmatic grounds. As we grow older we usually in large part feel that we are still the same person as in the past, an aspect of our being-in-the-world often endorsed by others who have known us for a long time. Different cultures have placed different emphases on identity. We have a private sense of who we are and we also have a social self, which is constituted by a set of

norm-governed performances from one setting to another. The self is both differentiated and persistent and can be looked at in a range of ways by any of us.

On that final point, the extensive historical exploration by Lebow (2012) in his book *The Politics and Ethics of Identity: In Search of Ourselves* unpacks what we mean today by "identity", prefacing his analysis by noting that it is "the secular descendent of the soul" (2012: 16). The distinctions Lebow wishes to make are indeed part of social ontology and so worth reflection.

He makes a distinction between our private reflective selves and our social selves and the fragmented sense of experience this creates. The "performative" aspects of selfhood and identity are the favoured interest of social psychologists and micro-sociologists. The enabling and dysfunctional interplay of our social performances (what Erving Goffman called "impression management") and our private experience, within identity politics, have already been noted above and in my introduction. Virtue signalling and "clictivism" confirm this point. Who cares about the need for complexity, caution, compassion, and respect for strangers (which we might reflect on in good conscience during our honest private moments), when public rewards of group membership await in the world of identity politics and its norm of frenetic passivity?

Be careful what you wish for: "the personal" in contemporary politics

Identity politics have been characterised by widespread self-righteous indignation and sporadic vitriol. This is a logical outcome of reducing politics to "the personal" and has its roots in the late 1970s, when two clear strategies emerged on the left, setting the scene for today's controversies about identity politics. The first was that antiracist activists (I was one of these) campaigned with some success for a policy of "no platform for Fascists". For example, in Britain, trade unions would pull the plug on electoral broadcasts by the National Front. The second strategy, and probably now most well known, came from second-wave feminists. Socialists in their ranks emphasised that "the personal is political" and more radical feminists went further, noting as well that "the political is personal". At the time, both strategies of blocking racist propaganda and emphasising that power relationships had personal daily consequences for women under patriarchy made complete sense.

If politics is now habitually personalised, even for what in the 1970s made reasonable sense, what if there is evidence of counterproductive outcomes? Antiracists and feminists certainly started with good intentions, but they may have taken us down a road to hell, with science being ignored, our imagination being puritanically constrained, and basic rights to express ourselves being trampled upon. Working-class voters have turned away from "loony left councils", opting for Eton toff politicians. The trade union movement is diverted on a daily basis by the virtue signalling expected now from the social groups vying for attention within identity politics, pushing more mundane workplace injustices into second place.

At this point another consideration is that the left, especially under the influence of Lenin and Stalin rather than Marx and Engels, has been accepting of two priorities: strong leadership and the ruthless treatment of those deemed to be the enemies of progress. Ruthless "vanguardism" has cultivated authoritarianism on the left, creating a norm of brutal intolerance. This has legitimised the moral absolutism demanded by the proponents of identity politics. It is one thing to use strong arm tactics to defeat the rich and the powerful (and, even then, anti-democratic tendencies and violence might be too readily and unjustly encouraged). It is quite a different matter if that moral absolutism is directed at ordinary people, who now are simply deemed to hold "the wrong views".

This point is germane to the main weakness of identity politics. Now the enemies of progress are not the forces of reaction, who control finance capital, operate in global crime networks, or, still, in old-fashioned Marxian terms, extract surplus value from working-class people in the industries of the West or the sweatshops of the East. Now the enemy is *anybody* who says or does the wrong thing, especially the first.

A critical reflection here is whether those with real and often hidden power in our lives are left under-scrutinised and are free to enjoy a mandate to control us. They are laughing all the way to the bank, as the anthropologist-turned-journalist, Sarah Kendzior, forensically demonstrates in her book *Hiding in Plain Sight*. Not only may identity politics now be a diversion from the deep ontology of **neoliberalism,** they may also be a complicit or self-reinforcing symptom. Its individualism and fetish for "lived experience", which is so readily commodified, thus might be a cause for alarm not celebration.

Since his death in 1950, the democratic socialist George Orwell has been co-opted at times across the political spectrum for his searing critiques of authoritarian statism and his uncompromising defence of freedom of expression. His books *Animal Farm* and *1984* are rich with prescient material about the dangers of authoritarianism in politics. In particular, "thought crime" stands out in its relevance, as a mirror to the legacies of both Stalin and Goebbels. The success of identity politics then might be seen, in part at least, as a celebration of the exposure of thought crime and the arrival of an Orwellian dystopia. Both Stalinism and Nazism were *mass movements* (Vajda, 1976). They cannot be accounted for by manipulation from the top alone, even though this was also part of the picture. The action of the baying mob is also required, as the rise of the crooked populist Donald Trump proved, documented by Kendzior just noted. Those at the top will always manipulate but they must have willing subjects in order to succeed.

Today, an alternative to the critical analysis of deep ontology, in order to puncture that mystification and expose the complicity of the powerless with the powerful, is the comforting but diversionary presence of identity politics. Ordinary citizens now "call out" and condemn their fellows stepping out of line, whose reputations and careers are disposable in the supposed interests of social progress. The traditional narcissistic politician, of any hue, with their rhetorical cliché of "wanting to make a difference", has been replaced by the online virtue signaller. They believe they are making a difference with a lazy series of clicks; at least the old-fashioned careerist politician had to work hard at his or her self-advancement.

Conclusion

We are all now under a constant pressure to self-censor our expressed thoughts (and we might even feel shame and guilt for simply *having* them privately). Imaginative transgression in our inners lives is now being crushed for fear of accidental social disapproval. We have entered an era of puritanical permafrost. Ordinary civility and decency have been discarded, like the latest disposable cheap top from Primark.

Although, as the saying goes, "people in glass houses should not throw stones", we are now surrounded by the daily noise of shattering panes, recalling the aftermath of Kristallnacht. Abuse is now normalised in a digital-age version of people being placed in the stocks and pelted with rotten vegetables. There is little wonder that Ashley Charles gave up in the face of the outrage fatigue created by this sport of the online lynch mob. In addition, offline violence (hard, not soft, power) used against individuals is even now the acceptable price paid to achieve diversity in society.

When a sixty-year-old woman, Maria Maclachlan, was punched in the face in Hyde Park in 2017 by a transwoman, Tara Wolf, she was simply standing alone and peacefully advertising a Woman's Place meeting to discuss sex and gender. When the police arrived, video footage showed Wolf's supporters denying that anything had happened. When the case came to court, the following year, Maclachlan was *ordered* by the judge to refer to Wolf as "she" in the proceedings. At this stage we see, in one exemplary case study, the triumph and limitations of identity politics in practice, the complicity of the mob, and the organisational capture of professionals by ideology, at the expense of factual material reality and judgemental rationality. If a modish ideology decides it is the case, then two plus two equals five and anyone disagreeing deserves social censure or worse. Orwell is spinning in his grave. This cues the next chapter, which addresses one of his greatest fears: authoritarianism will suppress freedom of expression and undermine our confidence in objective reality.

CHAPTER TWO

Identity politics and freedom of expression

Introduction

As Noam Chomsky, the libertarian American philosopher, has noted, "If we don't believe in freedom of expression for people we despise, we don't believe in it at all" (Aldridge, 2014). Freedom of expression has been one defining feature that distinguishes democracy[1] from totalitarianism of the left or right, a point I return to at the end of this chapter. A preliminary distinction worth noting is that freedom of expression refers to both words and deeds and so the relationship between these invites our critical reflection. Both words and deeds are part of both our **social ontology** and social epistemology. We are an interdependent species and so social obligations to others are ubiquitous in all societies, though the precise content of those obligations changes over time and place. Put differently, norms and mores vary but they *always exist in some form or other*. This is why we can so readily "get it wrong" when finding ourselves in a culture for the first time (which might cause either amusement or offence to locals).

---
[1] I return to versions of democracy in the final chapter.

Another preliminary reflection is that both words and deeds might be offensive but the first have been viewed as more problematic by moral philosophers because of their ambiguity. Offensive deeds (e.g., recorded evidence of physical violence) are more readily operationalised, detected, and appraised. By contrast, the common term "hate speech" poses challenges to law enforcers.[2] Does it mean anything that hurts or upsets others? If not, then how do we adjudicate on its occurrence in context, either as ordinary citizens or state officials? Is hate speech just the speech uttered by people we hate?

These are not abstract questions without practical significance because they recur within the debates of identity politics. For example, a few years ago a journalist challenged Germaine Greer about her second-wave feminist defence of sex and her refusal to accept that transwomen are women. Greer made the point she had no objections to men wearing dresses if they wished to, or calling themselves "she", but that would never make them women. The journalist pointed out that such a view would hurt the feelings of many people. Greer dismissed this with the point that all of us are upset or hurt by the views of others quite often but that is not a reason to suppress their expression. At one point, Greer noted that being an old woman involves being offended by what others say very often.

Or, taking another example, atheists routinely disparage a belief in God but a strong theist would deem their comments to be blasphemy, deserving of punishment. In theocracies this might mean being condemned to death. This highlights a fundamental political and ethical question: if any of us are offended about something, then what should be done about it? The social control of offensive speech is no simple matter, given that all solutions breed new problems, in relation to the content, the criteria of adjudication, the legitimacy of the adjudicators, and the just desserts of the offenders. And how do we distinguish a bigot from a

---

[2] In the UK at present this starts with the subjective opinion of the offended party, which is *ipso facto* subjective. This is then a difficult crime to prove, so on pragmatic grounds alone we might want to explore alternative ways of ensuring that citizens are civil to one another as often as possible. Anonymity on social media decreases that prospect significantly.

person with views we simply do not like? If they claim an evidential or ethical mandate for the views that offend us, do they have a reasonable case for articulating it to the world for our full appraisal?

For example, those in the Judeo-Christian tradition might honestly believe that homosexual acts are sinful in the eyes of God. For those outwith that tradition, such a judgement may seem unfair, unjustifiable, or at odds with the freedom of consenting adults about their sex lives. However, should the expression of such a religious belief still be defended? I think that it should, even though I do not agree with these religious moralisations, and I should have a right to say so. Similarly free citizens should be able to say what they like about God or satirise religion without being threatened with legal action or suffer harm or death (eventualities common in theocracies).

Is there a crisis of free speech?

Some on the left have denied identity politics has created a crisis about free speech. For example, the journalist Nesrine Malik, writing in *The Guardian* in September 2019, argued that today speech is *very* free, if we use the criteria of widespread unpunished trolling and violent threats against women and ethnic minorities on social media. Asserting that there is no crisis or that it is merely conveniently invented by bigots and reckless libertarians on the right could be our **empirical** starting point. However, note that this is a starting point; it is by no means the end of the process.

Malik's argument only holds some water if we *reduce* the crisis of free speech to the manipulations from those on the right, who might be confecting it in order to protect their prejudices. However, the new authoritarianism from below I discuss later has not only reflected a threat to the interests of the right (to be reactionary and bigoted with impunity). It has had a direct impact upon feminists trying to protect their gains during the twentieth century against male domination. In theocracies religious freedom warrants death and in liberal democracies, that fate might await anyone attacking Islam (see Box 2.1).

Turning to the cultural shift linked to what Malik claims is an illusory crisis, a caricature of a young **woke** generation steeped in the worthiness of identity politics is that they have become "snowflakes" in their expectations of "protected spaces" from speech or the written word that might upset them (O'Neill, 2018). Even if this is a caricature, the very *fact* that the scenario of "protected spaces" is being rehearsed for some people reflects a sensitivity about freedom of expression. This is manifest in other aspects of our recent cultural norms, which include academics self-censoring their own work and people now being proudly dishonest about their real names on social media. At one time, an alias typified criminality, not the honest citizen.

Whether freedom of speech should define, in part at least, the character of a democratic society is the point here about identity politics and its new expectations of thought control. My starting point then is a broad empirical claim that today freedom of expression is not habitually defended. Instead, it is knowingly and self-righteously *undermined*, with the assumption that this is a proud blow for social justice.

In Box 2.1 I expand on that recent empirical picture by giving examples of a new form of authoritarianism "from below". Most discussions in political science define authoritarianism as a "top down" process but this misses the point that for such regimes of power to be sustained, they require mass support and compliance. For this reason, I see authoritarianism as a dialectical process. It reflects the ongoing relationship between the expressed interests of elites, including oligarchs, kleptocrats, crony capitalists, and the opportunistic narcissists seeking election at the polls, and the masses they go on to rule. The latter gain existential security by being complicit in their own domination.

This might seem to be counter-intuitive (like "turkeys voting for Christmas") but the empirical evidence is quite clear. Authoritarian regimes of left and right have been sustained by mass support and so their mass psychology invites our understanding. The rise in authoritarian populism in parliamentary democracy in the past decade reinforces this psychological point: it can emerge from below, it does not have to be imposed by police terror but emerges from everyday ontological insecurities. Anxiety about our peers and concerns about our reputation or job security can drive self-silencing and social compliance. For example, the daily complicity of ordinary Germans in Nazi ideology in the 1930s came from this emotional setting.

Box 2.1 Moral absolutism, authoritarianism, and identity politics

If moral absolutism characterises much of identity politics on a daily basis, then those found guilty of transgressions will deserve their fate, according to those passing judgement. That might include losing employment, being "cancelled" from civil society, as well as threatened or actual violence. At times, this aspect of identity politics may draw attributions of "fascism" but this is misleading: whilst fascism is *ipso facto* authoritarian, the two cannot be simply conflated. There are many other variants of moral absolutism that do not fit this description. For example, evangelical Christians have aggressively lobbied abortion clinics and threatened clinical staff. The fatwah taken out against Salman Rushdie came from theocratic authoritarianism and dogmatic certainty. For this reason, it might be wiser to *specify* the type of authoritarian case by case in their **concrete singularity**.

In Chapter Six I discuss the refusal of Rosa Parks to give up her seat on a bus in 1955 in Montgomery, Alabama. In an ironical inversion of this scenario, in 2020 at the height of the Black Lives Matter protests, in a Washington DC restaurant, a woman, Lauren Victor, was cornered and intimidated by activists for refusing to raise her fist in solidarity. As she made clear to reporters, Victor sympathised with the cause but was perplexed about why she had to comply with the intimidators, who were baying at her, "White silence is violence." In the first scenario of Parks the authoritarian state sought to control an ordinary citizen's right to personal choice, whereas in the second with Victor, authoritarian leftists were imposing the same restriction.

In the world of celebrity there are sporadic reports of gender-critical writers being "cancelled" and then trolled on social media. These include J.K. Rowling, Graham Linehan, and John Cleese, with feminist groups noting that the extent of threats of violence (especially rape) were greater for women than men who are making the same logical or scientific point about biological sex.

A series of feminists have lost their jobs for simply articulating their views about gender politics or other matters about the rights of natal women. These include Sasha White who was fired from the Tobias Literary Agency in New York for her gender-critical comments, in 2020. The previous year in London, Maya Forstater was sacked by the Centre for Global Development for the same reason, though in 2021 she appealed successfully against this through the courts. In 2016 a survivor of sexual abuse, Kaeley Triller, was fired from her job in the YMCA in Washington state because she objected to men using the women's locker facilities.

In 2015 Natasha Chart was accused of bigotry and fired at Rewire News (formerly RH Reality Check) for attacking the sex trade, especially the evidence on the sale of minors for sex, and criticising the impact of gender ideology on lesbian and bisexual women. In May 2018 the San Francisco Public Library hosted an art exhibition from a trans activist artist and founding member of the Degenderettes of bloody shirts with the caption, "I punch TERF", as well as baseball bats and axes with barbed wire attached. On social media gender-critical women often receive a hostile meme showing a woman being hanged with the caption "Kill a TERF".

These recent attacks on feminists invert examples from the 1960s, when SCUM (the Society for Cutting Up Men), proposed violence to end patriarchy. Its most famous expression was from its manifesto's author Valerie Solanas who (non-fatally) shot Andy Warhol; both made films on the basis of the event. It remains contested whether SCUM was ever an organisation beyond its obsessively violent founder, as well as whether it triggered an unresolved discussion about "reverse sexism" or "misandry".

As an indication that this climate of violence linked to identity politics is not limited to differences of views about race, sex, and gender, we can also note the role of authoritarian religious groups. Two stand-out examples in France in recent years have been the murders by Islamist terrorists of the schoolteacher Samuel Paty in 2020, who was beheaded, and five years earlier the attack on the Charlie Hebdo offices where twelve people were shot dead, and eleven others injured.

What all the above examples show is the link between the direct action promoted in identity politics and its legitimisation of extra-judicial and authoritarian forms of justice (intimidation, threats, and actual violence).

The Maya Forstater case attracted particular interest from all sides of the particular culture war about gender and sex, which I consider more in Chapter Three. It included an intervention of legal support from those involved with the campaigning magazine *Index on Censorship*. They supported Forstater to help her win her appeal (Gimson, 2021). However, in order to be consistent in their position about freedom of expression, they also recognised that transgender activists had every right to articulate their case (Smeeth, 2021). Accordingly, in the wake of the Forstater ruling, which disappointed that lobby, the magazine printed a response from Phoenix Andrews, a transgender activist, who claimed in conclusion the following: "Speech is always more than just words. Forstater's win sets a precedent. It is a precedent that will harm trans people such as me" (Andrews, 2021:75).[3]

Andrews is on very weak ground, logically and empirically, here. Sometimes speech *is* just words. When and if ideas, written or spoken, are causally efficacious, which sometimes they can be, then we must be very careful to *demonstrate* that point case by case. Andrews cannot prove, rather than hyperbolically claim, a causal link between Forstater's genuinely expressed beliefs and personal harm. We all can come to our own conclusions in good faith, case by case, about the difference between emotive rhetoric and legitimate evidence. Offending people and harming them are different notions. J.S. Mill counselled us to avoid offending others where possible but only proof of actual violence against others arising from speech contravened his basic liberal defence of freedom of expression.

Strong generalisations, especially predictive ones in open systems, of "erasure" or people being "killed" by gender-critical arguments (rather than verifiable criminal acts, involving named victims and perpetrators) are untenable. They do not represent **judgemental rationality** but diversionary hyperbole. If transwomen pro rata are disproportionately the victims of violence, compared to biological women, then where exactly is the evidence? And if that evidence exists then how might the views of *this* particular gender-critical feminist be traced as the causal source of a crime against *this* particular person in the way being claimed by Andrews?

To put this spat between Forstater's supporters and her critics into a wider cultural context, religious texts arguably create a climate of prejudice against atheists but the latter, in line with the legacy of the Enlightenment, still defend religious freedom. We return again and again to the

---

[3] This piece was preceded by another from the gender-critical analytical philosopher Kathleen Stock (Stock, 2021).

ground rule defended by Noam Chomsky at the start of the chapter. We either defend people who express views we find offensive, or we do not.

The expectation of freedom of expression in modernity

For there to be a question about freedom of expression at all requires that we have communicable views to be expressed in the first place (to be permitted or disallowed). Our starting point in our **four planar social being** is that of our bodily capacity for language, first spoken and then written. This first plane of the materiality of our body is crucial. For example, those without language (the preverbal child or the older person with advanced dementia) lack the capacity to express their view. Similarly, if people are illiterate then they cannot express their views in writing (nor can they respond to the written views of others).

The capacity to reason in speech and to read and write are expressions of a form of human capability that if absent or impaired will undermine human flourishing (at both the interpersonal and individual levels). The evolution of our species did not *only* involve the increased capacity of individual problem-solving, as a function of our enlarged cerebrum; reasoning in other animals is now well demonstrated. We were different because we could codify those efforts and represent them first to ourselves and then to others. The latter process was then a *social* one, whereby thinking is learned, expressed, and judged in an interpersonal context.

Hunter-gatherers cooperated and learned how to learn together, including noting mistakes of one another and arguing about the best method to achieve X or Y. This involved individuals in small and large ways pitting one account against another to determine the *truth* of a situation at hand. Confidence in empirical reality or identifying what was *true* was thus derived from argument and consensus building, when faced with shared challenges (von Heiseler, 2020; Mercier and Sperber, 2011). The wisdom of the old could be passed on to the young via oral history.

It is here that we find the beginnings of science as an ongoing social activity (with the narrow confines of empiricism being seductive) but also argument and consensus building became the "glue" for democratic processes. We argue and then agree on what is going on and we seek to advance our individual and collective interests by arguing and sometimes then agreeing on what to do about it. We argue our case, listen respectfully to what others say, and then ally ourselves with those we agree with. We learn though that not all arguers are equal and that the loudest voice or the most prestigious in rank get their way more often. In order to participate in this social process, fraught with power play but also pregnant with the prospect of deliberative democracy, we have to have "a voice" as a precondition of participation. The latter is one defining feature of being a person and the springboard for our civil rights in any society.

For example, literacy is a basis of full citizenship and so it quite understandably became a common demand from political progressives, after the technological innovation of the printing press. At the same time, as Hoggart (1957) noted, high literacy levels in the populations of developed economies can still lead to the ideological drift towards the interests of ruling elites (via the content of mass culture). This might, and does, disrupt direct bonds of solidarity in working-class communities, previously built upon spoken communication in workplaces and neighbourhoods. Literacy then is an ambiguous capability, which can certainly help us in critical analysis but also seduces us as duped consumers ("because you're worth it").

What Hoggart noted in the 1950s about the printed page was amplified at the turn of this century by the internet. The moral philosopher Bernard Williams, in his book *Truth and Truthfulness*, picks up on the false promise of the latter (Williams, 2002). He argues that its postmodern context *seemingly* democratises communication but its norms have actually returned us to pre-Enlightenment times, with the global character of the internet making the situation even worse than in days long gone by. As he notes, in the Middle Ages at least people were forced to deal with their fellows more honestly in a real village, whereas "the global village" requires no collective accountability or moral integrity. Its anonymity destroys mutual respect and it has become the hiding place of scoundrels and cowards. From click-baiting to algorithms shaping our voting intentions, social media have become a catastrophe for democracy.

These reflections on where we are in modernity from those like Hoggart and Williams arose then in response to two considerations. The first was the impact of technological changes over time and the second was the change in wider ideological assumptions about democracy after the Enlightenment. A number of Enlightenment thinkers encouraged freedom of expression in opposition to the older authority of priests and monarchs. The latter would commonly simply direct the population to obey their instructions and disobedience led to punishment, including death. At this point, having a voice and being literate were not simply opportunities for ordinary people but also potential points of opposition to current power arrangements. If reason and evidence, rather than superstition, blind faith, and adherence to theocratic directives were to be encouraged after the Enlightenment, then this was reflected in the academy and championed by its participants.

Within the more general respect for freedom of expression (such as freedom of the press and religious dissent) academics were in a particular position to maintain and elaborate the implications of rational debate that used evidence and logic. It soon became evident that one particular form of logic was to undermine this broad intention: ad hominem reasoning. Whereas it was fair game in politics to disparage opponents and draw attention to say their stupidity, lack of morality, or other character flaws, this soon was discouraged in academic life. There, for freedom of expression to be effective, critical reflection had to be protected at all times.

This implied a rule of engagement in scholarly discussions in which peers were allowed to disagree with one another. What won a particular argument was not the named people involved but the strength of one rationale pitched against another. In the natural sciences, this largely entailed a focus on the presence or absence of empirical verification. A claim should not be made without the evidence to defend it. In the social sciences, arts, and humanities, where empirical detachment was more problematic than say in the laboratory or on the dissection table, respect for theoretical cogency or innovation was more prevalent. However, in all cases in the academy there emerged an overarching commitment to respectful discussion and debate. What became taboo was tackling the player rather than going for the ball.

With the postmodern turn in the arts, humanities, and social science in the 1980s, that taboo on ad hominem attacks disintegrated and was replaced (at least in the advocates of the new wave of reasoning) with a form of permission to personalise criticisms. Whereas Marxists had always been mindful of the ideological context of knowledge production, a basic respect for reason and evidence had been retained in principle. Indeed, the concern for Marxists was about the utility of knowledge for ordinary working people, rather than for the elites who controlled the means of production and dominated bourgeois power structures. However, the post-Marxian implications of the new logic derived from the "perspectivism" started by Nietzsche and the singular preoccupation of words and discourses by French post-structuralism went further.

Whereas Marxists would separate the role of ideology in clouding reason and evidence from the progressive *potential* of the latter, the postmodernists were to be more nihilistic and slippery in their approach. If everything was a discourse, then all that was left was more of the same in academic life (discourses on discourses). Truth claims and a confidence in the progressive role of evidence production could now be scorned in favour of "positionality", "situated reasoning", or "the undecidability of propositions". All of this unending relativism peaks with "epistemological privilege" (i.e., giving maximum credibility to individuals with particular experiences of oppression).

In the latter we find often now that legitimacy in academic life comes not from the older ways of intellectual probity, which defended reason and evidence, while eschewing ad hominem attacks on opponents. Those old habits were discarded with the postmodern turn, and the game changed: who was speaking and their character flipped, from being at the bottom of a hierarchy of persuasion in academic debates, up to the very top. This had the effect of blurring the distinction between opinion and evidence. At its starkest worst this meant that the good sense of an academic, who was "privileged" (say because they were male, white, "cis", or "straight", or some combination of these), could be ignored or denounced. By contrast, the random or politically expedient viewpoint of a person who had "lived experience" of X (the topic in focus) could or even *should* be considered sacrosanct. It was not just their *experiential account* reported honestly and usefully, in a form of biographical disclosure, which was to be respected, quite rightly. In addition, this was extended to all of their *views* about what was politically legitimate or desirable.

With the collapse of the taboo on ad hominem reasoning came a fundamental querying of the Enlightenment project. It also meant that ideological demystification (favoured by Marxists) to defend knowledge in the interests of ordinary people was taken a step further. All knowledge at all times was to be considered suspect unless it met the seal of approval of the self-appointed ideologues of identity politics. With this triumph of the postmodern turn a new generation of academics emerged which would defend this position, with dire consequences for Enlightenment liberals and Marxists alike (see Box 2.2).

Although the movement towards "wokery" in the politics of the left has been described as "cultural Marxism" by some of its critics, such as Jordan Peterson, there is much that is at odds with Marxism. This point is especially relevant in relation to the recasting of ideology as discourse, the rejection of **ontological realism**, and the disdain for, rather than confidence in, scientific progress. Marxism, amongst other things, is a *materialist* philosophy, whereas identity politics is dominated by **idealism**, especially the tradition of perspectivism, since Nietzsche.

The question of "cultural Marxism" might be a taken-for-granted dismissal from conservative commentators about identity politics, but they have plenty of ammunition about leftist authoritarianism and its contempt for bourgeois democracy and its liberalism. I now turn to its role in the twentieth century in the context of vanguardism.

Vanguardism and the twentieth-century left

Subsequent to the Russian revolution of 1917, Marxism became quickly yoked with the seminal ideas and strategic guidance of Lenin. Although Leninists, even today, appeal to an unsullied version of his political philosophy to insulate his role from the disasters that were to emerge on the world stage for the bulk of the twentieth century, his focus on vanguardism set the scene. Complaints from Trotskyists that Stalin distorted Lenin's intentions and that the permission of "tendencies" would have ensured socialist democracy, rather than totalitarianism, are dubious.

With hindsight, that magical thinking can be questioned legitimately. Surely *any* strategy which places power and authority permanently within a group deemed to have a form of higher consciousness than ordinary people, will ensure self-serving oligarchies. Appeals to leadership are not a problem provided that the leaders are readily challenged and replaced and the right to criticise and oppose them from any quarter is unconditionally defended. This ensures that leaders are honest and have the interests of the masses, not just themselves and their immediate elite group, in mind at all times.

Stalinism posed a serious problem for the left's credibility and this became worse with Mao and Pol Pot and their directives to control and kill ordinary citizens, who did not conform to the expectations of "the Party". Show trials, torture, and summary executions required one part of the population to turn readily on the other in a brutal manner. Not only was vanguardism a self-defeating strategy to ensure democratic socialism, even worse, it might and did encourage the cult of the personality. At this point the mass psychology of Marxist-Leninism became indistinguishable from fascism. Both required mass compliance of conduct *and* conformity to the ideological position of the state, embodied in the leadership of the party and its leader in particular. Those failing on either front deserved their just desserts, in the eyes of those who did conform in their actions and ideas.

It is here that the relationship between obedience to leadership becomes complex. The use of direct hard power by the state (summary executions, torture, imprisonment, psychiatric hospitalisation, etc.) is one obvious strategy. This was clearly evident under authoritarian regimes (Stalin's Russia, Hitler's Germany, Pol Pot's Cambodia, and during Mao's "cultural revolution"). However, daily conformity also relied on enough of the population to themselves *believe* in the political status quo and its defence. This legitimised the shaming of those not conforming and also provided the KGB, the Stasi, or the Gestapo with a rich resource of informants willing to do their version of civic duty to the Party, its leader, and the nation. The latter is important to recognise because authoritarian statism of right or left has appealed to primitive loyalty to blood and soil ("Motherland" or "Fatherland"), which I return to in Chapter Eight. As well as the primitive need for belonging there are other non-rational considerations, especially indignant rage.

Rage and identity politics

Rage is a good starting point for political action but in itself it is not transformative. Instead, it is corrosive and simply risks mindless violence. To be transformative it must be linked to calm reflection, self-criticism, and a respect for the views of others, even if we do not agree with them. And so this is why freedom of expression is a necessary requirement for social progress: it is not merely a vaguely liberal sentiment and individual right but a *necessary condition* for human flourishing in general.

The inherently divisive psychological process of mindless othering and the silencing of outgroup members is a conundrum for any onlooking moral philosopher. Are we *all* actual victims (say women, black people, or religious minorities) or potential ones (those of us reaching old age or developing a psychiatric diagnosis or becoming gay)? If we are, then is there a hierarchy of victimhood and, if so, how do we describe this and who is to take on that task and be the final arbiter of an imagined socially just future? What is the relationship between the psychological defence of splitting and the actual ontologically real divisions in society between oppressive and oppressed groups?

Another question raised is about intra-group differences, when identity politics tends to essentialise whole social groups and so stereotype individuals within them. In the 1970s a feminist diary cover had the joke (or was it?) "All Men Are Bastards!" Today all white people are privileged and transwomen lecture "cis" women about what it is to be female. Another version of this amalgam contempt for the outgroup enemy is the cannibalistic slogan "Eat the Rich" (derived from Rousseau). So, would Friedrich Engels and Jeffrey Epstein *both* be on the worthy menu of the starving masses?

The postmodern turn in the 1980s contained a post-Marxist shift on the left, rejecting or subordinating class politics in favour of identity politics. **NSMs** shifted the political focus from the workplace and parliament to domestic and public spaces in everyday life. What remained though, from the Leninist obsession with authoritative leadership, was an elite form of consciousness. The Orwellian outcome of "some animals being more equal than others" was the ingrained legitimacy on the left of *personalised* hatred of "the enemy" and who was to be hated was dictated by those of a higher consciousness. Traditionally this meant a contempt for the fat-cat rich and those working within the military-industrial context, who constantly undermined the solidarity of the international proletariat.

With the **emergence** of NSMs and identity politics this now became a highly variegated moving picture show. Now we might *all* be "the enemy" (whether we knew this or not or accepted it or not). Moreover, the authority of the Party leadership was now being replaced by those who are most "**woke**" amongst others (the critical social justice warriors); the rest of us ordinary mortals would now live in a constant condition of shame about our habitual failures of word and deed.

Confusion in the academy

If, subsequent to the Enlightenment, liberals and Marxists alike had looked to reason and science to resolve complex questions and encourage free critical thinking, then the name of the game had now changed with the regime of "wokery". Now the onus was on academics to justify and encourage a world in which diversity was beginning to displace equality as the hallmark of collective human improvement. The outcome of that new imperative is summarised in Box 2.2.

Box 2.2 The character of the postmodern academy

In September 2020, Jessica Krug, an associate professor at George Washington University, came out as a liar to the world with uncompromising self-abasement. A well-published expert on the African diaspora, who had claimed to be black, now confessed that she was Jewish and "white". Recalling the case of Rachel Dolezal, Krug partly accounted for the deceit by her childhood adversity. But beyond this mental health explanation, the existential option for academics in postmodern times was revealed. This avoidance of being "the enemy", by appropriating the role of victim to shelter within, implies that shelter is needed from a constantly hostile and judgemental everyday life. More than that, identity politics might now be the positive foundation for career building in the academy or in the corridors of policy formation. Self-surveillance and risk calculations about intellectual clarity and honesty meant that academics, like all citizens, had to "watch their Ps ad Qs", in order to maintain or improve their careers.

In the USA the Heterodox Academy has been conducting surveys about the degree of confidence on university campuses about freedom of expression. They found that there was self-censorship or inhibition about expression views known to be risky, according to current orthodoxies. In 2019, 1,580

> university students were asked how reluctant (versus comfortable) they felt in the classroom giving their opinions on politics, race, religion, sexuality, gender, and non-controversial topics. They were also asked about their views on the potential consequences that students feared, if they were to speak openly. Over half (58.5%) were "somewhat or very" reluctant to give their views on at least one of the topics listed above. Political views were particularly inhibited (32% of the sample being reluctant to offer a view on politics to peers and staff). White students were particularly inhibited about talking about race. Men were particularly reticent to talk about gender. Women were more inhibited than men when talking about politics and religion.

If the confines of the university have not ensured freedom of expression for all staff and students, then higher education has not offered us a model site or scenario for celebrating democratic ambitions after the Enlightenment. This then is a cue to look at democracy.

Freedom of expression and forms of democracy

The idea of democracy (society being run by and for the people) was first described in Ancient Greece. However, there are some cautions that have arisen from this truism. Its ancient advocates, such as Socrates, never intended the principle to apply to slaves, women, and children (Orwell's point that some are more equal than others). That defence of patriarchal elites, within a rhetoric of democracy, was retained and is still evident today. Also, democracy does not have to be *described* for it to be relevant in all human societies because the tendency is inherent to our species: it is part of our specific ontology. However, our collaborative interdependency has competed with intra-specific conflicts. I will now elaborate on these points in order to put identity politics into a longer historical and cross-cultural context, beginning with where we are today: the context of **neoliberalism**.

Individualism and neoliberalism

One stimulus (apart from the availability of the internet) for identity politics has been **neoliberalism.** This is true in two senses. First, the regime has now entailed the complex free play of powerful elites, driven by an unbridled greed for money and power. These overlap but their participants are often unaware of others in this regime of domination. The groups are involved in crony capitalism in the West, which hovers constantly on the boundary between legal and illegal means. They also involve organised crime operating across national borders, as well as the kleptocrats of Eastern Europe, who diverted state resources into their own bank accounts with the collapse of the Soviet Union. At times these groups are mediated and helped by the security services of nation states or by state-funded charitable projects. A consequence of this complex power play of so many forces, some legitimate and some criminal, hidden in the main from ordinary citizens, is that it shapes the programmes of elected democracies, via control of the mass media and the manipulation of support via social media. The latter is the common site for identity politics praxis (what Charles called "clictivism"—see Chapter One) and so its relevance is obvious in relation to our topic.

The decline in the market for newspapers, alongside the ready availability of social media for journalists themselves, has meant that costly investigative journalism has been displaced by the latter context. Given that, outlier viewpoints on social media (especially Twitter) become attractively controversial, at little or no cost to the mass media outlets with their fragile profit margins. Only a minority of the population is on Twitter and only a minority of those involved actually dominate its content. Social media, then, have not enlarged democracy but narrowed it. Mainstream media outlets, degraded by the convenience and cheapness of social media, then amplify the salience of a limited world. Part of that distortion is played out in the effervescent outrage from offended identities.

The second relevant aspect of neoliberalism is the ideological centrality of individualism. Whether one loves or loathes identity politics, what all can agree is that it is about the personal, and it is very personal. "This is my experience of who I am" is a necessary but not sufficient condition of "and I can be anything I want to be", which in turn is a necessary but not sufficient condition of "and you must accept who I say I am otherwise you are infringing my human rights". That final position in this narcissistic pattern of communication requires one more step to complete the amalgam of individualistic assumptions within identity politics: "I am oppressed and you are my oppressor."

An implication of this ideological formation is that social justice will be achieved in the world by individuals speaking and acting differently. Social progress becomes an experiential and social-psychological matter alone. The ontology of power has been reduced to the interpersonal (the second plane of our **four planar social being**), which is predicated upon the narrow assertion of biographical uniqueness (fourth plane). Apart from the fact that this is a reductionist vision of politics, it necessitates the suppression of freedom of expression, as probity about speech is the constant puritanical preoccupation of "social justice warriors".

Individualism (typified in US culture but, with globalisation, now prevalent in most places) does not have to take this form. For example, some theological moral strictures focus on the individual and their moment-to-moment choices in the eyes of an all-seeing God. This is a paradoxical individualism: God, not man, is central but individual agency is constantly on trial (the avoidance of sin). However, the economic context of neoliberalism has shaped individualism in a particular way, so that everything is a commodity, including the self. The latter is to be asserted and promoted proudly, partly as a consumer with rights ("getting what I paid for") but also being rightly rewarded by that regime ("because I'm worth it"). The egotism this spawns readily defines justice by whether or not an individual *feels* offended, and a price is then demanded of the offending individual.

What both the God-fearing and the God-less versions of individualism in the context of neoliberalism have in common is their indifference towards, or even disdain for, our interdependence in a world governed by *supra-personal* forces, which we do not control. They often control us and they are largely outside of our conscious awareness. Policies flowing from this insight might become the harbinger of socialism and neoliberalism is thus under threat. Moreover, why do we need to understand the complex ontology arising from our **four planar social being**, when we can achieve justice by simply raging at others and settling grudges against them, all in the self-righteous knowledge that we are defending diversity and human rights?

The positive and negative risks of direct democracy

If voting every few years in polls that are constantly skewed by commercial forces and media manipulation has brought parliamentary forms of democracy into disrepute, then the appeal of direct democracy becomes obvious. The poor turn-out at the polling booths is a sign of disengagement, with ordinary people feeling that elected politicians do not deliver the goods they all promise. An emergent alternative has been direct action from NSMs, as well as local co-operative initiatives in civil society.

As I noted earlier, there is a push from our genetic legacy in play here. Human beings are naturally co-operative and interdependent. Our attachment tendency is one of bonds with those proximate to us. This then is amplified in learning in the family and in friendships. We learn to give and take in our common interest. We learn that a division of labour is helpful in daily life when playing as children *before* a macro-economic arrangement rigidly imposes that in a particular form later in adulthood. We "take it in turns" and we relish team games. The latter allow us to sublimate our need to compete, not just co-operate, in order to survive. Scoring a goal is a prosocial alternative to killing a competitor. The victor holds up a shiny cup, not a severed head.

This co-operative impulse from our genes has been constrained then by other aspects of the history of our species. What we also know is that primates can be aggressive within their group to one another and certainly to outsiders of their own or others species. We share that complex emotional baggage from our primate history. Moreover, as psychoanalysts as diverse as Melanie Klein and John Bowlby have noted, from birth onwards we struggle with feelings of love and hate as well as ambivalence in relation to those we come to love and become attached to in our lives. Applying psychoanalysis to human groups, Bion and Foulkes described another layer of complexity. We bond in groups but they are also places where we might rely slavishly upon leaders or assume that they are places to fight and flee. We scapegoat individuals who are out of line. We might expel disturbing fears and feelings of hatred outwards onto those not present ("scapegoating out of the group"), as those already labelled as an enemy are ready receptacles for these feelings.

This intra-psychic and interpersonal complexity of being human shapes identity politics. It is a domain of politics that is *seemingly* simply about abstract or supra-individual notions of social justice but actually and additionally it is energised on a daily basis by our passions and anxieties. These give us the stomach for struggle and our solidarity in the groups of our choice, with the opportunity for one after another abreacted expressions of rage. But despite the performative aggression and power of the latter, these indignant displays of fury reflect deeper psychic forces of insecurity about staying alive and being accepted by others. When a trans activist shouts angrily that "cis" people can "literally erase" their existence, this is exemplified. It is not evidence-based but it is heartfelt.

The word "literally" today is used for its rhetorical value about justice and personal annihilation, not as a neat point about semantic precision or a contrast with the symbolic or metaphorical. Another example of this was in the debate about "deathmaking" articulated at length by Wolf Wolfensberger (2002) in his book *The New Genocide of Handicapped and Afflicted People*. A paradox in the debate about abortion was that some disabled people viewed it as the destruction of their own potential existence. The rights of the foetus were not then simply a matter of one version of identity politics (women's choice) but invited opposition from some disability activists (another version of identity politics), not just religious conservatives. We cannot understand identity politics without reference to this emotional (and often emotive) aspect of being human.

Thus the good news about direct political action is that it can draw upon the positive psychological aspects of care and co-operation that undoubtedly characterise our species. The bad news is that hate is also there, derived from a mixture of ubiquitous intra-subjective anxiety, the character of ingroup–outgroup tensions, and the legacy of unjust power structures we are thrown into in the society of our birth.

Freedom of expression as a necessary but not sufficient condition for deliberative democracy

The psychological processes which have characterised identity politics impede any society moving towards deliberative democracy. If we opt to suppress expression because it offends us, then we are faced with the challenge of operationalising what it means in practice. If we have laws on hate speech, then how are they to be framed and how are they to be policed? Echoing Chomsky cited earlier, this sober (albeit left-leaning) British judge, Lord Justice Sedley remarked:

> Free speech includes not only the inoffensive but the irritating, the contentious, the eccentric, the heretical, the unwelcome and the provocative provided it does not tend to provoke violence. Freedom only to speak inoffensively is not worth having.

That last sentence sums up the argument. Free speech will mean that quite often we will all be offended about something that somebody else says or does. Being offended reflects the reality of **epistemological relativism** in our species, as well as rule transgressions or behavioural nonconformity. People act in ways we disapprove of. We disagree with one another and sometimes that creates bad feeling. We might even disagree with ourselves over time (I frequently wince at aspects of the speech and conduct of my younger self). As ethical beings we might be mindful of causing offence (we vary in our circumspection in this regard depending on the size of our conscience) because with freedom comes responsibility. However, that caution about civility and concern for others should not override the higher order ethical obligation to give and receive viewpoints freely in the absence of intimidation.

Ignore it or argue with it, but banning offensive speech, or attacking the person who offends you, is ultimately not a sign of mature democratic reasoning. Instead, it is an immature demand to have your way about the world as you want it to be right now; it is a form of puerile narcissism. It has a pay-off of feeling part of the crowd but that does not make it morally defensible. Social media alloyed with identity politics encourages this recent norm of glib moralisation and the formation of the cyber-mob.

Freedom of expression in academic life and deliberative democracy

Freedom of expression is no more a panacea to ensure social justice than is the selective censorious push from identity politics. However, it is an irreducible *starting point* for deliberative democracy. Because it is not a panacea but only a good start, we can reflect on a couple of its weaknesses. The first, just noted from Mill, is that it might incite violence against others. This is not always simple to operationalise and police but it is a valid and important consideration.

A second weakness is that it is not self-evident that freedom of expression will ensure valid truth claims. It is only the *basis* for this process, not a guarantee of a fair outcome. Offering old-fashioned positivism as a corrective against the "perspectivism" and unending "positionality" encouraged by postmodernism is not an adequate answer to the dilemma of the establishment of truth claims.[4]

This points up the recent discussion of what we mean by a "post-truth society". That discussion has arisen from two major arenas of influence (some would say these are causally connected). The first is from the authoritarian statism of Russia. The top-down imposition of truth from the Russian state did not end with the collapse of the Soviet Union but continued as a cultural norm, with the staged managed transition to capitalism under Putin and other state powerbrokers in the KGB, with its superrich cronies, who stole public assets. In the USA ("the land of the free") the parallel process then emerged with Trumpism and the creation of the important concepts of "fake news" and "alternative facts".

In the case of populist politicians like Trump,[5] who accrue a reputation for massaging the truth or even simply lying, an ordinary observer who is sceptical (not even necessarily hostile) about his verbal performance may immediately identify his dissimulation. The fact that he then typically goes on as a rhetorician to accuse *others* of dissimulation (his fake news claims) means another rat is smelled. For psychoanalysts this is the domain of denial, dissociation, and projection being engineered for the protection of his ego and his instrumental goals in politics.

Our ethical judgements about truth are clearly bound up with the social process of interpersonal trust and this requires that we include, within our social judgements of others (and ourselves), our acculturated knowledge about human beings as being deceiving and self-deceiving at times. We are all cheats and liars but we also are human agents who

---

[4] I am using this term to cover both moral claims (e.g., it was wrong for the Syrian government to bomb its own civilians) and epistemic ones (e.g., the car crashed into the tree because the driver fell asleep at the wheel, not because the road was slippery).
[5] Another example of this was when Boris Johnson was accused by the ex-French ambassador, Sylvie-Agnès Bermann, of being "an unrepentant and inveterate liar". See also Bermann (2021).

learn how to spot dissimulation in ourselves and others in our particular cultural context. We vary in our capacity to deploy that quality.[6]

If naive realism (positivism) is flawed in its claims about epistemic truth, then Popper's scientific rationalism is one option. This is favoured by one group of those defending the Enlightenment project against postmodernism and critiquing identity politics (e.g., Pluckrose & Lindsay, 2020). They see science as now being *inherently* sceptical and so postmodernism simply throws the baby (of truth) out with the bath water (of unending **epistemological relativism**). Popper's case was certainly an advance upon positivism because he acknowledged instead that science was a social activity and as such was value saturated. He retained, though, a faith in the integrity of science to be self-correcting by its adherence to the rules of falsification and constant peer review and criticism. Popper's scientific rationalism (as the name suggests) is prone to being over-rationalistic. It does not encourage a deeper look at the non-rational aspects of value-driven social processes, including those involved in expert knowledge production.

Post-Popperians (such as the critical realists) have remained wary of that source of confidence about automatic scientific self-correction but their scepticism falls short of postmodern cynicism and nihilism. It is in that post-Popperian context that we also find the work of the social epistemologist Steve Fuller. Popper's faith in scientific self-correction is undermined by the interest work at play. That is, we are motivated for reasons of status, power or money to favour some forms of knowledge production over others.

Elites (commercial and academic) will tend to produce bodies of knowledge that suit their own interests, thereby excluding the bulk of the less powerful and less educated from a democratic say in the truth. Fuller's position is not one of full-blown postmodernism, instead his focus is on the need to examine power and the social dimension to truth exploration. Power shapes who gets to say what is true (a position similar to that of postmodernism) but Fuller does not deny that truth

---

[6] Apart from wider variations in lying in the population, some of us are more open to self-reflection than others. Psychotherapists encounter some patients who are "too defended" to embark on personal exploration in any depth.

claims must eventually have to rest in the world of ontology (material determination).[7]

His point about constraints on democratic involvement or exclusion from knowledge production, appraisal, and utilisation is then a fair one and cautions against us taking the legitimacy of expert knowledge for granted. This is a counsel of scepticism rather than cynicism and it is fair comment. Expert knowledge is not generated *merely* for self-interest, but self-interest certainly warrants examination. For example, in Chapter Three, I discuss the role of clinical and pharmaceutical interests in the maintenance of a transgender care industry. The scrutiny of socially produced knowledge can invite **immanent, explanatory**, and **omissive critiques**. This point can be applied to both lay and expert forms of knowledge production.

And if Fuller is correct to draw our attention to the complexity of reconciling lay and expert interests, when understanding how knowledge is socially produced (itself then a matter of power), then we also must consider another matter in relation to rationality. Non-rational and irrational processes are involved both within and between groups. This is true for both experts and non-experts. Moreover, rational and irrational viewpoints are communicated within these epistemic networks.

This concluding discussion is straying into the wider subdiscipline of the sociology of knowledge but its relevance to identity politics is clear. Group beliefs emerge from social processes and these are now enabled rapidly by social media. Whilst social contagion had always been relevant before this (gossip, rumour, parochial beliefs, urban myths, etc.) the internet now amplifies them for good or bad, mainly the latter.

Thus, whilst we are capable of judgemental rationality, this is an imperfect capability because we are not only rational animals. It is undermined at times by both intra-psychic and group dynamics. These

---

[7] In this sense, Fuller (2018) is closer to the first wave of social constructivism exemplified by Berger and Luckmann's *Social Construction of Reality*. That first wave respected material reality and the grand narratives of nineteenth-century sociologists such as Marx, Weber, and Durkheim. This can be contrasted with postmodernism and its rejection of those grand narratives and a respect for *causes* not just meanings. That second wave of radical social constructivism is what largely underpins identity politics today, though an exception to this is second-wave feminism, which retains a strong realist ontology.

include moral sentiments (a favourite of David Hume), not just the push from behind of the instincts of sex and aggression, which is discussed in the psychoanalytical canon. These are a matter then of **axiology**, not just epistemology and ontology: we value some things in life and feel strongly about them (Sayer, 2011). We experience passion, hatred, contempt, sexual desire, pride, murderous fury, and disgust (and more). These all alone or in combination might propel our decisions and actions.

If we were *only* rational beings, then we would not need psychologists or ethicists. We could rely instead on mathematicians and statisticians to make decisions for us in a passionless robotic state. This interplay of the rational and non-rational is one reason, amongst others, that we should exercise caution and **epistemic humility**, when seeking or claiming the truth in our lives and the lives of others. Such humility is at odds with the absolutist arguments common in identity politics, which I discussed in Box 2.1.

Conclusion

This chapter has introduced the enmeshment of identity politics with the taken-for-granted assumption that those causing offence in society should be silenced. That suppression is then deemed to be a public duty to ensure social justice. Counter to that view, I have reasoned that freedom of expression is a fundamental building block of democracy, along with others, including a tolerance of those with views we disagree with and a healthy mixture of respect for, and scepticism of, science.

Moreover, contested truths need careful and ongoing reflection in a spirit of epistemic humility. The norms of identity politics have allowed discreditable ad hominem arguments to be elevated into a favoured form of political practice, via the self-righteous fetishising of "epistemological privilege" and "lived experience". This has not supported humility and cautious reflection. Instead, it has engendered black-and-white dogmatic reasoning and moral certainties.

This has created a divisive scenario between those deemed to be morally worthy and those who are not. The former group are allowed an unfettered voice, whereas the latter are silenced and intimidated by being "called out", "no platformed", and "cancelled". Employment is lost and reputations scarred. Human beings are pitched against one another, with no clear positive outcome, but with casualties galore and structural inequalities in society being given barely a second glance. More on this febrile and personalistic zero-sum game in the chapters to come.

CHAPTER THREE

Sex and gender

Introduction

The fractious struggles between gender-critical feminists and their opponents are the main concern of this chapter, though matters beyond the disputes between women about their bodies and their meanings will also be addressed. For example, the validity of biological knowledge is in dispute now and so natural and social scientists are taking up their political and epistemological positions. Moreover, the psychological dimension to all of this contention is important to consider. An early champion of modern feminism, Mary Wollstonecraft, noted that girls are "taught from their infancy that beauty is woman's sceptre, the mind shapes itself to the body, and roaming round its gilt cage, only seeks to adorn its prison". This internal angst for girls was ripe for later commodification under capitalism and one factor in the **emergence** of a culture of narcissism. This tendency extended eventually to male appearance and the self-doubts, created by consumer capitalism, of their appearance too.

Arguments about the character of sex and gender have involved the regular expression of extensive personalised spite, discussed in the previous chapter. They have also illuminated a major philosophical division between realism and idealism. In the first camp are those who argue that sex is determined at fertilisation and *described* at birth or in prenatal scanning. In the second camp are those who argue that sex is *assigned* at birth and it can subsequently be reassigned, as both a right and a choice, if the person so wishes. Sex, like gender, is considered by transgender activists and their allies to be a linguistic matter, opinion, or perspective. Men who declare themselves as women can simply do so and others *must* respect that decision and self-declaration and, if they do not, then they are bigots. A transwoman is a woman and that is the end of the matter. This sort of gauntlet thrown down by gender ideologues raises the political stakes for all sides.

The realists argue that gender is a social construct but sex definitely is not. For them, a woman is an adult female. A transwoman is a person but not a female person because a woman is an adult female and that is the end of the matter. The idealists argue by contrast that both sex and gender are social constructed and both are a "spectrum". The realists argue that sexual dimorphism characterises humans, as it does other mammals.

During the 1970s, transgender activism, as a **new social movement (NSM)**, attached itself to another that was campaigning for homosexual equality. Although today the notion of "LGBT" is commonplace,[1] from the outset an inner incongruity was obvious. The alliance was held together weakly by the commonality of gender non-conformity. Even in that case, as we know, gay men are not necessarily conspicuously feminine

---

[1] In the UK the LGBT alliance associated with Stonewall has now fragmented, with the formation of the separate LGB Alliance. This was set up by ex-Stonewall leaders angry at the capture of the organisation by trans activists (see https://lgballiance.org.uk). The mission statement of the organisation reflects the position rehearsed at some length in this chapter, in relation to separating sex from gender, separating gender from sexuality, and the attack by gender ideology on women's and children's rights. A reaction from transgender activists, supported consistently by *Pink News*, has been to accuse this new alliance of being linked to neo-Nazis and homophobes (see https://www.pinknews.co.uk/2020/04/03/lgb-alliance-neo-nazi-homophobia-spinster-death-head-charity-co). *Pink News* dismisses gender critical feminists, including those who are lesbians, as the "female militia", reflecting the domination of the newspaper by gay men. In turn this has led gender critical feminists to informally dub it "Prick News". Whatever we make of these spats it is clear that the "T" in "LGBT" has been unambiguously divisive.

or "camp", nor are lesbians always masculine or "butch" in their demeanour and dress. Moreover, an underlying fracture line waiting to create a division was that homosexual people are same-sex attracted but sexual attraction is not the defining feature of being transgender. In the latter case, the central consideration is about experienced identity, *not* sexuality.

This has created secondary controversies, when "trans lesbians" have become offended if natal women refuse their advances. That offence is amplified when the "trans lesbians" involved have chosen to retain a penis. This physical point highlights the challenge of our bodies becoming a battle ground about defining the ontology of sex. Is a "woman with a penis" a woman and do they have a right to expect to have sexual relationships with "cis" lesbians? This controversy has been amplified by the evidence that some MtF transgender people are autogynephiles. This means they experience sexual arousal when viewing themselves as a woman, both in the sex act itself and in the fetishistic value of female attire.

Autogynephilia in adults is one reason why transgenderism has been understood as a clear form of mental abnormality by some health professionals. Another reason is the extensive discussion about the mental health of paediatric presentations (see later). Whether we are considering adults or children, in the case of people who believe that they were "born in the wrong body", is this just an unremarkable variation on healthy human life or is it a delusion or form of readily discreditable wrongheadedness? In most other daily contexts, people claiming something that others consider out of touch with reality or deceitful are deemed to be suffering from a delusion or lying. Thus, transgenderism highlights an anomaly in the routine social psychology of personal credibility. In this case, according to the political demands from transgender ideology, others are *obliged* to agree with statement that may lack credibility according to the evidence of their eyes. If a man looks like a man but demands to be called a woman, then the observer now *must* comply and not "misgender" the person observed. This very new metarule in social interactions being demanded from one version of identity politics is enforced by the informal policing of pronouns. Where noncompliance is identified then this might be raised to the status of hate speech and entail the intervention of the police. At this point injustice has been reduced to offence about language use in daily life.

The moral obligation of people to call a man a woman when, in all honesty, they perceive them to be a man, reflects a new and unusual authoritarian morality. The latter also is the case with the offence created when a lesbian (fairly understandably) is not interested sexually in a "woman with a penis". The latter scenario has generated a whole subcategory of pornography ("sissy porn" involving "chicks with dicks"), which is alluded to by gender-critical feminists as one contemporary source of both female oppression and autogynephilia. In response, transgender ideologues argue that the latter is a myth generated by transphobic researchers and clinicians, pre-empting any discussion of the ontological source of transvestism and its erotic dimension for some MtF individuals.

The credibility of this new moral framework for justice, about language use and sexual expectations, is compromised by the contradictions for transgender ideology. Transgender individuals are a mixture of those who flatly *deny* their psychological abnormality and are asking for no medical interference and those who are *preoccupied* with the process of medicalisation and extensive hormonal and surgical interference, given their acute gender dysphoria and the habitual self-loathing of their natal body. In the wake of medical transition, some transgender individuals accept that they are still not *really* now a member of the opposite sex. However, some are committed to the opposite conclusion. Thus the transgender community is not of one voice and so it is important not to conflate the dogmatic claims and demands of transgender activists with the range of views held by their fellows.

Divisions on the left, not just the right, about transgenderism

Transgender ideology has divided the left conspicuously. Indeed, if out of mischief someone wanted to invent a divisive topic, implicating such a tiny proportion of the general population, then this would fit the bill completely. Of all the topics covered in these chapters, this is the one that exemplifies the main problems from, and for, the left about identity politics. Bad feeling, self-righteous indignation, and an obsession with policing speech are woven throughout identity politics but they seem to be amplified far more loudly in relation to transgender people. This has been for a number of additive and synergistic reasons.

The goals of transgender activism are at odds with second-wave feminism, so two NSMs are at loggerheads. Second-wave feminists are gender abolitionists, aiming for a society in which gender is an irrelevance. By contrast, transgenderism wants individual gender choice to be central. In the dominant version of transsexualism, men become stereotypically feminine women, thus reinforcing, not challenging stereotypes, of femininity and masculinity.

This scenario raises contradictions in transgender rhetoric. Subjectively defined "non-binary" status is celebrated and yet the *objective* binary of sexual dimorphism is derided. Phenotypical stereotypes, and a frivolous preoccupation with outward appearance and dress, are part of transgender presentations. Thereby, ironically, a contemporary normative social binary is actually reinstated and the status quo about traditional gendered presentations is reinforced. Whilst inheritance is rejected as irrelevant in relation to sex (our XX or XY chromosomes), it is sacralised in relation to subjective experience; simply knowing that one has been "born into the wrong body" suffices and it categorically cannot be challenged by others. This knowledge about being "inherently" a member of the opposite sex is taken as a given, even in young children who *ipso facto* are cognitively and emotionally immature. Then there is the matter of gender non-conforming children and social contagion amongst teenagers. In response, the medical sterilisation of healthy children has been provisionally established as a mainstream feature of health policy and health service delivery, even if in recent times this has been hugely controversial.

The commodification of identities under neoliberal market capitalism has permeated so many domains of life in this particular case. Clinical professionals, from cosmetic surgeons and endocrinologists to clinical psychologists and specialist gender counsellors, build their careers around biomedical transition. This healthcare industry generates profits for Big Pharma, which produces cross-sex hormones and puberty blockers. Transgender activists have deliberately and surreptitiously planned to capture the policy formation across a range of organisations from medical colleges to political parties. Since the turn of this century that strategy has been highly successful and has been underpinned by a range of multi-million-dollar funders.

I will say more on these points later but another notable feature of the transgender controversy is that it is not *limited* to divisions on the left but is present across the political spectrum. As a policy phenomenon, transgenderism is reminiscent of eugenics at the end of the nineteenth century, which had its advocates of all political hues. The difference is that the latter broad consensus lasted for several decades in liberal democracies, until it unravelled in the 1930s with Nazi race science. In the case of transgender ideology, it became controversial within a much shorter period following its emergence.

At the time of writing, transgender ideology has by no means lost its authority in public policy but it is under constant attack from gender-critical feminists and scientific realists. The riposte from transgender ideologues and their supporters is that those attacks merely reflect bigotry and transphobia (the likely reaction, for example, to this chapter). However, this counter-attack, being a minimalist mantra, is soon threadbare for two reasons.

First, many liberal and leftist critics of transgender ideology more generally hold tolerant and progressive attitudes to their fellows and are not at all hostile to transgender people as *individuals*. Their explicit objection is to a range of implications of the authoritarian demands from transgender activists. Gender critics argue that their case is not about transphobia (implying fear of, and hostility towards, individuals). Instead, it is about the protection of the rights of children and natal women from the risk of patriarchal control and violence, as well as the reactionary erosion of freedom of expression, along with a contempt for natural science.

Second, gender critics are more than willing to have a clear and open debate with transgender ideologues about their points of disagreement. However, in response to these challenges transgender activists strategically adopt a "no debate" stance. This creates the strong suspicion that a debate would expose faulty logic and the absence of an evidence base for the core claims of transgender activism (more on this later).

With these introductory comments in mind, I will now expand on the themes in the sex/gender disputes noted at the outset.

The ontology of sex: forgotten lessons from high-school biology

A theme in this book is that identity politics has been overly preoccupied with only two planes of our **four planar social being** (relationality and our unique individuality) at the expense of the other two (the natural world we are part of and the socio-economic structures we are thrown into at birth and continue to inhabit). The postmodern turn intellectually justified this limited viewpoint about the totality of our existence in flux between birth and death. Third-wave feminists contributed to Queer Theory and the current push from within identity politics to erase the distinction between sex and gender. This reflects the failure of the recent tradition of philosophical idealism to satisfactorily address immutable biological facts. Indeed, within postmodernism, any claims about the latter reflected a new form of secular sin called "essentialism".

Critical realism, with its primary interest in **ontological realism** and the **intransitive aspect of reality**, by contrast *expects* the world to contain structured essences, which are permanent or evolve extremely slowly (say a rock formation). This was made explicit in Bhaskar's *A Realist Theory of Science*:

> God makes the spectrum, man makes the pigeon holes; so that genera, species, essences, classes and so on are human creations. I can find no possible warrant for such an assumption. Taken literally, it would imply that a chromosome count is irrelevant in determining the sex of an individual, that the class of the living is only conventionally divided from the class of the dead, that the chemical elements reveal a continuous gradation in their properties, that tulips merge into rhododendron bushes and solid objects fade gaseously away into empty spaces. (Bhaskar, 2008: 213)

Note how Bhaskar singles out at the start of his list sexual dimorphism as a basic fact about mammalian existence. Sex is immutable within our chromosomes, determined at fertilisation. A male can no more be turned into a female than lead can be turned into gold. Left without interference, most males will go on to produce sperm and most females to produce ova: sexual dimorphism is a structural precondition of the function of sexual reproduction for a species. It is an essential aspect of us as biological beings bequeathed by evolution.

Where statistical exceptions exist, such as intersex people or infertile men and women, their biological characteristics are *still* genetically fixed. What mutability there is, about these fixed characteristics, entails engineered cosmetic changes to disguise our sexual essence or (potentially) major medical interferences, such as a man having a transplanted womb. Even then the operation, if successful, would lead to a man with a transplanted womb, not a woman. Surgeries, whether they involve transplants, castrations, breast removal, or constructed vaginas or penises do not change our chromosomes, nor alter the fact that we were born male or female.

This same point applies to the use of cross-sex hormones. The latter can artificially generate secondary characteristics not typical of our natal sex. Testosterone given to FtM trans people will increase their aggression, stimulate facial and body hair growth, create new muscle bulk, and trigger male pattern baldness. However, the recipients will still have XX chromosomes and, unless deliberately removed, they will still retain a vagina, cervix, uterus, and ovaries. A transman will never die of prostate cancer and a transwoman will never die of ovarian cancer. Linguistic games in the wake of Queer Theory cannot alter this immutable reality.

The fact that these basic biological facts need to be stated and restated in debates about sex and gender is telling. We need to reflect on why what we learned in high-school biology lessons now is being discarded so readily by highly educated people (including some with medical degrees). The answer to that does not lie in biological science being in error for all this time but in identity politics and the climate of intimidation created in liberal democracies. I return to this later but first it is important to push on with another biological matter: the biomedical manipulations of gender non-conforming children.

Clinical iatrogenesis:[2] the sterilisation of physically healthy children

A specific contention in relation to gender politics has been how adults should respond to gender non-conforming children. Transgender ideologues emphasise that this is a children's rights question and that from a young age any child saying that they are distressed about being born in the wrong body ("gender dysphoria") should be "affirmed" in

---

[2] Iatrogenic impacts refer to the adverse consequences of medical interventions. All of the latter contain such risks to some degree but they may be justified by the health benefits accruing overall. In the case of interventions in this field there is no physical pathology to treat and so the ethical consequences of iatrogenesis are more serious.

their identity (a boy is now "affirmed"[3] as being a girl). Moreover, those children should have access to drugs to block puberty. This begins a pathway to other medical interventions of transition as the child gets older, including cross-sex hormones and surgeries.

The "affirmative approach" to paediatric transition began in The Netherlands in 1987 (de Vries & Cohen-Kettenis, 2012), followed by the UK in 1989 (Di Ceglie, 2018). What started as service innovation, with its effectiveness and risks being uncertain, within a decade became a service norm across many countries. Children referred to these clinics are physiologically healthy boys and girls and so a biomedical rationale (hormones and later surgeries) is offered in order to solve a *psychological* presentation of existential confusion ("gender dysphoria"). The triumph of this unevidenced natural experiment in healthcare is remarkable given its speed of adoption and its anomalous ethical rationale. A child who cannot marry, vote, buy alcohol, have a tattoo, or consent to sexual activity is now simply believed when they claim to be a member of the opposite sex and they are offered the right of access to life-changing biomedical interventions. They will be sterilised and their health will be put in jeopardy. The usual cautions about limited cognitive capacity in medical decision-making are discarded in favour of the child's right to identity affirmation and personal choice (Levine, 2018).

Whilst the "Dutch approach" about blocking puberty was aimed at "offering time to make a balanced decision about gender reassignment" (de Vries & Cohen-Kettenis, 2012), with time it became evident that children and adolescents prescribed puberty blockers invariably go on to cross-sex hormones (de Vries et al., 2011; Biggs, 2019). The latter author poses the question "do puberty blockers press the pause button on the body" or do they press the "fast forward button to cross sex hormones

---

[3] Although the term "affirm" is in common use in a clinical context, there is a deeper implication of "confirm": the person allegedly born in the wrong body is now ontologically confirmed (i.e., to become now who they "really" are). So according to transgender ideology they are not "really" (that is put in speech marks within the norm of postmodernist cynicism) a male or female at birth (that is merely "assigned"). However, they *are really* male or female (no speech marks note) because they believe that to be the case and that belief brooks no argument or critical scrutiny, as would be the case in other social settings, entailing the testing out of our ongoing interpersonal credibility.

and surgery"? (For a longer discussion of the ethics of paediatric transition see Pilgrim and Entwistle (2020).)

Those shielded from the grim and gory reality of "gender reassignment" may be unaware of the extensive destruction and reconstruction of healthy bodies, when surgeries are then added to hormonal interventions. The range of FtM procedures include double mastectomy, hysterectomy, vaginectomy, and phalloplasty. MtF surgeries may include breast implants, orchidectomy, penectomy, and vaginoplasty. All these carry the risks of procedural errors and hospital-acquired infections. The follow-up study of the original Dutch service experiment reported one young patient dying within a year of vaginal necrosis. Even when the procedures are initially completed with no immediate adverse physical effects, the transitioned person has to be committed to a life-long regime of hormones. These interventions are normally given in cases of acute illness (such as the treatment of prostate cancer) or offered to aid the menopause (HRT). Even in those short-term uses the hormones have adverse impacts on patients, so the risk to young people taking them for life are evident.

These physical risks and impacts are not the end of the story of iatrogenesis. Around ten per cent of young patients who have had puberty blockers, cross-sex hormones, and surgeries then regret the process and have to live with that unhappiness or seek a reversal ("detransitioning"). Here is an account from a conference presentation (Manchester, UK, 2019) by one such disaffected FtM patient:

> It doesn't make any sense to me why this is called "transition" or a "sex change" because it's not, it's castration. And now that I am trying to care for my health as much as possible I spend a lot of time on hysterectomy support sites and message boards for women. For women, because only women get hysterectomies and only women deal with the consequences of a hysterectomy. So, excuse me but what the hell are surgeons doing calling this "gender reassignment" or "gender affirming health care"? ("Livia". Detransition: The Elephant in the Room. Make More Noise. Available from: https://08e98b5f-7b7a-40c9-a93b-8195d9b9a854.filesusr.com/ugd/305c8f_34b673d3097c4df88bf9b9e8f6ed1006.pdf?index=true)

Another lobby against paediatric transition has been from within identity politics, not from feminists but gay men, aware that "gender dysphoria" is simply what they experienced during childhood and adolescence, as part of their emerging homosexuality (Everett, 2016). Accordingly, both gay men and lesbians are concerned that children and adolescents are being shepherded into medical transition as a false existential solution. Lesbians who were "tom boys" and gay men who were effeminate as children look back and see this false solution for what it is. They also understand that children can be readily swept along by social contagion, with autistic patients being vulnerable to this type of persuasion. The emergence of social media during the period of the trans health experiment has reinforced such trends. For example, in 2019 there were 27,000 (sic) "GoFundMe" accounts for "top surgery" (https://www.gofundme.com/mvc.php?route=homepage_norma/search&term=top%20surgery). A similar trend can be found in relation to breast binding by females who identify as transgender or non-binary (Sohn, 2019).

Even before the risks of surgery are encountered, hormonal interventions alone put children at risk (Saad, Blackshaw, & Rodger, 2019). Adverse outcomes include: compromised fertility and sexual functioning (Biggs, 2019; Martinerie et al., 2018) and stunting of growth (Catanzano and Butler, 2018). FtM patients are at risk of thickening of the womb lining and so typically hysterectomies are medically (not psychologically) required after two years of taking testosterone.

Many states in the USA allow surgical, not just hormonal, interventions for gender non-conforming children. In December 2020 the use of puberty blockers was interrupted by an English judicial review that noted that poor cognitive capacity, in a context of an experimental (i.e., evidence-free) treatment, meant there should be oversight by the courts of new cases in England. This landmark judgement forced into the open a debate about the ethics of paediatric transition, which previously had been shrouded in a climate of intimidation. (Critics inside and outside of healthcare, prior to the judgement, were dismissed as being transphobic.)

The emotive divisions that have emerged about this topic were epitomised by this Twitter exchange. The first point is from the BBC journalist Deborah Cohen, reporting the findings, and the second is made in response from a trans activist, "Amy the First".

> DC (Apr 2, 2021) Enough's enough. In the last 24 hours ... hannahsbee & I have been called dishonest journalists, unethical, accused of killing children, liars ... All for highlighting the lack of good evidence for an intervention used on kids & reporting on whistleblowing concerns at an NHS service.
>
> Amy the First (Apr 3, 2021) Because you are dishonest, unethical liars who would rather see trans kids dead than get the healthcare they need. There is plenty of evidence for the intervention they get. You're nothing but fucking transphobes.

The claims that gender critics "literally kill" trans people is part of the postmodern norm of identity politics and its reliance on the notion of "epistemic violence", which I return to when discussing race in Chapter Five.

To summarise in this section, the expanding trend of treating gender non-conforming children with hormones, and young adults then with surgeries, is an experiment based upon little or no evidence about effectiveness. Indeed, what evidence there is suggests that these interventions simply put children and young people at risk in both the short and long term. Gender non-conforming children have a totemic status for transgender ideologues. That is why the latter have put so much effort into influencing both healthcare and educational policies, within a general trend of organisational capture (a cue for the next section).

"No debate" dogma and the political economy of organisational capture

Any potential debate that was respectful, in depth, and considered between the warring factions about transgenderism would be difficult but not impossible. However, at the time of writing it is being blocked deliberately by transgender ideologues. The "no debate" position has been adopted quite deliberately and is rationalised by a refusal to pander to the putative prejudices of gender-critical and scientific-realist critics. This pre-empts the outcome and reflects an ontic fallacy or begs the question.[4]

---

[4] The term "begs the question" has come to mean, in the vernacular, to invite a new question (or maybe more). However, traditionally philosophers used the term to point to

That is, transgender ideologues assume in advance that people are born into the wrong body and such an existential state *without question* creates the right to be recognised as such, at all times, by those who are not in that state. Any questioning of that assumption is not permitted and if it is ever expressed then it is automatically deemed to be bigotry, rather than a rationale worthy of a hearing.[5] The confirmatory bias of the ontic fallacy entails transgender ideologues simply asserting an ontological position (some people *are* born into the wrong body), pointing to the evidence for this in the subjective accounts of many transgender individuals (the epistemic justification). This is a self-sealing rationale that permits no discussion.

A problem here is that gender critics and scientific realists break the seal because they simply do not *accept* the ontic fallacy being claimed, nor are they willing to be cast in the role of bigots. This has necessitated transgender ideologues creating a strategy to ward off such attacks, in order to generate a rhetoric that is more than simply name calling or slurs ("TERF" "transphobia", "bigots" etc.). The strategy is enshrined in sources such as the Yogyakarta Principles and advice from the law firm Dentons (see later). This becomes obvious in the ways in which transgender activists conduct themselves publicly, when coming together in groups such as Stonewall and Gendered Intelligence. The broad strategy they adopt is to speak but not debate[6] and to maintain a "low profile" in backroom organisational activity in order to influence or capture policies by stealth. When needed, they call upon the intellectual resources of Queer Theory and third-wave feminism to argue that the debate demanded by gender-critical feminists is an irrelevance and obstructive to the rights of transgender children and adults.

---

unchecked *a priori* assumptions than can lead to biases in logic. This is why the ontic fallacy and confirmatory bias are useful to explore in any contentious area of public policy.
[5] The usual slogan of "transphobia", when faced with any challenge has been displaced sometimes in academic discourse with the term "anti-trans". These mantras are vacuous and their brevity signals the deliberate refusal to countenance that transgender ideology, like any other, might be open to legitimate critical scrutiny.
[6] An example of this is that when trans activists are asked to present their position on radio shows, such as BBC Radio 4's *Woman's Hour*, they do participate but it is on the strict condition that they will not have a live debate with the gender critics also participating. The latter do not make the same stipulation.

Reviewing this picture of "no debate" and its strategic origins as part of transgender ideology Brunskell-Evans (2020) explains the interlocking power of different forms of advice and justification. For example, Stonewall[7] set up a dedicated "Diversity Champions" scheme, to embed trans-inclusive policies in as many organisational settings as possible. Apart from promoting the "assigned at birth" position in its materials, it redefines homosexuality as "same-gender" not "same-sex" attraction. Stonewall also campaigned to remove the single sex exception clause of the *Equality Act 2010*, again signalling a strategic removal of the concept of sex-based policies in favour of gender diversity. This focus on policy capture by Stonewall has not gone unchallenged. For example, Transgender Trend was set up in 2015 to resist the assumptions of trans-inclusivity in educational materials.

The rhetorical justification for the Stonewall policy can be found in the Yogyakarta Principles issued in 2017. This is a human rights document issued by transgender activists that opts to conflate sex and gender, such that sexual orientation and gender identity are treated in the same way. An implication of this is that a sex-based approach to human rights is simply deleted. That same pattern was seen in the difference between a Memorandum of Understanding on conversion therapy[8] in the UK that was issued in 2015. It was revised two years later after transgender activists within its working party (from Pink Therapy and the British Psychological Society) simply added in the notion of gender identity.

---

[7] See first footnote. Stonewall retains a trans-affirmative position but many of its members left in protest to form the UK LGB Alliance, pointing out the misogyny and homophobia that are part of the retained policy.

[8] The term "conversion therapy" was applied originally to efforts on the part of psychological therapists to reorientate gay men into being straight (aversion therapy was typical). The 2015 version of the Memorandum of Understanding limited its consideration to this problematic and largely discredited aspiration. However, two years later trans capture was evident by the altering of the wording of the document, which added "gender identity" to "sexual orientation" in its clauses. This conceptual mixing of apples and oranges meant that transgender ideologues could now accuse therapists who were exploring unique biographical accounts of transgender children of acting unethically. The irony is that it is *biomedical transition* that is a real form of conversion therapy, because it turns healthy bodies into medically manipulated phenotypes, often reflecting social stereotypes of femininity or masculinity and bodily presentation.

These trans-capture initiatives have led Brunskell-Evans (2020) to conclude that the transgender social movement is a *men's* movement because it is dominated by natal males. Other indicators of the operation of patriarchal forces within the movement include: the willingness to use violence and intimidation; the emphasis on transwomen being at the same risk as natal women in society; the demands to have access to women's prisons; the demands for MtF transgender individuals to compete in women's sports; the disparaging use of natal female anatomy to dismiss sex-based rights ("cervix havers" and "menstruators"); and the aggressive expressed entitlements of "trans-lesbians" (i.e., penis-retaining natal males). On the last point, this claimed right from some men to be lesbians is without reference to the common-sense point about desire. Lesbians desire to have sex with women, not men.[9]

When we turn to the top funders of trans-capture the same pattern is evident of male domination. Three key figures have been Jennifer Pritzker, Jon Stryker, and George Soros, who are all billionaires. The first was born James Pritzker and having been married to two women and siring children announced in 2013 that James was now Jennifer Pritzker.[10] Jon Stryker is a gay philanthropist whose charitable contributions include extending the human rights of transgender people. George Soros is probably the best known of these three philanthropists. He has made regular contributions to trans-advocacy organisations in the USA.

Some gender critics such as Jennifer Bilek[11] have reasoned that the trans movement is commercially driven but a caution here is that of economic **reductionism**. With that caution in mind, there is no doubt that two key drivers of the trans movement are, first, its billionaire backers, just noted, and, second, the beneficiaries of the trans healthcare industry. The latter include pharmaceutical and surgical equipment suppliers, as well as the whole trans-care workforce of endocrinologists, surgeons, and psychological assessors and therapists.

---

[9] I am grateful to Beatrix Campbell for pointing out to me the elephant in the room.
[10] For a flow chart of the role of transgenderism in the $29 billion Pritzker family empire see: https://www.the11thhourblog.com/post/follow-the-money-how-the-pritzker-family-makes-a-killing-from-the
[11] See https://uncommongroundmedia.com/stryker-arcus-billionaires-lgbt

Apart from the financial push for transgender policy influence, the movement has had specific strategic advice on how to ensure capture of policy-making processes in organisations and political parties. The key document of relevance here is that produced by the international law firm Dentons in conjunction with the Thomson Reuters Foundation called "Only Adults? Good Practices in Legal Gender Recognition for Youth". The firm provided the document on a pro bono basis, having taken advice from nine LGBT organisations across Europe. The point of the document was to facilitate, encourage, and offer strategic advice in one common legally informed source for gender activists.

The report recommends that children should be allowed to change their legal gender without the involvement of medical professionals or parents. It also notes that the state could be called upon to take "action" against parents who attempt to interfere with this direct request from children. It also advises gender advocacy groups to be secretive during their lobbying. Its conceptual starting point (again begging the question) is taken from the notion supported by Stonewall that we all have an "innate" (sic) gender identity. In the context of UK law, it recommends that the policy aim should be to "eliminate the minimum age requirement" at which children can change their legal gender "on their own volition, without the need for medical diagnoses or court determination". This would remove the requirement for eligibility criteria overseen by healthcare professionals. For example, even the minimal requirement of reported gender dysphoria should be eliminated in law according to Dentons.

The strategy of remaining "under the radar" is spelled out in the document, with trans-advocacy groups being advised to "avoid excessive press coverage and exposure", because the "general public is not well informed about trans issues, and therefore misinterpretation can arise". This is a barely veiled way of suggesting that debate might well expose any new demands to fatal scrutiny by the public. The evasion might reflect the challenge of defending, in-depth and persuasively, a set of assumptions that are based on ideological dogma not science and which invite questions about both misogyny and homophobia. If the trans-affirmative stance about laws and organisational rules is so readily justified morally and scientifically, then why do its advocates have to hide from public scrutiny? Why is the "no debate" stance adopted if there is nothing to hide? In answering these questions, the additional rationalisation that the problem is that the public is ignorant and bigoted would surely be tested out by having a full debate.

The combination of billionaire finance noted earlier plus this strategic advice has proved to be effective, at least on a short-term basis for the transgender movement. This has been made manifest in the viewpoints expressed by mainstream political parties. The point made by Brunskell-Evans (2020) that this reflects a triumph for patriarchy is borne out in the way that this has divided women against one another (see Box 3.1).

Box 3.1 Trans-capture in British politics and the divisions created among women

I noted earlier that trans-affirmative and gender-critical arguments can be found across the political spectrum. This is reflected in the move towards the first position in British political parties and the resistance this has created from within. In the UK this picture became apparent when the potential revision of the *Gender Recognition Act 2004* was being discussed. That legislation from a Conservative government deleted the distinction between sex and gender, allowing people over the age of eighteen to self-identify as a member of the opposite sex and acquire a certificate that records their natal birth in the way they wish. In 2004 this required though that the person must have demonstrated their gender dysphoria to medical experts and to have lived for a period of two years as the opposite sex. By 2015, again a Conservative government created a new committee on women and equalities chaired by Maria Miller. This explored the prospect of further liberalising the GRA, when in 2018 Miller's work on the Select Committee was extended by the new chair Penny Mordaunt. At that time the Conservative prime minister Theresa May spoke publicly about the need to de-medicalise transgender to allow unfettered self-ID. However, a push-back emerged in 2020 under yet another Conservative government, when the new minister for women and equalities, Liz Truss, expressed concern about the impact of the GRA on natal women. This division in Conservative ranks was mirrored in a different way inside the government opposition during the same period. The Labour Party had lost many members who left in protest over its acceptance that MtF members were eligible to be Women's Officers in local branches. Gender-critical feminists remaining in the Party objected to the appointment of (MtF) Lily Madigan in 2017 to a local women's officer post and to be head of Labour Students in 2019. In the wake of the 2020 General Election all three female candidates for the Party leadership supported the revision of the GRA and they signed a petition condemning the gender-critical group Women's Place[*] for being transphobic. During this period, evidence of dissent was less obvious in the small Liberal Democrat Party, which maintained a consistent gender-affirmative position and support for self-ID. What is noticeable about this cross-party picture is that it divided women against women; men rarely were visible in the debates. For example, Keir Starmer, who defeated the three female competitors in the leadership election for the Labour Party in 2020, did not sign the petition condemning Woman's Place. The three defeated candidates (Rebecca Long-Bailey, Lisa Nandy, and Emily Thornbury) did sign the petition. Subsequently, Starmer called for a considered debate about the GRA, without committing himself strongly to any position. Ironically the party which was set up in 2015 to represent women alone (the Women's Equality Party) from the outset welcomed MtF transgender members. When, in 2018, its advisor on violence against women and girls, Heather Brunskell-Evans, raised critical questions about sex and gender, she was removed from her role. This punishment encouraged her to provide a deeper understanding of the emergence of transgender ideology, expressed in *Transgender Politics* (2020) and cited earlier in this chapter, with the main conclusion that the transgender movement is a men's movement.

---

[*] This UK organisation was formed in 2017 in the wake of the *Gender Recognition Act*. It has five broad aims: women have the right to self-organise; the law must work for women; an end to violence against women; "nothing about us without us"; and sex matters.

To summarise this section, a trend within identity politics is that transgender ideologues have self-organised in a preparatory manner to capture the policy-making process. A range of organisations have planned to influence the latter by stealth and by appealing to the idea that transgender people are always oppressed and never oppressive. They promote paediatric transition as a positive boon to children rather than a pathway to lifelong sterility and iatrogenic harm. They promote the idea that access to women's spaces (from prisons to sports events) is a self-evident right for transwomen because they are simply women like all others. They promote the idea that mental health problems in the trans population are generated by the stigma and oppressive acts of others, evading the possibility that a personal preoccupation with "being born in the wrong body" might arise from a wide range of psychological and social processes case by case. Instead of this concession to the complexity and multiple psychological ambiguities of existential confusion, simplistic reductions are imposed on others, who *must* "affirm" identities, which are deemed to be self-evidently "inherent" or "innate".

The routine right of us all to believe or disbelieve those we encounter in life is now overridden by the authoritarian strictures of affirmation. Consequently, "misgendering" becomes a hate crime rather than a perfectly understandable occurrence, when we are socialised to differentiate those around us. We learn, in good faith, the conventions of discerning male from female, old from young, sick from healthy, tall from short, clothed from naked, sitting from standing, etc. This denial of everyday common-sense perception is part of a wider idea promoted that "cis" people are not in a position to understand or judge trans people, because the latter have an inviolable epistemological privilege.

Both the obligation to call a man a woman and to affirm an identity a person asserts about themselves are at odds with common-sense attributions, made in good faith, by ordinary sensible observers. They are at odds with our general way of understanding the beliefs we hold about ourselves and one another. Beliefs are based on logic and **empirical** credibility, both within ourselves and when we communicate with others. We are constantly balancing credulity with scepticism in our inner worlds and in relation to others in a process of **judgemental rationality**. Transgender ideology demands dogmatically that this routine sociopsychological process is simply abandoned.

Conclusion

The problems common in identity politics and discussed in subsequent chapters are present in extreme form in relation to transgender activism. Science is defied or ignored. Debate is denied and freedom of expression held in total contempt if it does not accord with those policing it.

Sterilised children are depicted as a triumph for diversity and a harbinger of social progress. The gains of decades of struggle about sex-based rights are scoffed at and deemed passé. Male sex offenders enjoy their time gratefully in women's prisons. Lesbians are accused of bigotry for not finding the idea of having sex with a "woman with a penis" attractive. A whole industry has been created about "trans healthcare" boosting the profits of the drug companies and ensuring the career pathway for legions of endocrinologists, surgeons, and mental healthcare workers. This highly questionable scenario is defended as being sane and fair by political leaders and those managing public and private organisations. Policy capture in these domains of public life is hiding in plain sight.

CHAPTER FOUR

Antisocial sexual identities

Introduction

If gender non-conformity was the initial point of a precarious affinity between gay men, lesbians, and transgender persons, then this is not the case for those discussed in this chapter. Instead, the common features reflect a claimed victimhood, in the face of social censure or criminalisation. In part, those hostile pressures might reflect the dislike from many in the general population of *all* minority sexualities, for example in relation to homosexuality.

That generic distaste for any challenge to heteronormativity, from socially conservative citizens ("the moral majority"), provides a specific and welcomed opportunity for some dubious minorities to protest about *their* unjust treatment. In practice, they are offered a Trojan Horse for their demands for citizenship and acceptance. For example, paedophiles can say "see how we are persecuted and criminalised, just like gay men have been throughout history". More generally we see the tendency of any criticism of identity politics to be conflated with right-wing bigotry, but this can leave the left floundering in their stance towards the groups discussed in this chapter. This is a function of the wish to celebrate diversity in all its forms, which I now argue is an untenable and unwise desire.

Diversity and individualism: be careful what you wish for?

The sacralisation of diversity and "lived experience", which has been a feature of identity politics, now guides policy formation but it also opens a can of worms. Linking open-ended "diversity" to "equality" in employment and other practices signals benign worthiness. It also implies the moral failure of those people who are ignorant of, or opposed to, all forms of human diversity. Indeed, the reason that equality and diversity training is justified in principle is because it is a form of moral education and re-education. This new version of earnest common sense (*doxa*) is seemingly self-evidently worthy.

Much of the time, diversity training laudably promotes civil rights. However, when it becomes a blanket endorsement of human difference then there is a problem. This is because we are a social species and therefore all human societies have norms. Whilst norms might be variable, across time and place, normativity *of some sort* is ubiquitous. Some sexual minorities indulge in forms of conduct that may well be offensive in *any* society and so they will stress-test the acceptable limits of unending diversity. Obvious ones that come to mind here are incest, bestiality, and necrophilia. In which social context would these be considered tolerable and a victory for human liberation or a contribution to human flourishing?

For those from established, and so traditional, moral communities, generally some form of (Kantian) checklist is offered to remind everyone of what is and what is not acceptable and permissible. Those, such as the Biblical Ten Commandments, lay down rules to follow about being good or bad. Like identity politics, these religious moral codes were and remain primarily concerned with the personal and the interpersonal. This exhortation to goodness can also be found in the Eastern ways, though there, for example in the case of Buddhism and Taoism, God does not feature. Instead, there is an emphasis on offering orientations towards the "right" sort of daily habits and our empathic consideration of others. This is more advice on living the good life rather than a focus on sin.

All this religious guidance about what is permissible and desirable in our lives changed with the postmodern turn. Amongst other things this queried "grand narratives" and so scientific or religious authority now held little or no sway in guiding our lives. But this was not the same as saying that there were no longer moral imperatives. Two began to stand out and the dogma from the past was replaced with another (hence the unending virtue signalling I explored in earlier chapters).

The first postmodern moral stricture was negative refusal: there was now a cynical obligation in relation to *any* given external authority. This resonates with the strong individualism of the anarchist tradition and some forms of existentialism. The second was positive: our constant unbridled choice as an unquestionable right. This is replete with ambiguity because it can be found in post-Marxian existentialism (Sartre's dictum that we are condemned to choose) but it is also in the moral order of the market (**neoliberalism**). Choosing subjects are all choosing consumers, of course provided that they have the money available to spend.

It is not surprising that the philosophical justifications of neoliberalism can be found in the brutal individualism of those like Ayn Rand. Through our free decision-making in the marketplace, we choose to become who we want to be ("because I'm worth it"). This soon can become "I can choose to be anything I want to be" or "I am what I say that I am, and you must simply accept that as an unquestionable fact". I drew attention to this aspect of transgender ideology in Chapter Three. We see here, then, a general vulnerability in all forms of identity politics, where individual assertion for freedom (autonomy) and unchallengeable self-definition might also reflect narcissism and even solipsism ("it's all about me").

Angry misogyny: the incel movement

One sexual identity that defends itself in a state of fulminating individualism is found in the incel movement. This refers to men who cannot find sexual partners and this is declared then as a denial of their human rights. This triggers what they consider to be legitimate anger against women and even other men who do form sexual relationships. This sense of angry entitlement has also been reported at times amongst gay men (see Want To Understand Straight Incels? Talk To This Gay One. | HuffPost UK (huffingtonpost.co.uk). Occasionally in the mainstream mass media a woman "comes out" as an incel (Women can be incels too | Gender | The Guardian, 2018).

The latter correspondent noted ironically in conclusion in her letter that this did not lead to her committing a massacre. This refers to the most striking extreme outcome of the incel movement. In 2014, Elliot Rodger murdered six fellow students at the University of California and then killed himself. In 2003, the massacre of fourteen women in Montreal by Marc Lépine explicitly targeted those thought to be feminists.

Lépine and Rodger now hold a martyr status in the incel community. Incels are in constant online contact to support one another in their justifications of murder, rape, and the angry taunting of female peers. Misogyny then dominates the mind-set of these angry young men, though a wider misanthropy is also evident. Their actions are not merely anti-social in any context, they are also self-defeating and at times suicidal.

One of the many contradictions, within the variegated world of identity politics, relates to the matter of biological **reductionism.** Unlike Queer Theory, which simply deletes biological ontology as being relevant (self-identity is everything), this is the opposite with incels. They, like all other social movements, seek out, and so will find, an explanatory account for their rights, or to account for their existential state. In this case they appeal to evolutionary psychology to explain the latter and this has something in common with some radical feminist accounts of the strong driver of testosterone.

One appeal incels make is to the notion of "strategic pluralism",[1] which assumes that women are the strategic gatekeepers of sexual activity. They then tend to look for "bad boys" to impregnate them (for their strong genes) and "good boys" to settle down with to share child rearing.[2] The other consideration, within this biological account from incels, is the differential impact of testosterone levels, which explains why mammalian males are determined to impregnate females, if needs be forcefully.

We see this behaviour in both mammals and birds. In humans we call it "rape" and generally it is a matter of condemnation, shame, and criminalisation. In consensual sexual intercourse, a lawful residue of this sexual physiology is that a man has to utilise a *degree* of aggression to ensure intromission, ejaculation, and potential impregnation. For this

---

[1] https://incels.wiki/w/Strategic_pluralism
[2] The long-term dominance of "good boys" can be found in apes. For example, male gorillas that are nurturant and protective towards their young are more successful in their group hierarchies.

reason, all occurrences of sexual intercourse are violent acts of sorts. Any man, straight or gay, will testify to this biological compulsion to penetrate,[3] a point that has woven in and out of feminist critiques of patriarchal domination.

Incels argue that men *have to* be more sexually appetitive than women, as the latter statistically have a greater reproductive success[4] in their fertile years than do men. This then displaces the patriarchy thesis from feminism with an alternative: men *have to* impregnate more for reproductive success, and this drives their sexual demands. By contrast, women more often have the passive contentment of being sexual gatekeepers (see previous point). This also affords their upward social mobility ("marrying up" or "hypergamy").[5] This logic then renders heterosexual men as the victims of the arbitrary or manipulative power of women. This cultural trope was epitomised in the 1934 film *Tarzan and His Mate*, when Jane, played by Maureen O'Sullivan, advises us that, "the best weapon a woman has is a man's imagination".

Thus, incels challenge the feminist characterisation of patriarchy by these explanatory accounts, when justifying the legitimacy of their identity claims and sense of entitlement. Aggression against women is seen then as a "natural" outcome of our evolutionary history as a species: "A man's gotta do what he's gotta do." Variants of this display of male "responsibility" were commonplace in US culture in the twentieth century, attributed at different times to macho roles from John Wayne, John Steinbeck, or Charlton Heston. The incels of today are honouring this cultural trope, and their bullish patriarchal display readily legitimises criminal violence, a cue for the next section.

On the borderline of social acceptability: BDSM

If incels have a sense of (frustrated) entitlement, which to them then warrants spitefulness and might culminate in sexual and non-sexual violence, this pattern also resonates, in "the BDSM community". Differentiating itself from incels, the predominant message in this

---

[3] An in-joke amongst some young men is that having a penis is like being chained to a lunatic.
[4] https://incels.wiki/w/Reproductive_success
[5] https://incels.wiki/w/Hypergamy

"kink" group, which contains both straight and gay people, is about consensual violence.

The celebration of the free mixture of sexual enjoyment, power play between people, and the giving and receiving of pain, as with the incels, has been elevated into a human right. Despite the focus on consensual acts in the rhetoric of BDSM, its practice hovers constantly at the borderline of actual violence. Indeed, that edginess is part of the fun for this group. Being transgressive is the main *point* of the exercise and so the prospect of "going too far" is always tantalisingly near. An example of this, which became a cause célèbre for sexual libertarians, was the "Spanner Case" (see Box 4.1).

Box 4.1 Operation Spanner: nailing foreskins to wood

Operation Spanner was the name of an investigation by the Greater Manchester Police during the 1980s. Sixteen gay men were prosecuted successfully for causing actual bodily harm and unlawful injury to one another, even though it was accepted that the violence was agreed voluntarily by all participants. In 1990, they were found guilty at trial and a subsequent House of Lords judgement ruled that consent was not a valid defence against interpersonal violence. This case stimulated the formation of opposition movements from sadomasochists from within the gay community (Countdown on Spanner and The Sexual Freedom Coalition).

Many participants were identified in the investigation about the BDSM culture, so the sixteen men prosecuted were a sample. That network of sadomasochists extended nationally (sixteen police forces were involved). At the centre of the police investigation was a tape of their activities, acquired in 1987, which included a record of whipping and burning with hot wax. The most gruesome scene was of a pierced foreskin being nailed to a block of wood and then the penis was cut repeatedly with a scalpel. This and other tapes permitted the identification of the individuals prosecuted. Whilst the defendants might have gained sexual arousal from what was presented in evidence, for those not so inclined it produced disgust and incredulity.

The arguments about the role of consent in sexual violence, such as that depicted in Box 4.1, rumble on today. They become particularly contentious in rape prosecutions, when the defendant asserts that there was consent on the part of the complainant.

In other cases, the antisocial character of sexual violence is less ambiguous. The expression of that human right to forms of violent practice can lead to murder, as indicated in Box 4.2. The focus on consensual practices in BDSM (including "safe" words when the "slave" wishes to stop) at first sight preserves the social acceptability of this sexual orientation. However, the scenarios described in Boxes 4.1 and 4.2 invite **judgemental rationality** in contrast to judgemental relativism. The latter is at the centre of both identity politics and the norms of diversity training today, as well as poststructuralist celebrations of BDSM as a form of practice that resists social conformity (Holmes, Murray, Knack, Mercier, & Federoff, 2017). Some feminists, such as Andrea Dworkin and Audre Lorde, were critical of the normalisation of sadomasochism in gay culture. For example, here from Lorde (1988) we find:

> Sadomasochism is an institutionalized celebration of dominant/subordinate relationships. And, it prepares us either to accept subordination or to enforce dominance. Even in play, to affirm that the exertion of power over powerlessness is erotic, is empowering, is to set the emotional and social stage for the continuation of that relationship, politically, socially, and economically. Sadomasochism feeds the belief that domination is inevitable and legitimately enjoyable.

There is a clear incompatibility at times then between feminists about whether eroticised power play is to be celebrated as emancipatory or is to be condemned for its wider implications for the oppression of women (Keith, 2016). Although Lorde is included as a contributor to the third-wave feminism of the 1980s, her views on this particular topic are at odds with those such as Butler, Rubin, and Califia, noted later.

Apart from murder and injury waiting in the wings, when those involved with the conformity-resistive enjoyment of BDSM transgress their *own* rhetorical norms, the particular personalities of those involved bear examination in their **concrete singularity**. That is, it may well be *logically possible* that sexual sadists more generally in their lives are kindly, compassionate, and protective of the autonomy of others. However, it is *psychologically probable* that this is not the case.

This matter of our private sexual lives reflecting our particular personality structure is explored well in *The Anatomy of Human Destructiveness* (Fromm, 1973) and *Escape from Freedom* (Fromm, 1941). The case study offered in Box 4.2 resonates with Fromm's exploration of the psycho-biographies of De Sade, Hitler, and Stalin. This reminds us of the need to reflect on "the personal" and its constitution at times of desires that are then rationalised, or even celebrated, as liberating ideologies by politicians and intellectuals; a point I return to in the final chapter.

Box 4.2 The murder of Elaine O'Hara by Graham Dwyer

The remains of Elaine O'Hara were discovered on Killakee mountain near Dublin in 2013. Her killer, Graham Dwyer (a respectable architect with no criminal record), had been involved in a sadomasochistic relationship with his victim; O'Hara had a psychiatric history and had been bullied at school, which was relevant to her vulnerability and her fatal exploitation by Dwyer. Given her mental health problems, on first discovering her body it might have been assumed she had committed suicide. However, soon other nearby evidence came to light of bags of leg restraints, handcuffs, and a ball-gag (i.e., the paraphernalia of the BDSM subculture).

Murderer and victim met up via a BDSM website and embarked on their spiral of sexual violence in 2008. Laptop evidence gathered by the police found homemade images of the couple involved in routine acts of sexual domination and violence. Texts exchanged between the "master" and "slave" indicated that Dwyer routinely fantasised about stabbing women during sex. This was ratified subsequently at the trial by a previous partner who had borne him a son.

After a break in the relationship, it was resumed in 2011 with its fatal outcome, just after O'Hara had been discharged from care after a recent psychiatric episode. It came to light in his trial that Dwyer knowingly exploited that particular context of personal vulnerability, in order to plan and commit his sadistic murder. He never confessed to the crime and he denied ever knowing his victim, when first interviewed. After being obliged by the evidence to confess to the existence of the relationship, he then argued that its kinks* were always consensual and he had nothing to do with her death.

The case raises a fundamental question about the possibility of separating sadistic interests, enacted in allegedly consensual intimate contexts, from the likelihood that sexual sadists are prone to a wider antisocial orientation to others. Dwyer brazened out the charges and showed no guilt or remorse for his actions.

---

* The notion of "kink" now has many connotations. Although mainly associated with BDSM, it might also refer to people dressing up as animals ("furries"), which may or may not have a sexual element or antisocial dimension. This same ambiguity applies to the sexual element in cannibalism as an extreme eventuality of sadomasochism. When this occurs, it tends to be reported by the police as murder with a sexual element.

The sexual crime summarised in Table 4.2 may be less well known in popular culture than the *Fifty Shades of Grey* film trilogy.[6] This began in the same year, 2015, when Dwyer was handed down a life sentence in the Dublin court. By the turn of this century, BDSM had become a respectable expression of diverse sexual identities and it had its high-profile academic champions. One of these was the third-wave feminist and Queer Theorist Gayle Rubin. Her essay "Thinking Sex: Notes for Radical Theory of the Politics of Sexuality" (Rubin, 1992) included a positive endorsement of the demands of NAMBLA (North American Man/Boy Love Association). Rubin argued that:

> for over a century, no tactic for stirring up erotic hysteria has been as reliable as the appeal to protect children. The current wave of erotic terror has reached deepest into those areas bordered in some way, if only symbolically, by the sexuality of the young. ... The laws produced by the child porn panic are ill-conceived and misdirected. They represent far-reaching alterations in the regulation of sexual behaviour and abrogate important sexual civil liberties. (1992: 268)

---

[6] In the popular hacking thriller *Mr Robot*, there is a sadomasochistic subplot. The heterosexual woman in focus is depicted as a murderous narcissist, rather than merely a passive and submissive object of male desire. Thus, in popular culture, BDSM retains an ambiguous fascination for now.

The ultra-libertarianism in some feminist and LGBT groups about sexual contact with children did not disappear with Rubin's writings. For example, the International Lesbian Gay Bisexual, Trans and Intersex Association (ILGA) today still calls for the lowering of sexual consent to ten years of age. The ILGA website notes that it is:

> a worldwide federation of more than 1,600 organisations from over 150 countries and territories campaigning for lesbian, gay, bisexual, trans and intersex human rights. We want a world where the human rights of all are respected and where everyone can live in equality and freedom: a world where global justice and equity are assured and established regardless of people's sexual orientations, gender identities, gender expressions and sex characteristics (SOGIESC).

This motherhood-and-apple-pie imagined future offers a simplistic assumption. This is that an open-ended amalgam demand about equality and diversity is possible. However, universalism is incompatible with the diverse demands and internal contradictions of identity politics. This is why eliding "equality and diversity" naively comforts social progressives, but it also mystifies them. The paedophile's freedom is not compatible with a child's right to be left unmolested. The transwoman's right to enter women's spaces offends second-wave feminists.

Thus, the ILGA statement unwittingly highlights the ideological tensions that exist *between* versions of feminist politics, as well as *within* groups divided about the politics of gender non-conformity. (See the split-off of the LGB Alliance from Stonewall in the UK discussed in Chapter Three.) "Paedosexuality", being part of the + of the unendingly elastic LGBT+ concept, can be a matter of pride or disgust, depending on which group one listens to in the febrile self-righteous world of identity politics.

I return to NAMBLA and other pro-paedophile groups later but here Rubin's chirpy celebration of BDSM practices is the focus. She was not merely a run-of-the-mill practitioner of these but a self-righteous warrior for sexual liberation. For her, BDSM was, like all forms of transgression, a blow for social progress and human freedom. This was the period when postmodern Queer Theory was flexing its muscles and enjoying the exercise. Along with Judith Butler, Rubin is often credited with being its academic innovator.

The stand-off within feminism in the 1980s between anti-pornography campaigners like Dworkin and sexual libertarians like Rubin was to define the "sex-wars" in its fractious ranks. Some sex-positivist feminists, such as Nina Hartley, even enjoyed lucrative careers in the porn industry. More recently lauded feminists, such as Roxane Gay (2020), in the celebratory "kink" fiction tradition, have fantasised about a man slapping, strangling, and scarring his wife with a razor. The perpetrator in Gay's story turns out to be a transman, just to enlarge the sexy domain of "kink", now legitimised in the wake of the mutually reinforcing strands of Queer Theory, postmodernism and neoliberalism.

Thus, feminist thought has certainly come a long way since the 1970s. A subplot in this drama within feminism reflects a conundrum for identity politics. Is porn simply another expression of patriarchy or are sexually free participants in the trade striking a blow for women's liberation? And is that liberation reduced now to unending choice for women, rather than their collective release from patriarchy? These questions became more complicated when we consider BDSM. Is the latter more than likely to be oppressive in straight relationships (with women the victims) but is it clearly a celebration of sexual freedom, when the participants are lesbians (who *ipso facto* are all women)? Alternatively, are some lesbians internalising patriarchal oppression in their cruel and domineering practices?

These questions are made more pertinent when we put them in the context of the **empirical** evidence on intimate violence. The rates of the latter are approximately the same in heterosexual and homosexual couples (of both sexes), with some estimates placing non-straight people as *more* at risk of assault (see https://williamsinstitute.law.ucla.edu/publications/ipv-sex-abuse-lgbt-people). Even with some methodological caveats about sampling to note, there is simply no evidence that intimate violence is *singularly* about male-on-female attacks.

The data is clear: lesbians can and do assault one another, as do gay men. Also, in straight couples, women assault men at nearly the same rate as vice versa, prompting discussions about feminist interpretations (Straus, 2011; cf. Johnson, 2011). (The consequences of serious harm or death tend to be less for male victims because of physical strength differences between the sexes.) All of this complexity is at odds with a superficial and misleading popular discourse that women are the sole victims of male violence, thereby excluding other permutations of victimhood.

Thus, hard power seems to find its expression in a proportion of *all* human intimacy. The use of corporal punishment of children in families is another example of this point. It would seem that the capacity for intimate violence might be dominated by patriarchal power but that cannot be the whole explanation. To understand that complexity, we need to look at other **generative mechanisms** in the personalities of victims and victimisers. Bullies (male or female) are bullies for a reason and victimised children often find themselves re-victimised later in life. Some may flip at times between being victimisers and being victims.

Rubin and her sympathetic colleagues within third-wave feminism provided their definitive answers to these questions about sex, power, and domination: it was all about liberation and fighting the social forces of sexual repression. Along with her partner Pat Califia, Rubin founded the lesbian BDSM society Samois in 1978. By the 1990s, Rubin was a celebrity in gay BDSM culture. She was asked to judge the annual gay men's leather competition organised by the BDSM magazine *Drummer*. In 1992 she became a director in the Leather and Archives Museum in Chicago.

Rubin's partner Califia worked as a columnist for *Drummer*. She became Patrick Califia in 2000 after embarking on biomedical transitioning. Fluidity and transgression then were personified in the lives of Rubin and Califia, including their ongoing celebration of the personally liberating powers of BDSM practices. The presumption of the norm of being consensual in BDSM culture became much more problematic to claim by advocates of paedophilia, endorsed in the earlier note by Rubin. That endorsement suggests that sexual liberation at all costs is far more important than a serious consideration of the exploitation of human vulnerability.

"Minor Attracted Persons" (MAPS): the paedosexual identity

Sexual activity involving children is not limited to men (and the occasional woman) whose primary sexual preoccupation is one of paedophilia. The latter term in the vernacular is used to refer to contact with those under the age of consent but in sexology it refers to prepubescent children. An attraction to older children is called "hebephilia", though this term is little known and so rarely used. Both of these are sexual *orientations*.[7] When they are enacted, they then constitute child abuse, and in most jurisdictions, also criminality.

The ambiguity about antisocial features of child sexual abusers is part of the picture to understand. On the one hand, paedophile advocate groups emphasise the presence of unremarkable citizenship in their ranks and this in one sense is fair comment. Those molesting children and consuming online images (including in vivo abuse which might be interactive in its form) come from every stratum of society. On the other hand, the psycho-social profile of serial child sex offenders is characterised specifically in two ways. First, they are likely to seek out roles that give them access to children. Second, serial offenders are more likely to have a general history of interpersonal violence. These features reveal that they are egocentric planful characters with antisocial tendencies. Arguably then, they are both normal and abnormal in their psychological functioning.

Child sexual abuse (CSA) is not limited to adults with a primary sexual interest in children. About a third of this occurs between children themselves and some adults committing sexual crimes against children do so opportunistically and episodically. That ambiguity is complicated by the scenario of male sex offenders who form relationships with women in order to gain access to child victims. Some women become confederates of child sexual offenders or offend alone but it is estimated that over ninety per cent of these crimes are at the hands of men. Elsewhere I have offered a book-length critical realist critique of the fashion within social constructivist social science to dismiss child sexual abuse as a moral panic (Pilgrim, 2018a). Here I summarise those arguments.

During the 1970s, prior to the feminist "sex wars" noted earlier, a range of libertarian intellectuals defended sexual contact with minors. For example, in France, this list included Michel Foucault, Jean-Paul Sartre, Simone de Beauvoir, Roland Barthes, and Louis Althusser. They (unsuccessfully) lobbied their government to remove the age of consent

---

[7] This point causes offence in some quarters. However, I think that they *are* orientations and to describe them as such is not to endorse them in practice. What matters is whether they are enacted. When that occurs then children are violated.

for "non-violent" sexual acts. The presence of de Beauvoir on the list has proved an embarrassment for feminists at times, when they hear of her involvement, not just in this campaign but also with Sartre in sexually grooming young female students. (Sartre enjoyed deflowering virgins and de Beauvoir was bisexual.) In 1943 she lost her licence to teach in France after an investigation of her relationship with a seventeen-year-old pupil: a case of "hebephilia". Her license was eventually reinstated.

During the 1970s in the Western world several pro-paedophile groups emerged, including the North American Man Boy Lover Association (NAMBLA) and, in the UK, the Paedophile Information Exchange (PIE). Their argument was that "intergenerational sex" was a positive experience or, at worst, harmless for children and that any aversion to it was simply a "moral panic". They claimed that any distress experienced by children was an artefact of police investigations and the disruption of their loving attachment to the adults involved.

In the UK, arguments justifying paedophilia as a positive identity did not peter out after PIE tried and failed to convince politicians to lower the age of sexual consent. For example, Yuill (2004), in his PhD study of the contemporary identity movement, contrasted what he describes as the "hegemonic CSA discourse" (i.e., the mainstream view shared by most people at present about child protection) with another one. This was an organised resistance from paedophile activists and their academic allies. Yuill draws on Queer Theory and poststructuralism as a framework for his analysis.

Yuill argues that the pro-paedophile social movement reasonably disagrees with the common assumptions of most people today that adult–child sexual contact is wrong and harmful. The latter views, the argument goes, have been maintained by a moral panic logic. Yuill goes on to propose that there are legitimate arguments from pro-paedophile group, including the rights of children to join "boylover identity groups", in order to discover the "positive and beneficial aspects" of relationships with men. This position is in line with that offered by Rubin and ILGA discussed earlier.

Prior to the postmodern turn, the book *Perspectives on Paedophilia* (Taylor, 1981) was edited by a PIE member. It contained contributions from three other members who were established academic researchers (Ken Plummer, Peter Righton, and Morris Fraser). Their PIE membership was not declared in the book nor confessed later, but it was discovered by others (including this author). Righton and Fraser were later to be convicted for their offences against children or for the possession of indecent images.

Plummer has no similar criminal record, but he continued during the 1980s to publish defences of sex with minors, pointing out that paedophiles were a persecuted sexual minority. For example, Plummer (1981) suggested that, "by applying sociology to the field of paedophilia we may partially relativise it, humanise it, normalise it, and politicise it." In later years Plummer self-censored his pre-1990 publications about the topic on his own website. He did not apologise for his membership of PIE (he was its insider ethnographer) but he did say that his research was not intended to harm anyone.

Whilst Taylor, Righton, and Fraser were conniving liars, when not declaring their involvement with PIE, this was not the case with Tom O'Carroll. Both in the 1970s, and still today, he has ditched the hypocrisy of those allies and made quite explicit the moral and political case for paedophilia. Despite repeated convictions for sexual offences against boys, he retains his position as articulated in his book *Paedophilia: The Radical Case* (O'Carroll, 1980). Being "out" as an activist is rare though; most keep under the radar and make occasional attempts to capture the policy apparatus, using civil libertarian arguments about their persecuted identity status.

The sociologist and sexologist Jeffrey Weeks in his book *Sexualities and Their Discontents* (Weeks, 1985) relayed the arguments of the PIE group within Taylor's edited collection. By now the position of Weeks was reflecting the postmodern turn and the **emergence** of identity politics, with its emphasis on comprehensive diversity of sexual expression. The extent to which those variations warranted social acceptance and citizenship was now being reflected in the academic writings of lesbians, who were "into BDSM", like Rubin noted earlier, and now from gay academics such as Weeks.

Weeks, though, began as well to introduce some cautions to unending transgression in sexual life. First, he noted the feminist concern with patriarchal power over women and children, as most pro-paedophile groups are male-dominated. Second (and an elephant in the room) was that the mental capacity of an average child is less than that of an average adult. That routine discrepancy of cognitive competence undermines our confidence that adult–child sexual contact could be between equal participants. As a discursive tactic, pro-paedophile groups use the term "participant" rather than "victim". This rhetorical convenience preempts any moral attribution of wrongfulness.

The importance of moral panic theory in paedosexual rhetoric

For those supporting free love for "minor attracted persons" (MAPS), the assumption of a moral panic is absolutely central. Thus, it is important to check whether that assumption is valid in relation to the topic. The issue here is not whether moral panic theory in its entirety is useful in social science but whether it specifically explains public concerns about adult–child sexual contact. Here I use an **immanent critique** for this purpose. I will define a moral panic, list its expected features, and then discern whether child sexual abuse complies with those expectations and, if so, to what degree.

Moral panic theory began in the early days of the symbolic interactionist wing of the Chicago School of sociology and so is linked not to postmodern forms of radical social constructivism but a less nihilistic version. In symbolic interactionism the traditional grand narratives of sociology were not rejected, and social causation was accepted as an important aspect of power in any society. For example, what was called "primary deviance" (say criminality or mental disorder) might have a range of traceable objective causes. Accordingly, deviant acts were not *simply* a product of the agency or choice of knowing transgressive individuals but might be shaped by a wide range of supra-personal forces that are beyond the insight of the actors involved.

Within that Chicago School tradition, Waller (1936) had noted that social problems began with real-enough features but those were *amplified* by emotional public reactions. These were capitalised on by politicians and others who became "moral crusaders" and "moral entrepreneurs". This amplification then maintained secondary forms of deviance in a society.

After the Second World War, Stanley Cohen popularised moral panic theory, after studying the youthful violent spats between "Mods and Rockers" in broad daylight in the seaside towns of southern England in the 1960s (Cohen, 1972). In that first edition of his classic text *Folk Devils and Moral Panics*, Cohen defined a moral panic in this way:

> A condition, episode, person or group of persons emerges to become defined as a threat to societal values and interests; its nature is presented in a stylized and stereotypical fashion by the mass media; the moral barricades are manned by editors, bishops, politicians and other right-thinking people; socially accredited experts pronounce their diagnoses and solutions; ways of coping are evolved or (more often) resorted to; the condition then disappears, submerges or deteriorates and becomes more visible. (Cohen, 1972: 1)

This definition was elaborated later by Goode and Ben-Yehuda (1998) to include the following expected characteristics:

1. Concern—it is assumed that a moral panic is harmful to people and society more generally.
2. Hostility—a condemnation of a transgressive social group creates an "othering" process, whereby some groups are designated as "folk devils" to use Cohen's term.
3. Consensus—there is a widespread agreement that transgressive acts and their agents do pose a real threat to contemporary social mores. That position is developed and maintained by moral entrepreneurs and crusaders and a professionalisation of expertise to respond to that particular threat. The transgressive minority group, in comparison, is voiceless and powerless.
4. Disproportionality—the public and political reaction to the putative threat is disproportionate and thus unwarranted.
5. Volatility—moral panics are ephemeral not permanent concerns.

If we combine the definition from Cohen and the features expected from the conceptual summary from Goode and Ben-Yehudi and apply them to adult-child sexual contact then we can note the following in reverse order:

CSA is not a volatile concern but has been dealt with by policymakers in a sustained and even enlarging way within countries and globally.

UNICEF has pointed out that the largest threat to children from sexual exploitation is the patriarchal norm of child brides in developing countries (UNICEF, 2015). This picture is also the case in some states in the USA. Developed countries offer long-term strategies for dealing with CSA (e.g., Council of Europe, 2007). The "hegemonic" CSA discourse then is not at all ephemeral and so this criterion of a moral panic is not fulfilled.

The public response to CSA is not disproportionate. CSA is an underreported crime, with some estimates suggesting a nine-fold underestimation of incidence (Children's Commissioner Report for England, 2016). Under a third of cases are reported to the police (Finkelhor, Hammer, & Sedlak, 2008; Radford et al., 2011). Of the latter, only a proportion are successfully prosecuted and so cases recorded empirically are less than the *actual* cases. The internet has been a game-changer. Online offending has outstripped public awareness of its scale and the difficulty the police have in dealing with this trend. Even some moral panic claim-makers themselves have expressed curiosity that online sexual offending has *not* become a moral panic (Jenkins, 2004). Again, this criterion of a moral panic is not fulfilled.

Pro-paedophile groups and policy libertarians are not at all voiceless or powerless. They are not a priori low status "candidates" for being "folk devils", as is the case with other moral panics (for example, about deviant groups in poverty). The only predictor for that candidature is being male; the other usual predictors, such as low social class or young age, are missing. We find perpetrators in *all* social groups. Those abusing children might be ordinary parents or respectable non-family members, such as teachers, priests, sports coaches, health and social care professionals, and even celebrities. These are around us all "in plain sight". Moreover, conservative elite groups have often sought to *suppress* moral panics, not "whip them up". Respectable organisations such as the BBC have been found lacking, when dealing with CSA. In their midst was Jimmy Savile, the most prolific sexual predator recorded in British criminal history. Thus, this criterion of a moral panic is not fulfilled.

There is certainly hostility about CSA but it is by no means clear *which folk devils are being identified* for public vilification. Sometimes the mass media have targeted "stranger danger" and blithely ignored the more mundane and prevalent threat to children in ordinary family and neighbourhood settings. At other times the mass media have also attacked child protection workers, such as paediatricians and social workers. Sometimes they have offered us serious and illuminating investigative journalism. Indeed, this ambivalence of the mass media about child sexual abuse was noted by Cohen in the final edition of his book in 2002. Again, this criterion of a moral panic is not fulfilled.

There is overwhelming evidence that CSA is harmful. The evidence for this was conceded eventually by Cohen and he then he turned his attention away from moral panic and towards what he called but "moral stupor", "chilling denial", and the "passive bystander effect" (Cohen, 2001, 2002; Jay, 2014). The evidence about harm is now unequivocal. Victims are exposed to immediate physical risk (anal bleeding and sexually transmitted diseases in boys and girls, and unwanted pregnancies and vesicovaginal fistulas in girls). In the long term, mental health impacts are clear. Survivors are over-represented in all diagnostic groups, including psychosis, posttraumatic stress disorder, and borderline personality disorder (Cutajar et al, 2010; Read 2003; Ogata et al., 1990). The health economic costs to the State of investigating CSA and dealing with its consequences for perpetrators and victims are measurable and considerable (Saied-Tessier, 2014). This criterion of a moral panic is not fulfilled.

Thus, apart from the first criterion of a strong emotional reaction in the general public to adult–child sexual contact, none of the other "boxes are ticked" about paedophilia reflecting a moral panic. This being the case, we might then ask how such an assumption has been maintained (moving from an **immanent critique** to an **explanatory critique**). I think three factors need to be considered that have become interwoven to sustain the moral panic claims and permitted paedophile advocacy groups to retain their putative status as an oppressed sexual minority.

First, which I noted at the start of this chapter, those groups emerged in a political context of NSMs, which included those of other sexual minorities. The new expectations within identity politics expanded citizenship for sexual minorities and this created a Trojan Horse for pro-paedophile advocates. The latter were mainly a splinter of Gay Liberationists in the 1970s, who were then joined by men sexually interested in girls and the odd lesbian. That emergence was met with ambivalence from within gay politics at the time, with some defending paedophiles and others wishing to reject them indignantly.

Second, some academics aimed to defend a moral panic position because they were themselves paedophiles or celebrated "man-boy love" in print. This was the case for those adopting leadership roles. They could use their academic confidence to create a credible policy position. Leaders in PIE appeared on national television to put their case and influenced organisations like the National Council for Civil Liberties to defend their cause. Academic status then became a political lever.

For example, the academic social worker Peter Righton was an advisor to the National Children's Bureau, worked for the Institute of Social Work, and wrote extensively on child protection. He was prosecuted in 1992 for the possession of indecent images of boys (with no custodial sentence). Another example was the child psychiatrist Morris Fraser, who published articles on disturbed children during the political "troubles" in Northern Ireland in the 1970s. Subsequently he was convicted in both the USA and the UK of sexual offences against children.

The editor of *Perspectives on Paedophilia*, Brian Taylor, was a senior lecturer in sociology at the University of Sussex and under the pseudonym "Humphrey Barton" was the "research officer" for PIE. Now deceased, he had no recorded offences against him but he offered a defence of man-boy love in the *Sociological Review* (Taylor, 1976). Note, for emphasis, that PIE membership for many of the contributors to Taylor's edited collection was not reported in the book. This reflected the underhand tactic of capturing the policy-formation process.

The third factor that might explain the growth and maintenance of a moral panic position, especially *after* the 1980s, was the postmodern or linguistic "turn" in social science: strong social constructivism became the norm. This meant that a range of confident certainties held by normal social research were problematised. Realist arguments by traditional quantitative researchers were brought into question. Radical social constructivism meant that earlier versions from symbolic interactionism (the source of moral panic theory) could be boosted in confidence now by postmodern social science. Suddenly arguments about the seemingly *obvious reality* of child sexual abuse became suspect and open to scorn by academics.

The moral panic logic about paedophilia remains today in some parts of academic social work (Clapton, Cree, & Smith, 2012). Some sociologists also reassert the moral panic position on CSA (e.g., Furedi, 2015).

The latter author, in his chapter "The moral crusade against paedophilia", recalling the conclusion of Plummer, asserts that paedophiles represent a "permanent focus of moral outrage". He goes on to say that "according to the cultural script of virtually every Western society child abusers are ubiquitous" and the moral panic about paedophilia is "symptomatic of a world view that risks losing the capacity to understand the distinction between fantasy and reality". That rhetorical flourish at the end implies evidence would be revealed to defend the claim. He does not offer evidential grounds to claim that those concerned with child sexual abuse cannot distinguish fantasy from reality.

The assertion of a "moral panic" to wish away any reasonable objection is reminiscent of the claims of transgender activists that any request to examine reason and argument are automatically transphobic. That comparison has been made by journalists like Owen Jones that fears about transgender ideology are an unfounded moral panic in the tradition of the historical persecution of all sexual minorities (Anti-trans zealots, know this: history will judge you | Transgender | The Guardian).

This logic can also be found in some quarters of my own profession of clinical psychology. For example, Quayle (2016) argues that a concern about online offending is a "misdirected moral panic", though the author concedes that this is a diversion from directing our more needed attention to in vivo offending. She, like Furedi and Jones, resorts to the language of moral panics for rhetorical purposes.

All these writers avoid judgemental rationality, preferring instead unfounded rhetoric. In particular (and this weakness is common from moral panic claim-makers) they confuse a moral *concern* with a moral panic. Concerns that children are being abused and harmed, physically and psychologically by paedophiles, might be simply *warranted*. Indeed, this was why Stanley Cohen later became less interested in moral panics and more interested in wilful moral blindness about child abuse, when he referred to "chilling denial", "moral stupor", and the "passive bystander effect" (Cohen, 2001).

In the final edition of his book, Cohen revisited a defence of Enlightenment values and regretted his earlier (philosophical) idealism in response to positivism in social science. His reawakening about the project of the Enlightenment, with its confidence in reason and evidence, came when his own research on torture in Israel was dismissed by the authorities there. Suddenly, rhetorical dismissals had been turned against *him* and this was a salutary experience, as he admitted to his old friend Laurie Taylor (Taylor, 2007).

Conclusion

Examining antisocial sexual identities alerts us to a central problem with identity politics and the modish diversity training in its wake. If all identities are to have the same moral value, then what is the difference between a woman in poverty and a rich paedophile? If our answer is "nothing" and we respect unending judgemental relativism, which is the implication of the ethos of the postmodern respect for diversity of perspectives and all personal accounts having equal value, then this creates moral chaos. If we have no anchor points to judge how we might assess what is worthy in our lives and what is not, then diversity in its entirety might be respected. However, we may then pay a very high ethical and political price.

If, on the other hand, we assert humanistic values, within an approach of judgemental rationalism, then we would look to certain principles. These would include respect for others who are vulnerable. For example, in the case of paedophilia and sadism we would condemn their inherent preoccupation with the exploitation of power discrepancies. In the case of incels, their blocked and angry sense of entitlement is the key indicator that power, not sex, is the starting point for their antisocial stance to others.

Whether it was those like Rubin and Califia celebrating BDSM, or O'Carroll and Taylor extolling the harmless beauty of "intergenerational sex", the ideological role of academic arguments becomes evident. It is obvious in these cases that these writers started with their own sexual interests and then found convenient intellectual rationalisations[8] in

---

[8] The term "rationalisation" is used in psychoanalysis to describe a human tendency to justify an argument that is conveniently desirable for the individual, whether or not the argument fits with the facts or is open to quite legitimate dispute. The outcome is "ego-syntonic". In cognitive psychology it is aligned with the notion of primary "confirmation bias" and in critical realism with the "ontic fallacy". At a collective level it might operate as "ideology" or "*doxa*". "Rationalisation" was used in a different sense by Max Weber, when examining bureaucratic rationality in modern societies.

their defence. In this post hoc logic, if they can argue that these practices should not just be tolerated but also *celebrated*, as forms of sexual liberation, then anyone casting a doubting glance will simply be accused of narrow-minded bigotry. Conveniently, the problem then is not the antisocial perpetrator but their puritanical critics.

The case of BDSM is a useful point of reflection on why we value or disvalue some forms of intimate conduct in our lives. I described it as a "borderline" case because it encourages us to reflect on competing values. Should we tolerate, unendingly, consensual actions between adults (whatever their type or character) or sometimes might we condemn them for ethical reasons (as in the critiques of Dworkin and Lorde) and if so, why? Answering that question, whether in agreement or disagreement with these particular feminists, encourages precise moral reflection, whereas identity politics tends to displace considered reflection with immediate black-and-white answers, a point I will return to in the final chapter.

Whereas the cases of incels and paedophiles are for me open-and-shut cases of antisocial identities, rationalised by their advocates, selectively using science or social science, the case of BDSM is more debatable. I tend to favour the doubts expressed by Fromm, that basically such a sexual proclivity is likely to reflect an antisocial orientation to others in the non-sexual realm. Basically, they are not likely to be very wholesome individuals in their dealings with others.

These ambiguities, about some antisocial personalities cynically enjoying the shared privilege of diversity in society of the prosocial majority, are glossed over by the binary logic encouraged in the norms of identity politics. The latter implies that all diversity is good, and that it should be protected in its entirety. We all then need training to explain this in our state of perpetual ignorance, moral failure, and "privilege". Those challenging that position are immediately deemed to be morally deficient in their judgements.

The binary of "you are either for us or against us" is a running theme in identity politics, which contributes to the silencing of those of us who wish, in good faith, to posit an alternative viewpoint, based on either evidence, or values, or both. With regard to the topic of this particular chapter, in what sense do antisocial sexual identities contribute to collective human flourishing? My personal answer would be "not very much".

CHAPTER FIVE

Racial politics

Introduction

It is common now to accept the claim that race is a concept that has no scientific basis; it reflects a pseudoscience driven largely by nineteenth-century eugenics (Sussman, 2019; Rutherford, 2020). Critical realists emphasise this historical point when considering racial politics today (Pilgrim, 2008; Alcoff, 2005; Carter, 2000). In this context, skin colour and other physical features (such as height, hair type and colour, facial features, and body shape), which visibly differentiate some groups of human beings from one another, often continue to be manifest in the power play between groups of people. Those on the right arguing for the greater control of immigration unambiguously point to skin colour as the empirical guide for their policies.

Religion or nationality sometimes are a code for the same prejudice. Today in the UK, being Muslim is a code from the xenophobic right for people with brown skins (in the private vernacular of casual racism, "Pakis"). This shift is because direct racism is now legally constrained by the *Race Relations Act 1976* (extended in 2000). This blurring of racial and religious identities, to afford or impede citizenship, is not new, a point I return to in Chapter Seven. Collective belief systems, which compete for moral and political authority, can in turn be exploited politically, as in the partition of India by the British. In these circumstances the pacifistic pretensions of religious leaders become absurd, a theme explored in Amartya Sen's *Identity and Violence* (Sen, 2006).

Even before the notions of being "white" or "black" became politically significant in modernity, the enslavement of captured Africans was rationalised on grounds of religion. Western Christians could dehumanise them on a priori grounds for being heathens. When slaves were then Christianised in their enforced relocations, a new category was required to justify their continued treatment as being subhuman. The boundary between white and black then emerged out of self-interest for the white ruling class. By and large, racism arose *from* colonialism and the commercial adventurism of slavery, not the other way round (Gerbner, 2018).

Biological and social ontology

The biological ontology of race may well be open to question on good grounds (see later) but the **social ontology** of race remains powerful. It can be described empirically and invoked to examine racial discrimination in a range of ways in modern post-colonial societies. In turn these can be the basis of political solutions, as well as the reactionary incitement of violence.

Whether we consider the Australian "whites only" policy, the Nazi destruction of European Jews and Roma, or the Windrush scandal in the UK,[1] physical indicators of race as a social reality today are the touchstone of understanding. It is not only the perpetrators of these forms of enacted racism that rely on those physical indicators, so do their victims and critics.

How can sports organisations demand that we "kick out racism" or the new social movement of Black Lives Matter argue their case unless there

---

[1] The ship the *Empire Windrush* brought black Caribbean migrants to Britain in 1948. They were a labour force necessitated by post-war construction, finding their way into state employment in the main in healthcare and transport. In 2018 it was reported that many of that generation and their offspring were being expelled from the UK even though they were British citizens. The fact that they were black made the point about racism at the centre of government decision-making.

is a working empirical and ontological consensus on who *is* black and who *is* white? For James Baldwin to tell us that "To be black and conscious in America is to be in a constant state of rage", required that he saw himself as a black person and so did others. During the 1970s in England, why did black soccer players have bananas thrown at them and not the white players? Winding the clock forwards, why do far-right football fans still make monkey chants at them and why in the recent past have they been occasionally racially abused by their white fellow players?[2]

If, on the one hand, the study of race is a pseudoscience but, on the other, race is the basis for policy preferences on the left, not just the right, then that seeming contradiction has to be explored. One resource for this task is our **four planar social being**. The salient physical differentiations noted above informing our current social ontology and *realpolitik* have an evolutionary history and this requires an exploration of **ontological realism**, in the first instance in relation to the first plane (our embodied existence in the material world).

Biological variation within a species does not warrant *categorisation* into "races" but, for a range of judgemental reasons, it does warrant *differentiation* according to physical appearance (phenotypical variation). The latter exercise then reflects both **epistemological relativism** and **judgemental rationality**. This has led in the USA to a range of positions about the "just one drop" approach to mixed-race citizens. An outcome of this is that a light-skinned citizen may still opt to call themselves "black".[3] The phenotypical appearance of a person (an **empirical** aspect of reality) is then the basis for discussions about race as an epistemic matter.

---

[2] The 2012 incident between John Terry, the England and Chelsea captain, and Anton Ferdinand informs a BBC a documentary on this, which revealed the limits of relying on personal accounts without a full exploration of their social and economic context. The latter is hinted at but personal distress is the limited focus (BBC One—Anton Ferdinand: Football, Racism and Me). In 2019, England players were racially abused during their game against Bulgaria. In the same year, complaints about racism to the England FA increased, compared to 2018 (Racism in football: "FA not doing enough to support victims of racism"—CBBC Newsround).

[3] This point applies to the question of whether Barack Obama is black. He was raised largely with a sensibility of having a white identity and learned as a young adult to take on the sense, ways of speaking, and demeanour of blackness in the US cultural context of his time. As a child, Obama would have had no idea that he was to become not just the President of the United States of America but its first *black* President.

In a field, the odd black sheep attracts our attention (empirically scarce events or deviations from the norm become noticeable). In the case of dogs, their genetic history might be traceable singularly to wolves, but we see empirically how extensively differentiated they are now (compare say a bulldog with a poodle), largely under the influence of deliberate human intervention.[4] This leaves us with a core noun description of a species (dog) with an adjective to denote a type or "breed" or subspecies ("poodle" rather than "bulldog"). This is why some racists will use the notion of "breed" to draw that analogy about phenotypical variation with the human species (Norton, Quillen, Bigham, Pearson, & Dunsworth, 2019).

The relationship between phenotypical variations and genotypes was discussed in Chapter Three in relation to sex and gender. I cited Bhaskar to confirm that genotypes are the ontological evidence of sex being determined at fertilisation. The same is true for species differentiation, if we use the criterion of the capacity for sexual reproduction (bequeathed by genetic configuration). Generally, biologists have agreed that this is a strong ontological basis for species typing.

As Homo sapiens migrated, over thousands of years, gene–environment interactions amplified phenotypical variations. In particular, climatic factors during migration engendered changes in melanin production, providing the biological mechanism as underlying the social ontology of race (Gibbons, 2014).[5] However, that underlying complexity gives no comfort to the glib expectations of racists.

A woman with a white skin may produce children with a black partner who may be white like their mother, black like their father, or

---

[4] This highlights that the transitive dimension created by human language and praxis can create alterations in what we normally think of as the intransitive dimension (unalterable givens in the external world). Human action can impinge on the naturally given world; climate change is the most blatant and species-threatening consequence of this power.

[5] Melanin changes in relation to climate accounts for one important aspect of phenotypical variation. In addition, "genetic drift" accounts for other variations in appearance; this is when due to random and complex genetic interactions in each generation, variegated appearances emerge. The use of DNA tracing by physical anthropologists indicates that features that we now would broadly call "Caucasian" only began to develop in Europe about 8,000 years ago.

variants in between (the appearance of "mixed race" in the vernacular). Many people, including white supremacists proud of "their race", have phenotypical appearances that disguise a complex and hidden genetic inheritance. This can be embarrassing for the far right. For example, after his death, DNA samples from Adolf Hitler revealed evidence of both his African and his Jewish ancestry.

To conclude in this section, within the species of Homo sapiens there are family and regional resemblances in people. However, despite those intra-specific variations, all human beings are still human; they are not dogs and regional differences in typical appearance does not mean there are human "breeds". We now find ourselves with the confusing habit, across the political spectrum, of semantically confirming race as an obvious social construct, when it has no clear-cut ontological referent in our genes. What *do* exist are empirically obvious phenotypical variations, linked to complex gene interactions, and some of these, especially skin colour, connote historical power relationships that are reinstated in the present in social interactions and in tendencies of discrimination.

Those with African-typical skins exist in the Caribbean, the Americas, and ex-colonial European countries because of the history of slavery and colonialism. In another example, the much-marginalised Roma people of Europe quite understandably resemble people from the Indian subcontinent (the source of their itinerant migration northwards in the fourteenth century). Skin colour is then a current empirical marker of social history and identity politics is one emergent response to that basic fact. Whether it is an *adequate* response is my interest in this chapter. In particular, how far can we comprehensively explore social and economic processes by limiting our understanding to experienced identities and "lived experience"? This question cues the next section.

Plane three: socio-economic structures

Moving from the first plane of our embodied connection to the natural world, as part of **four planar social being**, to the third, today's identity politics has its intelligible roots in part in the objective conditions of slavery, colonialism, and patterns of migration. The human stories of enslavement, death, and torture that are valid testimonies to those economic conditions boost the legitimacy of a narrow identity politics approach to understanding the politics of race. However, on their own they do not exhaust our understanding of complexity. They may point to current social structures and past global politics but these cannot be fully illuminated by those stories because we have to push on methodologically by examining politics and economics in the mists of time.

For example, most African American people today can point to the slave status of their forebears. In turn, this hints at the need to understand colonialism. However, some of the slave trade did not entail colonialism, as it involved offshore trading in West Africa. Those particular white slave traders were *not* colonisers. They were just brutal exploiters of human beings as commodities; much like today, modern slavery is about direct commercial exploitation by criminals, not proud political adventurists, representing nation states. Any of us can only appreciate that complexity of slavery by studying economic history; qualitative sociology will not suffice (Gardner and Tirthanker, 2021).

Also, racial minorities structurally are more prone to poverty. As disvalued groups, the enslaved and colonised were typically impoverished (with obvious individual differences within this trend). Take the example of health status (both physical and mental). Black and minority ethnic communities in majority white societies have a tendency to higher rates of ill-health. However, a proportion of this (to be determined from context to context) is because they are also *poorer* than white people on average. This poverty is also reflected ecologically in urban areas with black and ethnic minority groups tending to live in poor housing in polluted areas. Toxic pathogenic locales tend to have a higher ratio of black and ethnic minority populations.

Moreover, the cultural stigmatisation of previously colonised groups plays its role as well in this complexity. For example, in Great Britain one ex-colonised group, the Irish, had higher rates of ill-health following Irish independence. This could be accounted for by a mixture of relative poverty and prejudice, even though the Irish are overwhelmingly white skinned.[6] An example of ongoing racism against the Irish is that in 2018 it was reported that a large holiday camp firm in Britain had issued

---

[6] After the Second World War in Great Britain, signs in boarding houses—"No Irish, no Blacks, no dogs"—were reported. Some disputed the authenticity of these claims, though further academic reviews confirmed their existence. This resonated as well in the USA

a memorandum listing forty Irish surnames to be used as exclusion criteria for guest applications.[7] All of this consideration of the third plane of our **four planar social being** reminds us that personal accounts *as testimonies or grievances* (the moralistic character of identity politics) should be treated with caution. Instead, the norms of identity politics encourage us to rush to judgement and expect a short cut to social justice. I return to this dubious logic later.

The vagaries of anti-racist identity politics: virtue signalling and statue toppling

When we turn to the highly salient role of race in identity politics, biology is so distrusted that its relevance is discarded. It is as if the eugenic past and the summary conclusion that race is a myth created by pseudoscience means that it is closed down as a consideration; the debate is over on the left.

The risk of biological **reductionism**, which is real enough, means that biology might be simply ignored or denied. But this would ignore the biological reality of intra-specific differences emerging from regional differences historically in gene–environment interactions. Middle-distance runners from Eastern Africa excel more than those from Eastern Europe. These real biological differences within our species are occasionally reflected in differences in morbidity. To concede these differences is not to slide into pseudoscience or eugenic logic but simply reflects scientific honesty and sensible public health policy. From sickle cell anaemia and phenylketonuria to differences in severity of COVID-19 symptoms, there is clear evidence now that there are intra-specific differences in *biological* vulnerability, though note that these are more widespread in relation to sex rather than race (Moalem, 2020; Dyson, Atkin, & Culley, 2014).

---

with "NINA" employment warnings (No Irish Need Apply). See https://www.irishpost.com/life-style/infamous-no-irish-no-blacks-no-dogs-signs-may-never-have-existed-14
[7] Reporting of this at the time focused on it referring to Irish travellers as an ethnic group from Ireland, that separated from other Irish during British colonialism. In Ireland itself they now have a separately recognised ethnic status.

If biology has fallen out of favour on the left, it should at least have retained a respect for socio-economic structures. However, and reflecting post-structuralism, within the postmodern turn, the personal and interpersonal became a preoccupation and words displaced material reality as the political focus. To be clear, I am not arguing that the personal and interpersonal preoccupation of "critical social justice warriors" contains no valid points about the legacy of slavery and colonialism. However, this discursive focus on words and symbols is an incomplete basis for a persuasive and comprehensive account of the **emergence** and maintenance of racism. At the same time, although incomplete, it still raises legitimate matters because the ideas we hold or meanings we attribute to events in our lives shape our conduct.

If many white people prejudicially fear black people and cross the road when they see them approach, or a security guard pointedly follows a black person around in a supermarket, these are real events. Those real habits today have a real social history. They might have a cumulative "weathering" effect detrimentally impacting on the immune system of those subjected to them (Geronimus, 1992).

Moreover, those events emerge from the real power of racist ideology because ideas are causally efficacious. We can view these ideas as social constructs but the latter are real and potentially and actually impactful (Elder-Vass, 2012). For example, if European gentiles have inherited a set of cultural stories about all Jews being inherently mean and cunning and those stories are treated as valid truths, then anti-Semitism awaits. If those generalisations extend to assumptions that Jews are preoccupied with world domination as well (via their leadership of both communist movements and capitalist corporations) then anti-Semitism is deemed to be a political necessity and so the death camps await.

The failure of identity politics in relation to race then is not because a case is not being made but that case is based upon an *overly narrow set of considerations*. This distorts our analysis and turns to the need for a range of exercises, including a detailed historical analysis of colonialism and slavery and its societal legacy. That legacy has been described as "structural racism" and it operates at a suprapersonal level (individuals may or may not be aware of its operation). Thus, whether or not this affords personal racism (the daily concern of those committed to identity politics), it operates anyway to sustain racial inequalities.

One example is the lack of intergenerational social mobility in black people compared to white people, in white-dominated societies. Another example in the USA was the systematic criminalisation of ex-slaves in the southern states of the USA in order to maintain the social control of black people by the white dominant group of all social classes. Justice was purportedly for all American citizens but it operated in the post-slavery context in an inequitable way, explicitly legitimising "redneck" white bigotry against black people (see Box 5.1).

Box 5.1 The death of Emmett Till and the life of Rosa Parks

Emmett Till was a fourteen-year-old African American boy who was murdered in Mississippi after being accused of offending a white woman in her family's grocery store. A few days after the (contested) incident, in August 1955, he was abducted, beaten, mutilated, shot, and then dumped in the Tallahatchie River. At his funeral his mother insisted on the coffin being open for the world to see the boy's injuries. A rapid trial of his two white murderers, in front of a white-only jury, led to a not-guilty verdict. Newspaper reporting of the murder and the protection of his white murderers created a peak of angry awareness both in the black population and in white progressive opinion. The continued cultural separation of the northern and southern states during the 1950s was now becoming evident, even though black and white troops had fought together during the war against fascism, still a fresh memory from the previous decade. However, despite that shared war effort, black and white combatants were separated in the US military; a norm that only ended in 1948.

In the same year as Till's murder, another event also made this point about post-war civil rights in the USA. A black woman in her early forties, Rosa Parks, was on a bus in Montgomery, Alabama and was told to give up her seat to a white passenger. She was already in a section designated for "coloureds" but the rule was that black passengers should relinquish their seat for a white passenger if told to do so. Parks refused, but she was not politically naive. She had been attending activist meetings about civil rights and later recalled that her stubborn refusal had been galvanised by her anger about the recent murder of Emmett Till. When the police were called, she was arrested and then found guilty of being in violation of the city code defining segregated spaces based on race. The incident triggered civil disobedience (a bus boycott), which was to act

> as a model for peaceful protest under the leadership of Martin Luther King Jr in the next decade. This was not the first bus boycott but the most well-known today. All had been a response of resistance to the Jim Crow laws enforced in the southern states of the USA from the 1870s until the 1960s. These ensured that black and white citizens (allegedly "equal but separate") were segregated in education, transport, and in restaurants and bars.

The tracing of the particular way that those in power in the USA dealt with the aftermath of slavery, with its totemic cultural position after a civil war, is an important academic task in order to inform the political struggle for racial equality today. Case studies such as those of Emmett Till and Rosa Parks emphasise the need to consider history, culture, economics, law and regional differences in the USA seriously. That considered multi-disciplinary reflection can be contrasted with the unreflective acting out by social justice activists guided by their version of identity politics.

The clearest example here is of the angry toppling of statues. We can throw statues of slave traders into the river or we could retain them in situ (or maybe carefully place them in a museum) in order to discuss what they tell us about history. Compare the preservation of Auschwitz as a place to visit for us all to learn from about anti-Semitism and genocide and the disappearance of a statue of slave trader into a river for ever.

As Adams (2020) has noted, iconoclastic vandalism erases history and this encourages ignorance not enlightenment. If the destruction of cultural artefacts is fair game for the left, then their moral case for indignation when a statue of Nelson Mandela is defaced or destroyed is logically undermined. Imagination and education might be a sounder strategy to adopt about statues and speech we do not like (see Chapter Two). Whilst the first slave-trader statue to hit the water and sink had a totemic value for social progress (like knocking down the Berlin wall), paradoxically it is the *preservation* of these icons from the past that offers us current lessons. The answer to speech that is offensive to us should be more speech, not less (see Chapter Two). Similarly, the answer to offensive symbols inherited from a past age is not their destruction but their contemplation, discussion, and the learning they afford.

A more obvious example is a church. In England there are many of them, some very old. Comparing the less ornate ones created by the serial wife-murderer,[8] Henry VIII, when his followers systematically stripped them of the cultural symbols of Rome, with those that survived this political vandalism, allows us to reflect on an important period of British history. If all of these churches had been demolished, then the learning would have been lost.

In a similar vein, note how ISIS, in its military adventurism, has focused on the destruction of ancient cultural artefacts in Iraq and Syria that were deemed to offend the strictures of Islam in order to make a point about their moral superiority to non-believers. However, it only reinforced the view of the latter that they were right to oppose Islamic fundamentalism and arrogant patriarchal violence. Vandalism is a sort of politics but whether it is intelligent politics is a different matter. In practice it seems to lead to barbarism and unedifying stupidity, whether it is from theocratic bigots or authoritarian secularists on the left.

Anti-racism and neoliberalism

If offensive symbols can be a source of learning, so can virtuous symbols. Virtue signalling is central to identity politics, which is a point made recurrently by libertarian critics of right and left. Rather than excluding self-righteousness from political discourse (another form of banning or statue-toppling) we can take stock of its emergence and current functioning. Where did it come from and why is it embraced by so many today, including by power elites themselves?

As far as the left is concerned, one partial answer to this question (apart from its general proneness to authoritarianism) is that during the twentieth century political struggles mainly led to stories of heroic defeat. We can list, amongst other, to demonstrate this point: the betrayal of the Russian revolution and the eventual collapse of the Soviet empire; the General Strike in Britain; the failure of the German left to halt the rise of Nazi power; the victory of Franco in the Spanish civil war; the assassination of Martin Luther King; the betrayal of social democracy by Tony Blair and his acolytes, etc. By the turn of this century the left

---

[8] The ongoing embodiment of the "Merrie England" of the past was that he was a jolly soul, not a serial killer (which of course he was). His legacy includes the Church of England and its Bishops in the House of Lords.

was tiring in its traditional efforts but then postmodernism offered an answer: justice could be achieved simply and quickly by deconstruction, discourse analysis, and the celebration of minority voices with their *specific* campaigns for justice.

If power is really all about words (what should and should not be said by whom) then the struggles are simplified and made easy. They still require struggle and protest (though, with clictivism, not that much). They might achieve *immediate* results if there is enough moral sympathy across society, including from the rich and powerful. Anticipated market sensitivity is relevant to the latter. For example, bosses in UKTV stopped the availability of the "German" episode of the classic British comedy *Fawlty Towers*, even though there had been no demands for the ban. Another example of the importance of marketing strategy is the Black Lives Matter campaign. Other than white supremacists, who would be churlish or blinkered enough *not* to celebrate the emergence of this particular new social movement? For this reason, business bosses are aware of majority customer opinion and respond accordingly (more on this later).

If we look at the history of the Black Lives Matter campaign, its focused demand, which has required repetition because of a lack of effective corrective action, has been that police brutality should stop against black people. In practice, this overwhelmingly has meant *young black men*. The movement was started by three black women in 2013, mindful of the disproportionate force used by the police against the latter. The problem with this demand to reduce or eliminate police brutality is whilst that is completely legitimate and laudable, it is individualistically focused (the named victims) and it is open to the charge that *other* social groups could make the same claim but are being ignored. For example, the very poor (whatever their colour) are brutalised by the police. Young men, whatever their colour, are more likely to be subjected to coercive control by the state than older men or women.

The coercive social control of the *lumpenproletariat*[9] is not limited to black people but racism certainly plays its part in amplifying that

---

[9] This term has been replaced in recent times in British sociology by that of the "precariat". Its original meaning came from Marx and Engels when describing the lowest or poorest part of the social structure of capitalism. The unemployed or unemployable were

tendency. Moreover, the fatal consequences of police victimisation are overdetermined if they carry guns. The deaths of young black men are more likely if the police are armed, for two reasons. First, they may be fatally shot by the police and second, the confidence of carrying a gun enables police officers to increase the level of force utilised, which increases the risk of serious injury or death. In the USA, deaths of young black men (the focus of the Black Lives Matter campaign) have reflected both of these scenarios.

The pattern of the coercive social control of the *lumpenproletariat* is the wider context here then—it is partially but not wholly a matter of race. This point is reinforced if we move our attention from policing to psychiatric coercion. The same pattern repeats: the poorest in society are detained in psychiatric facilities but young black men are disproportionately represented *within* that trend. This point also applies to those who are moved to higher levels of security, secluded (the psychiatric term for solitary confinement), and highly medicated, with the risks to health that entails (Rogers & Pilgrim, 2020).

Thus, a clear caution about highlighting that *black* lives matter and police brutality is that: (a) it is not all black people but mainly black *young men*; (b) this is not just about the police but also implicates other official agencies, with coercive powers of detention and behavioural control, often staffed by black people who are acting as agents *of* the state; and (c) black people are often poor and *all* the poor are managed brutally at times by agents of the state. This highlights the tendency of identity politics to narrow our political focus, with some analytical and strategic cost. In the case of psychiatric detention, race reductionism (see later) was preceded in feminist critiques, suggesting the women are labelled and treated more than men. However, if we look at the coercive use of psychiatry it is men, not women, who are over-represented (Pilgrim, 2008). Thus, any wider sociological understanding of social

---

mainly held in suspicion by Marxists who saw them as uneducated, reactionary, selfish, and without exposure to the trade union and class consciousness that can emerge in the struggle between capital and labour (see later footnote on football supporters). Some neo-Marxists rescued their political value and creativity (see, for example, *One Dimensional Man* by Herbert Marcuse). Many new social movements and their ambitions have been aligned since the 1960s with that more optimistic position.

group membership and its variegated pattern of harsh control by agents of the state requires an examination of **intersectionality** in its *causal* sense, which is outlined in Box 5.2.

> Box 5.2 The ambiguous utility of intersectionality
>
> At first glance, intersectionality offers a way out of one form of reductionism. It was developed with this in mind by Crenshaw (1989) who pointed out the limits of feminism as focusing only on the oppression that comes from being a woman. For example, being a woman and black and lesbian and old brings with it a scenario of marginalisation in society for individuals that is more than the sum of its parts. So far so good as an account of the synergistic logic about the range of interactions in social systems of power discrepancies. Indeed, just as Black Lives Matter invites a social and historical curiosity about slavery, when recording the deaths of black men at the hands of agents of the state today, so too does Crenshaw's elaborated form of feminist analysis. However, the shortcomings of this form of political analysis and strategising is also evident because of its tendency to psychological reductionism and individualism. Whist social and historical curiosity is *invited*, it is neither guaranteed nor required by identity politics, because intersectionality retains the focus on *identities*. The emphasis is on *experienced oppression and intersecting identities evidenced by a series of individual case studies*. This limits our understanding of ontology to relationality and individual personalities. This culminates in a limited analysis prompting special pleading in political demands, which can be contrasted with others, with no clear criteria for arbitrating between competing claims.
>
> For example, in Britain in the past few years, senior female academics (including those on vast salaries if they are university Vice Chancellors) have campaigned for a closing of the "gender pay gap". Whilst the overall goal of that campaign is completely legitimate, those pleading for it, and very keen to offer themselves as examples of victimhood of the "he" "glass ceiling", are palpably financially advantaged, compared to the low-waged cleaners and porters (note, male and female) working in universities. That contradiction can only be understood if we move our focus away from the relational and the personal alone (evidenced habitually by individual case studies) to social structure (in this case in relation to aggregate evidence about the inequalities flowing from differences in positions of class). In 2018 the top ten UK universities had Vice-Chancellors

who were paid in excess of £400,000, with the *average* salary across the sector being £350,000. This average figure was over double that paid to the British Prime Minister in the same year, with the top earners, *including women*, approaching triple the figure. Under a third of this elite band were women but there was an upward trend, prompting those in the group to celebrate the feminist victory (see https://universitybusiness.co.uk/news/breaking-through-the-he-glass-ceiling). During the same period, over ninety per cent of Vice-Chancellors were white, with only three non-white representatives (note, two of whom were women) (see https://www.green-park.co.uk/news/94-percent-of-vicechancellors-at-top-50-universities-are-white/s3307). If we were to use race, not gender, as the focus then it would be the "white" not the "he" "glass-ceiling".

If we reflect a little more on the implications of the case study offered in Box 5.2, then we can see that intersectionality certainly has its merits. They lie in the need to attend to simultaneous **generative mechanisms**. These causal processes involved in a complex picture of the emergence of oppression include our particular internal worlds and the contingent interpersonal contexts we pass through and are party to between birth and death. However, the risk is that we limit our attention to these processes alone so that "identities" (vulnerable and oppressed versus privileged and oppressive) are our *only* basis for understanding power. If we are seduced by this offer, then we will keep producing answers that are at best partial and at worst misleading.

Take the ambiguous example of "privilege" understood sociologically. We can focus on it as a social process (plane three of our **four planar social being**). We can gather empirical evidence that it really exists as a tendency or demi-regularity (an ontological matter about structural and institutional racism). We can also examine its impact in fine grain, interpersonally (Plane 2). For example, is there evidence that black people *are* treated with suspicion more in public spaces than white people and spoken to differently or ignored ("micro-aggressions")? We can also use evidence then in a quasi-judicial manner about particular incidents within that tendency. That is, we may opt to *deduce* in *this* instance that *this* black person was being treated prejudicially by *this* white person. We can also assume that the latter carries around with them a quantifiable human feature we call "privilege".

We can discuss privilege in all these ways and all of the time it starts to take on a slippery quality, unless we check with those discussing it what they mean. I return to this point later when considering "white privilege" but here am noting that identity politics will tend to provide a blinkered or narrow focus on the last scenario of individual attributions. Social justice becomes what is said to whom by particular individuals and so is a form of psychological reductionism. The latter does not threaten the socio-economic status quo but actually strengthens it for reasons I discuss in the final chapter.

From causality to the kaleidoscope of subjectivities

My emphasis here upon the need for ideological critique about the socio-economic context has resonances with some of the early phase of critical race theory, during the 1970s when its emphasis was materialist (Bell, 1973). It is quite appropriate that we address the material inequalities of non-white people in a post-colonial historical context and understand the ideological function of policies today. The aggregate social disadvantages of black people in the USA can be empirically described, analysed, and policies of remediation proposed.

However, during the 1990s, once critical race theory moved its focus from the extra-discursive or suprapersonal realm, with its emphasis on multi-factorial material causality, to a postmodern obsession with identities, perspectives, narratives, and standpoints, then different priorities followed. These were about words and words about words (see Box 5.3). A particular focus was on identifying hate speech and dealing with it, naming-and-shaming anyone (including black people themselves who had internalised racism), diversity training in public and private organisations, academic self-censorship or heated contention about the curriculum, public virtue signalling to divide saints from sinners, etc.

The dominant and dominating moralistic drive within identity politics, in the context of race relations, leads to divisive goals and in-group–out-group dynamics. This is reflected explicitly in some of the outputs of critical race theory, which focus on the unending failure of white people ever to come up to scratch as worthy human beings and the need for separatism. The most extreme version of the latter was the emergence of Black Nationalism as a social movement. This secessionism (splitting off black from white people) pointed up another consequence of identity politics and a paradox in relation to race.

The legitimisation of separatism, especially in relation to ethnicity meant that Black Nationalists not only found white people to be permanently beyond redemption, they also at times defended and espoused anti-Semitism to justify their state of victimhood.[10] When the latter did emerge, it revealed the importance of ideological considerations beyond the social construct of race. Just as the slave owners weaponised Christianity, separatist Black Nationalists at times invoked Islamic dogma and with that the distrust of, or contempt for, Jews. (I return to the divisive role of religion and its valorisation in identity politics in Chapter Eight).

Box 5.3 "Racism" and other terms since the postmodern turn

Any discussion of race today played out using the rules of identity politics has to be understood in the context of the postmodern or linguistic "turn". The notion of "racism" is only one relevant current in this sea of postmodern wordplay, which now informs diversity training. For example, the emotive word "violence" deserves a brief and separate note here. Its common-sense use refers to acts of actual and demonstrable physical aggression purposefully directed at individuals (as in murder, grievous bodily harm, torture, or sexual assault) or groups (as in genocide or the bombing of civilians, which is commonplace now in warfare).

A general risk within the norms of identity politics is that causal links between an ideological context that encourages eventual violence as a *trend* are declared to be self-evident in *particular cases*. This is dubious logic and can lead to implausible interpretations. For example, in 2019 a trans woman and activist, Julie Berman, was murdered in Toronto. A "self-identifying non-binary" man, Colin Harnack, at the scene was immediately charged. Trans activists then reported this to be a direct and unambiguous result of the transphobia of feminists. This logic of explaining the murder at the hands of a *man*

---

[10] The secessionist tendency within the black power movement was not clear cut. For example, a key member of the Black Panthers, Fred Hampton, was murdered in Chicago by local police at the behest of the FBI on 4 December 1969. Hampton's main danger to the US state was that he was a credible revolutionary socialist, prompting his extrajudicial execution.

by the ideological position of unidentified gender critical feminists is, to say the least, open to legitimate questioning.

Thus, we need to be aware that soft power is a function of words or ideologies, whereas in the case of hard power it is indexical about actual events. It points to an objective aspect of the world; it is not merely a way of speaking, even if the latter might at times be causally efficacious. A white slave owner raping a black slave is a different expression of power than a white person in their daily verbal habits casually stereotyping black people. This reminds us of the matter of freedom of expression discussed in Chapter Two. As J. S. Mill noted, words can hurt and even encourage harm but the proven outcome of actual violence needs to be demonstrated to warrant the dogmatic suppression of their expression. This echoes the respect for freedom of expression from Karl Popper, who advised that the war of words is part of democracy and conflict resolution; it is always better than the war of swords.

In Chapter Two, I drew attention to the incident in the Washington restaurant where the young woman was being terrified into raising her fist in the BLM demonstration, with the angry moralisation "white silence is violence". This scenario of mob harassment was self-justified with that final phrase. As the psychoanalyst-cum-existential psychotherapist R. D. Laing put it in his hyperbolic metaphor from his *Politics of Experience*, "we are all murderers and prostitutes". Identity politics denies that insight and divides the world digitally into those who are self-evidently good and those who are not.

With the risk of these digital simplifications in a mind, a range of writers have analysed how these ideological forms of power are exerted to sustain inequalities and increase the *risk* of violence differentially to some social groups (Spivak, 1988; Dotson, 2011). The notion of "epistemic violence" came from Bourdieu, within his wider theorisation of ideology and power. His emphasis was on the degrees of legitimation of credibility in various social groups. The notion of "structural violence" came from Galtung (1969), who examined the societal conditions of possibility that increased the risk of actual violence to some social groups and not others (poverty, racism, and sexism are the most obvious ones). Looking further back, the term "social murder" was coined by Friedrich Engels in *The Condition of the Working-Class in England*. He made the point that under capitalism the ruling class create the conditions under which the poor die young on average: as capitalism has persisted, then so too has that tendency.

The ontic fallacy of white privilege

The discussion in Box 5.3 highlights the logical distinction between conditions of possibility that create tendencies of harm to some social groups more than others, and the speculation about a direct causal link in particular cases. Related conceptual spin-offs, then, in relation to this chapter, are "structural racism" and "institutional racism". These concepts also remind us to check on the logical proof that trends in social or economic processes (Plane 3 of our **four planar social being**) have led to interpersonal events (Plane 2) that in turn clearly led to racial oppression in this particular person (Plane 4). The speculative link between these three planes, which may or may not be approached sceptically case by case, raises the contested matter of "white privilege", which is now discussed.

If there is no clear-cut biological evidence to define race, but only an acknowledgement of phenotypical variation and some subpopulation variability in proneness to health and illness, then where does this leave the social ontology of being *white*? Does it include Ashkenazi Jews or Turks? Does it include those who have a black-skinned parent but actually look white? These open questions arise because a core tenet of critical race theory, which today is part of the daily discourse of identity politics, is that of "white privilege" or simply "whiteness" and the inverse political credibility then created by this skin colour.

In the introduction to this chapter, I noted the historical ideological roots of whiteness and blackness in colonialism and the weaponisation of Christianity. That historical scenario is the (questionable) basis for making judgements *today* about racial justice in a new social context, by focusing reductively on the vague notion of "privilege". The latter (be it male, white, able-bodied, cis, sane, or any other identity category) means the voices of some people have now been deemed to be past their sell by date and so can be discarded. This emerges not because of the logical, evidential, or ethical validity of what is being said but because the views come from the "wrong" people, according to the diverse and self-appointed quality controllers of identity politics. The chaos this creates in routine moralisations is obvious for us all to see. Is the female university Vice Chancellor in Box 5.2, who earns twelve times the amount in salary of the male cleaner in her building, suffering because of his "privilege"? And if she is black and he is white, is she doubly oppressed by *him*? How do we "do the math" if she is white and he is black? Is "privilege" a *commodity* held by some of us but not others and can it be quantified? If so, how do we do that?

If we scratch the surface of the hyper-individualised concept of "privilege", there are no objective criteria to calibrate it unequivocally. There is certainly clear evidence at the *aggregate or group level in some contexts* that there is racial discrimination and injustices (the structural racism I noted earlier). Also, in highly racialised times in the USA and South Africa in the recent past there has been explicit segregation and restrictions on citizenship for non-whites. Thus, there is no doubt that over time some *racial groups* have dominated and disadvantaged others. However, this is not the same as saying, or proof, that individuals in their **concrete singularity** carry around a high or low quantity of "privilege", according to the colour of their skin (or some other notion valorised in identity politics).

When that assumption is simply asserted, as not just a theoretical possibility but an actual and presumably measurable ontological property, and then a powerful white person (who does really exist) is pointed to as evidence of confirmation of the whole generalisation about white people, then this is an **ontic fallacy** or "division fallacy" (Malik, 2018; and Shackel, 2005).[11] "Whiteness" and "white privilege" are simply asserted, as if they are factually *non-problematic general truths*. This a priori logic then triggers permission for the daily moralisations of identity politics about white people, for simply being white and being adjudged for saying "the wrong things" or being unaware of their privilege. It is not clear

---

[11] Shackel (2005), in his critique of postmodern slippery thinking, calls this the "motte and bailey" fallacy or argument. This is when an arguer deliberately confuses two positions—one readily defensible, with one far less so. In this case it would, for example, be the claim that this poorly educated white man is a racist (judged by his speech and deeds) and therefore all poorly educated white men are racists. It is a form of inductive reasoning used for rhetorical purposes. If challenged with this point, the arguer retreats into saying that the general argument still remains a possibility. The fallacy rests on vague assertions and constant hints of guilt by association about an individual case in order to support a general argument that is already presumed in advance to be valid—hence the **ontic fallacy**. All of identity politics relies on this dubious logic to some degree but Reed (2020) explores the point specifically in relation to race.

what exactly is achieved by this, other than moments of satisfaction or shame in our dealings with one another, with skins we were born with and would have to work very hard to alter.[12]

The ontic fallacy creates what Adolph Reed (2018) calls "race reductionism". Recalling the arguments of Hobsbawm and Sivanandan I cited in the introduction to the book, Reed argues that race reductionism is favoured by some liberal middle-class black people. They can then constantly or episodically claim their *personal* disadvantage, compared to their white peers. This leaves their own cultural and economic advantage compared to poorer people *of any colour* unscrutinised or evaded.

This preferred narrative within identity politics in the USA, which in extremis accounts for *all* social inequalities by ineluctable white supremacy, obscures the matter of class politics. It places all black people on tramlines of victimhood, leaving whites as the ubiquitous oppressors; class disappears as a causal and complicating variable. This vague assumption is made without reference to the complexities of capitalism or to the prospect of genuine changes to it through reform or revolution. As Reed (2018: 108) notes:

> In the antiracist political project white supremacy/racism is—like "terrorism"—an amorphous, ideological abstraction whose specific content exists largely in the eyes of the beholder. Therefore, like antiterrorism, antiracism's targets can be porous and entirely arbitrary; this means that, also like antiterrorism, *the struggle can never be won*. (Emphasis added)

Reed notes elsewhere, when being interviewed in 2020 about race reductionism that:

> Race should be treated as an historical phenomenon comparable to others—a category I call "ideologies of ascriptive differentiation"—that comes into existence at a certain point in relation to specific patterns of social relations and institutions.

---

[12] Playing around with racial surfaces is a minefield. Witness the case of Rachel Dolezal and the disapproving shouts of "cultural appropriation" at white people growing dreadlocks ("wiggers") or European chefs daring to create dishes of the East.

"Race" is more often taught in universities in a way much closer to how Victorian era racists used it. (https://daily.jstor.org/ adolph-reed-jr-the-perils-of-race-reductionism)

Here we see, then, the invocation by Reed of the Plane 3 of our **four planar social being**. He is a black academic from the left and he despairs of a line of argument which shores up **neoliberalism** and is a counsel of despair for ordinary black people. In part of his argument, he joins with the ranks of conservative black intellectuals who reject race reductionism.

These black libertarians include Thomas Sowell, Shelby Steele, Glen Loury, and Walter Williams. They go further than Reed and highlight the cultural responsibility of black people in the United States to change their own norms to become more prosocial and politically creative. Thus, black critics from the right and left here agree on the error of race reductionism, but the right focus more on personal agency and moral responsibility (Plane 4), whereas leftists like Reed retain a holistic focus from the tradition of historical materialism (and by implication all four ontological planes).

The conservative commentators oppose special pleading from black groups in relation to affirmative action. They also point up the real advances (that should be acknowledged and celebrated) of the abolition of slavery, the end of the Jim Crow laws, and the reforms gained from the civil rights movement. According to these conservative black intellectuals, the *denial* of this sort of demonstrable progress from the critical social justice left (most of whom are white not black) encourages young black people today to mechanistically replay a narrow victim narrative, set on tramlines from the past of slavery. That nihilistic narrative of collective predestined victimhood leads to the moralistic strictures of diversity training and complaints of ubiquitous white privilege, as the focus of constant irritable political complaint. Echoing Reed from the left, "the struggle can never be won".

Moral re-education, via diversity training, reinforces this diversion from the structural question of class for the left and from the demand of self-responsibility for the right. Moreover, as Williams (2021) in her critique of diversity training has noted, there is no empirical evidence that the rationale of race sensitivity in workplaces, within that training, actually works. Notions such as "unconscious bias", if they are causally efficacious, would be mitigated by such training. Williams notes to date that this has not been demonstrated empirically and so is an act of faith not a fact. This empirical contention is important, because it would mean that diversity training may not only be a waste of resources (and a confected industry); it might actually just demoralise people of any colour and engender distrust between us all. In other words, its social impact would be negative not positive.

My concern goes further: even if the (positive) impact on anti-racism were eventually to be demonstrated unequivocally, then it would still be a form of psychological reductionism and mystify our needed insights into structural racism. Within racial identity politics, white people are invited to be in a state of lifelong personal self-doubt and guilt about who they are, and they are held in suspicion, when they are well-meaning anti-racist allies of black people. Some white writers on this topic simply assert that all white people are racists and any attempt to query this generalisation itself reflects their lack of insight and confirms the point (DiAngelo, 2018). This is reminiscent of the "no debate" position adopted by transgender activists, discussed in Chapter Three: any request for debate is deemed *ipso facto* to reflect bigotry.

A variant of this position, from Ibram Kendi in his long autobiographical account, is that *all of us* are racist, including black people (Kendi, 2019). The fact its punch relies upon a personal account confirms again the rhetorical salience in identity politics of epistemological privileging. Although Kendi explores many important extra-discursive points about racism and intersectionality, the bottom line is that he makes an appeal from *his own concrete singularity* to prove his case. Ultimately that plane is valorised out of all four in our **four planar social being**.

Other black writers are less inclusive about racism as a general human challenge and return to the position of DiAngelo, locating society's ills in white privilege. That sort of account can be found in *Whites on Race and Other Falsehoods* (Uwagba, 2020). This is a much clearer example than that of Kendi of how politics is compressed into the two planes of the interpersonal and the uniquely biographical. The early promise of intersectionality addressing complex simultaneous generative mechanisms is ultimately lost in this narrow psychological preoccupation.

Complex causality about a racist society is reduced to the racist thoughts and actions of individual white people, whether these are wilful or unconscious.

Apart from these writers reductively evading two of the four planes of our **four planar social being**, there is a never-ending challenge created in identity politics generally about this focus on the secular version of sin. Kendi plausibly deals with this by saying that we are all sinners and conceding intersectionality in some detail, whereas DiAngelo and Uwagba focus on the moral failures of those with white skins. These arguments only retain credibility if we have an a priori belief in the comprehensive causal role of just *one* variable (be it sex, gender, race, sexuality, or whatever). However, if that logic is demonstrably dubious, and an ontic fallacy is being promoted, then the proponents of single variable logic are vulnerable to the charge of not just being wrong but also hypocritical.

As with the opulent female Vice Chancellors, still claiming personal victimhood (see Box 5.2), there is a hollow ring to the claim that epistemological privileging is the only game in town. For example, Uwagba came from a middle-class, privately educated background; she is an Oxbridge graduate and successful "influencer"[13] on social media. By criteria of wealth and education (i.e., social class) *she* is highly privileged. Once we go down the highly personalised road of moralistic calculations then none of us can be excluded; Kendi is therefore much stronger on this point than Uwagba.

These ambiguities about special pleading for this or that dominant or singular variable within identity politics leaves any fair-minded person perplexed, on a moment-to-moment basis, about how to mathematically calculate who is oppressed about what in daily life. The latter is now governed by the febrile naming-and-shaming approach favoured in identity politics. Not only is that emotive context not the best one to "do the math", we might also reasonably ask whether the task is valid in principle.

The questioner, within the personalistic meta-rule of identity politics, will then matter more than the question itself and its unfathomable

---

[13] The attribution of "influencer" about this writer reflects the narcissistic norms of neoliberalism and the moral vacuity of social media.

answer. The question posed by a white person will be immediately held in suspicion. However, what then happens if a black person endorses and replays the *very same* argument to the very letter? Would it suddenly become valid rather than discreditable? These questions highlight the problem of recasting suspect ad hominem reasoning as hyper-valid truths rooted in epistemological privileging and "lived experience".

And if we do add up all of the millions of these daily naming-and-shaming incidents about variants of privilege, then how exactly do they contribute to human flourishing? And how do other forms of privilege allegedly at play (say based on sex, age, ability, gender, sanity, or sexuality) mitigate or amplify putative white privilege? Where is our moral calculator to make precise judgements when comparing one contingent interpersonal event with the next contingent interpersonal event, with all these intersecting identities (many conceded by Kendi) co-occurring variably across time and place?

Structural racism versus moralisations

These questions about the proof and quantification of white privilege demonstrate the vulnerable credibility of identity politics in general, not just in relation to race. In this swirl of moralistic triumphalism, judgemental rationality has been displaced by judgemental *relativism* defended by forms of epistemological privilege that cannot be gainsaid. This fault-line in identity politics is exposed in part by the very logic of intersectionality discussed earlier, despite its promising start.

Once multi-factorial complexity is defended (quite correctly in the eyes of critical realists) then we should not end up with either simplistic political analyses or with glib policy solutions based upon surveillance, self-surveillance, and angry moralisations. The asserted notions of measurable personal privilege (prefixed with "white", "cis", "male", "straight", or whatever) are simplistic and dubious reductive claims, creating variants of an ontic fallacy. "Calling out" and naming-and-shaming are not the easy road to social justice, indeed unintentionally they may form a roadblock.

Some writers on whiteness and white privilege do offer more elaborate holistic accounts. These retain the notions but link them very clearly and properly to structural racism. I would include here *some* aspects of Kendi's work (though overall in my view it is too personalistic) but also see Bhopal (2018) and Patel (2021). These authors focus clearly on the importance of structural racism and warn against psychological reductionism.

It is only when the notion of racism is tightly limited to meanings in the interpersonal and biographical planes that we encounter the ontic fallacy. The critique I noted above of Reed pinpoints this error of reasoning within identity politics; hence his claim that identity politics suits the interests of the black middle class, who can special plead for their inevitable victimhood, to gain advantage *within* a better off demographic.

To illustrate the political importance of shifting from the personal and interpersonal alone about racism, to the higher order question of structural racism, the criticism of a Conservative government report in March 2020 in the UK is salutary. This was commissioned by Boris Johnson as one response to Black Lives Matter protests. The core group reviewing the topic were all, bar one, non-white but within days it provoked extensive criticisms from a range of quarters, including some black academics who complained that their advice was co-opted for legitimacy, but was not properly represented.

The report focused on how Britain was now on track for being a well-functioning, post-racial, multi-ethnic society[14] and that what problems remained were mainly because of *personal shortcomings and family dysfunction*. This chimed with the arguments of conservative black intellectuals like Sowell, Steele, Loury, and Williams from the United States noted earlier, which then backgrounds the explanatory value of structural racism. This is what divides libertarians of left and right in relation to their shared concern with the mutually agreed error of race reductionism. The left concedes and emphasises structural racism, whereas the right problematises or discards its analytical value.

Critics of the report were particularly aggrieved that the well-established evidence pointing up educational, housing, and health gaps between white and non-white Britons was ignored in the report or misinterpreted. For example, the report argued that racial disadvantage

---

[14] In the European context, at present there is evidence that Britain is *less* racist than most nearby countries, if we use survey data of the experience ordinary people (Discrimination in the European Union, 2019).

could be accounted for largely by socioeconomic inequalities. When the rich get richer under neoliberalism, the poor get poorer, and this retains the *pre-existing gap* between white and non-white.

This discussion invites class back into the calculation, exposes the generic impact of neoliberalism on socio-economic impoverishment, and allows us to explore why non-whites are recurrently disadvantaged economically *compared* to whites, as subpopulations. It is that subgroup tendency that is vital to our understanding of racial inequality, which points us to the capitalist system and its ongoing vagaries to both survive and to oppress and harm some groups of people more than others.

Even when racial disadvantage is apparent in the data, locality, not just class background, needs also to be taken into consideration. Also, the BAME demographic description is not uniform. There are differences within this group about, for example, poverty levels and aspirations for commercial or educational advancement. In other words, there is racialised structural inequality, but its character is complex. It does not warrant the logic of identity politics and give a green light to glib moralisations.

This point about empirically variegated tendencies of advantage and disadvantage as *social rather than personalistic* phenomena (say in relation to health, housing, and education) is separate from, and at odds with, attempts to explain away racial difference by family dysfunction and personal shortcomings alone. It is also at odds with the moralistic discourse of left identity politics, which in a different version turns the personalistic focus on white privilege and unconscious bias. These forms of reductionism, from the right or the left, short-circuit the need for a judicious understanding of the complexity of **laminated reality**. For example, look at the uneven impact on black people in the USA, as the Obama government bailed out the banks after the 2008 crisis, leaving poorer homeowners to suffer personal ruin (Cooper & Bruenig, 2017). Given the latter were *proportionally* more black than white, this created an aggregate tendency confirming the structural racism thesis.

An important implication of this interpretive dilemma about reports of racial disadvantage is that the empirical complexity requires both ensured free debate *and* caution about seeking justice via moralisations about individuals. For example, it was not self-evident that the report in the UK was a Conservative whitewash, whatever its a priori ideological loading and its post hoc interpretation. It raised some important challenges of making sense of the pattern and extent of racism in Britain, particularly bearing in mind Reed's caution of race reductionism noted earlier. Some white groups are notably disadvantaged (especially travellers and, so too, in recent history, the Irish). Regional difference in the UK could account for some of the inequalities reported. Some ethnic minority groups are *over-represented* in higher education.

Thus, this is a complex picture that cannot be pre-emptively understood by invoking single explanations. Even the use of structural racism as a totalising explanation is questionable if it is used crudely. In other words, it requires **epistemic humility**. The reductionism of "white privilege" is certainly an unconvincing explanation but also from the right, the "cultural failure" explanation favoured by conservative black intellectuals fails for the same reason. In different but complementary ways, the two sides over-emphasise individual human agency. The left focus on individual black victims and individual white oppressors, whereas black conservatives focus on bootstrap-exhortations and a critique of their own cultural norms of anti-social fecklessness.

At best, the preoccupation with "white privilege" raises a *starting* consciousness about the empirical evidence for racial disadvantage and its historical roots. At worst, it offers a simplistic solution to the latter in unending moralisations, ricocheting irritably between mutually accusing citizens, and encouraged by diversity training. Its solemn and enthusiastic incorporation into commercial rhetoric is a clue about this glibness. "We need to root out racism, where ever we find it on or off the field"—to quote the football commentator solemnly offering his earnest advice, as players take the knee—is easy to say. It requires about the same effort as "clictivism" but is being broadcast to millions in a few fleeting seconds. As a momentary moralisation it is a highly partial basis for both analysis and strategy. Unlike the cost to customers of cable sports channels, words are cheap.

The role of football as an industry exploiting young BME talent and the understandable desire for upward mobility into a rich but short career, as well as the profits from gambling generated by the global interest in the game, bear serious examination. So does the role of the capitalist elites who have monopolised their control of media outlets and are happy to promote sport spectatorship as a bland opiate of the people.

And then we have the global super-rich (including kleptocrats) who buy football clubs, like they buy tower blocks, art, diamonds, yachts, or empty office blocks, while the homeless sleep rough outside.

The list goes on about the complexities of the sociology of soccer. But who needs to be bothered by that complexity when safe and passing moralisations, which in and of themselves would find no objection from any fair-minded person, can be scripted at the start of a televised game? The whistle is blown to start the game and the anti-racist sentiment soon fades from the viewer's mind but **the actual** background complexity of sport as a commercial and cultural commodity continues unexamined.

Beyond this commercially convenient virtue signalling, we can return to the complexities of structural racism and its *aggregate tendencies*. These may be persistent, but they are also challengeable and mutable, if the political will is there. The empirical picture is complex, though, and deserves proper academic and political consideration, to avoid the binary logic and prejudgements favoured in identity politics of the left or right. Young black people *tend* to progress less well in the educational system than their white peers, though in recent times in Britain poor white children are entering university at a lower rate than their black peers. This tendency was reported by the Parliamentary Education Select Committee in 2021 (https://publications.parliament.uk/pa/cm5802/cmselect/cmeduc/85/8502).

Also, some of the educational data on inequality is accounted for by locale, not race per se. *Where* families are, not their race, might be more important as a generative mechanism. Black children are bullied more, but so are other children who are socially different. The complexity of social ontology needs calm reflection and interdisciplinary respect by legions of researchers.

The **emergence** of these race-inflected tendencies implicates a multi-factorial picture in all levels in our **four planar social being**, not just two. The challenge for the left, as Reed noted, is to avoid a tramline logic of unending victimhood determined by skin colour. It is also vital to defend free debate about making sense of complexity, given all my caveats about broad tendencies just noted. The generative mechanisms involved are more than racism alone, whether personal or structural, but it is an important consideration amongst many. Another caution (and to restate the need for free debate about race) is that the concrete singularity of cases of structural racism in one country will be different to another.

For example, in the USA, the post-slavery, post-civil rights context is different from British society, where racism and ethnocentricity are today being played out in a different way. I return to this point in Chapter Eight, along with a greater consideration of ethnicity. In the USA, with its plantation culture and its financial gain to the rich in Britain, genocide preceded the slave trade, as noted here by Martin Luther King Jr:

> Our nation was born in genocide, when it embraced the doctrine that the original American, the Indian, was an inferior race. Even before there were large numbers of Negroes on our shore, the scar of racial hatred had already disfigured colonial society. From the sixteenth century forward, blood flowed in battles over racial supremacy. We are perhaps the only nation which tried as a matter of national policy to wipe out its indigenous population. (King, M.L. (1963) "Why the Negro Won't Wait," *Financial Post*, 27 July)

There are some who might question whether the final sentence might also apply to British colonialism in Australia. These ambiguities remind us that racial politics have been played out in different ways in different countries as modernity emerged. To understand these differences, we need to develop a historical sensibility about socio-economic complexity, drawing upon a range of interdisciplinary resources. Identity politics is not up to this task, with its overly narrow focus on the personal and the interpersonal and the moralistic preoccupations this generates in the immediate present.

Conclusion

I have deployed a **four planar social being** framework of understanding to contemporary racial politics. This allows us to consider the natural world, relationality, socio-economic processes (past and present), and our unique biographies as human agents, when we reflect on the adequacy of identity politics, with race as its focus. Whilst we should give due weight to the personal and the interpersonal (Planes 2 and 4 from the list above) if we overburden them with expectations of analytical adequacy or political inspiration then we are whisked away into a self-righteous world of authoritarian moralisations, speech suppression, and guilt-ridden self-surveillance. This scenario obscures, it does not clarify. A discussion of empirical complexity and uncertainty, in a spirit of **epistemic humility**, is replaced with reductionist simplifications. At times it can divert our attention from structural racism and its discussion in relation to poverty in general. It divides people against one another, with no clear evidence that this encourages social justice and human flourishing. It supports, rather than challenges, neoliberalism.

CHAPTER SIX

Mental health politics

Introduction

This chapter examines the **emergence** during the 1970s of groups of current and ex-psychiatric patients protesting about the limitations on their citizenship. The debates about the rights of this **new social movement** (NSM), variously called the "users' movement" the "consumers' movement", the "ex-patients' movement", or the "survivors' movement", relate to competing views about the rights and wrongs of deprivation of liberty without trial and the interference of bodies without permission.

A focus of contention is whether these infringements represent false imprisonment and assault by agents of the state on the one hand or, on the other, they are wholly legitimate actions in order to offer the mentally sick ameliorative treatment or even cure. We have, then, opposing views about an ethical approach to madness (Pols, 2001). There has been widespread negligence on the part of state paternalists because they have failed to routinely ensure the legally expected "principle of reciprocity", that is, to be humane and ensure effective amelioration, in exchange for loss of liberty without trial (Szasz, 1963; Eastman, 1994).

Accordingly, critics can then describe routine psychiatric detention in similar terms to torture or cruel and degrading treatment

(Pūrasis, 2017). This objection is not, then, about the abuse of psychiatry but its *use*. Biomedical psychiatry tranquillises and contains madness, it does not cure it. The natural course of madness in particular individuals is highly variable, whether or not they are medicated or electroshocked.

With regard to the medical group working on behalf of those sane by common consent, much hostile attention has been given to them by the protesting NSM (Crossley, 2006). However, this might imply that if the psychiatric profession were to be abolished tomorrow, then tensions about citizenship from those who are unintelligible or incorrigible in our midst would disappear. A variant of this demand relates to the removal of all of the coercive apparatus of the "mental health workforce", involving involuntary detention in locked facilities, forced medication, and solitary confinement, which in this context is dubbed euphemistically "seclusion". That wider demand, rather than a focused one to remove a single vilified profession, gets to the nub of why this particular NSM has emerged and why it has joined the ranks of identity politics.

The recurring debate (with or without the presence of modern psychiatry) is whether mad people will *ever* be permitted a form of citizenship equivalent to their sane peers (Rogers & Pilgrim, 1989). After all, in pre-psychiatric societies the mad had often been met with a repressive response from those around them (Westermeyer & Kroll, 1978). Chained and derided, the mad have never had an easy time.

Modern biomedical psychiatry has been *biddable* within this long history, but it is only one part of it. Accordingly, removing the profession would not be a guarantee of social progress. Its diagnostic codifications and routines of involuntary treatment are one version of state-endorsed repression, but others could readily be invented (Bean, 1980). Complaints that in authoritarian cultures, biddable psychiatrists do their very worst, point up that in more liberal ones, their complicity is there but merely in a softened or cautious form (Cohen, 1989; Bloch & Reddaway, 1977). Hard power is still there in both scenarios, however we may sanitise it with administrative terms, such as "being treated under the Mental Health Act".

This double standard over being honest about psychiatric coercion became clear in relation to the case of Princess Latifa of Dubai. She was kidnapped and held captive by her own father when she tried to leave the country. The explanation was that she was a suffering from bipolar disorder and was being treated at home. Her forced detention and tranquilisation caused a major international scandal. However, the practical elements of her treatment were no different to what happens on a routine daily basis to ordinary psychiatric patients, under "mental health law": forced detention; coercively administered drugging; and solitary confinement ("seclusion").

Below I trace the conditions of possibility for this contestation about citizenship. Those who are both psychologically different *and* then disvalued according to contingent social norms are the current **empirical** starting point. Ultimately other questions, such as whether medicine is being applied inappropriately as a form of social control and why applying medical solutions to psycho-social problems is futile, are important. However, they arise as secondary considerations to the core questions about rule infraction and its warranted control in any society, which then jeopardises the citizenship of mad people.

Citizenship and insanity

If we fail to keep the coercive control of insanity as our central focus, then the broader notion of "mental health politics" will tend to drift to bland and readily answerable questions. This safer territory involves those who have never been, and probably never will be, detained psychiatric patients. That is, the majority of people who are treated for psychological problems by chemicals or conversations remain free citizens, even if for varying periods of time they are unhappy ones; the generic inoffensive term for their experience is "psychological distress".[1]

These so-called "common mental health problems", which are mainly variable mixtures of expressions of fear ("anxiety disorders") and sadness ("depression"), encourage us to normalise our common distress

---

[1] It is common in progressive circles to use the sympathy-inducing catchall term "distress", as a straight euphemistic swap for "disorder". However, this semantic reduction glosses the question of who is distressed and whether the social disruption, created by rule transgressive conduct, is being backgrounded and obscured. This point applies also to wilful self-starvation. The anorexic child is distressed at being expected to eat. The parent is distressed that their child might very well soon die. Calling *everything* "distress" is a reductive mystification of a complex psychosocial field. At least the term "disorder" invites us to clarify what is *mental order* contingently, if we are minded so to do.

and remove the stigma associated with its confession.[2] After all, we are all in our particular ways tired of living and scared of dying. The boundary then between normality and distress really is very porous. However, the psychiatric profession has been involved overwhelmingly, *when employed by the state*, rather than privately where its skills are anxiously sought and gratefully, in the coercive control of unintelligible and socially disruptive individuals. Distress is a secondary consideration to the search for social order and attempts at rule enforcement by "mental health professionals".

A blurring of the normal and abnormal in anti-stigma campaigns, and the encouragement of more and more of us to "come out" about our distress makes much sense and it reflects the notion that distinctions are not binary but reflect continua. Psychological models within both the psychodynamic and cognitive traditions quite correctly identify this rationale. For example, Freud and his followers espoused the idea that we are all in our particular way ill and that the term "psychopathology" was relevant to us all, no exceptions. Similarly, cognitive models have more recently confirmed that abnormal phenomena (fear, sadness, delusions, hallucinations, etc.) can be understood by the same psychological **generative mechanisms** as those of normal ones (Bentall, 2003).

Notwithstanding, this advantageous logic of bringing the abnormal back into the fold *conceptually* by these psychiatrists, clinical psychologists, and psychotherapists, the *practical* social consequences of going beyond the pale in rule transgressions remain. This also has implications for the enthusiastic wide support for "mental health campaigns", affecting those with "common mental health problems", as well as anti-stigma policies.

For example, in the late 1970s the British mental health charity MIND collaborated with a popular BBC TV programme *That's Life* to

---

[2] What are traditionally accepted as "true mental illnesses", such as "schizophrenia" and "bipolar disorder", were until the middle of the twentieth century marked off quite clearly from the more common "stress reactions" to life (Fish, 1968). With diagnostic expansionism under revisions of the *Diagnostic and Statistical Manual of the American Psychiatric Association* (DSM) and the International Classification of Diseases (ICD) of the World Health Organization, a vast range of deviations from social norms became "mental disorders". This eventually reduced the "pool of normality to a mere puddle" (Wykes & Callard, 2010) and shy people became patients (Lane, 2008).

highlight the dangers of major tranquillisers. These are drugs given to psychotic patients, inside or outside of hospital, aimed at reducing the presence of auditory hallucination and encouraging rational conduct. They are hit and miss in their impact and when they fail, prescribers tend to add in other drugs ("polypharmacy") and increase dose levels ("megadosing"). This then creates serious risks to patients of movement disorders and occasionally even death as the cardiovascular system is shut down (Kellam, 1987). The stigmatising impact on the appearance of patients is socially relevant, as they tremble, shuffle, and have jerky movements.

What happened to the joint forces of the BBC and MIND is relevant for this chapter. Instead of the exposure of this problem taking off as a public scandal about the damage being done to vulnerable psychiatric patients, detained and forcibly treated, the programme was inundated with reports of patients who were not under the jurisdiction of psychiatry at all. These were those who had been prescribed *minor* tranquillisers by their general practitioner for symptoms of anxiety.

These are called "anxiolytics", mainly from a drug group called the "benzodiazepines" (with trade names like "Valium" and "Librium"). They are very effective at calming us down in the short term; for example, they are administered as a one-off intervention, just before we have surgery. However, as soon was becoming evident, they cause more problems than they solve if used beyond the very short term. We habituate to the drugs, meaning that we need more of them to maintain the same calming effect. This creates a pathway to addiction as withdrawal is distressing. A particular rebound effect includes panic attacks.

Those inundating the TV programme with these accounts were the canary in the coal mine about an emerging iatrogenic scandal: the widespread addiction in society to benzodiazepines, prescribed for symptoms of anxiety or insomnia and furnishing Big Pharma with profits (Gabe & Lipshitsz-Phillips, 1982; Bury & Gabe, 1990). The point here, then, is that the campaign to highlight the iatrogenic scandal of *major* tranquillisers failed and was displaced by one of patients detrimentally affected by other psychiatric drugs (*minor* tranquillisers), leaving the clinical norms of coercive psychiatry in "specialist" services unscrutinised.

The division between the sane and the insane was thus marked. The concern of the general public and the medical profession itself with psychotic patients, who are the recipients of major tranquillisers (also called "anti-psychotics"), was as at best indifferent and at worst negligent (Brown & Funk, 1986). These patients were both poor *and* mad, so there was little mass sympathy for their plight, compared to those "hooked" on prescribed minor tranquillisers. The low social status of psychiatric patients was thus thrown into relief and a contempt for their citizenship highlighted.

The story of the fear of madness is one of contested citizenship. The subtext from the discourse of sanity is that the mad deserve their fate for their transgressions. It is for the best that they are segregated legitimately, out of sight and out of mind, and, if required, their actions forcibly constrained. This is a cue for the next section.

Being mad and being burdensome

To be mad typically is the necessary but not sufficient condition for deprivation of liberty without trial. Many people are walking around amongst us, hearing voices not heard by others and holding strange and fixed ideas (delusions) that bemuse others when spoken out loud. It is the way that they do or do not then *act* upon those perceptions and thoughts that is the key to understanding why risk, to self or others, determines the shape and priorities of so-called "mental health services". So-called "mental health legislation" exists to regulate that risk and guide agents of the state in its legitimate management.

Risk to others, when the criminal law is broken, is managed by a set period of imprisonment. Wrongdoing is punished but, as important, any immediate danger to others is considered about incarceration. Judgements about criminal deviance are made by the courts, on the basis of proven past conduct and the accused has access to legal advocacy to argue for their innocence and liberty. That rationale does not apply in the case of non-criminal deviance but where risky conduct is the focus. In the case of psychiatric patients, it is the *prospective* risk in the near future that dominates decision-making. Legal provisions exist then for psychiatric agents of the state to use their delegated discretion.

The psychiatric patient is assessed for a risk of the equivalent of "future crime", which determines the period of their detention (not the finite decision made by a court about criminality). Moreover, patients who are admitted to psychiatric facilities involuntarily, unlike the criminal, do not have legal advocates actively arguing for their liberty. Thus, risk management in modern societies is not governed by consistent rules of constraint or protections of civil liberties (see Box 6.1).

Box 6.1 Inconsistency in the state regulation of risk

When I taught undergraduate social science students about mental health legislation, I would begin by arguing that there should be a curfew law, so that those under the age of twenty-five could not leave their homes between dusk on Fridays and dawn on Mondays. The thought experiment was warranted, I argued, because blocking young public binge drinking would reduce, amongst other things, attendance at accident and emergency departments, road traffic collisions, sexual and non-sexual violence (domestic and in public), sexually transmitted diseases, and unwanted pregnancies. There would also be a substantial cost saving to the state, in relation to police and health care involvement. I asked the class their thoughts and the overwhelming response was that the suggestion was ridiculous and unfair. Most of them were under twenty-five, so the provocation was intended.

I then asked whether we should have mental health legislation. Most (but not all) agreed, on the grounds that people who were mentally disordered should be controlled and looked after. I noted in response, citing evidence, that the rates of actual harm to others was very small from patients with a psychiatric diagnosis (compared to some other social groups). Suicide is not ipso facto evidence of mental disorder; people often kill themselves for reasons that make sense at the time, quite logically. Also, in most jurisdictions with "mental health law", suicide per se is not illegal.

We can only make sense of discrimination against psychiatric patients, about risk to self and others, if we judge their deviance in a different manner to other forms of risky conduct in society.

These young students might have had their own motives for reserving the right to drink alcohol, excessively and at will, but their support of the need for special legislation to control psychological abnormality probably goes beyond their own age group. It is contentious for the very reason that people *know* that it is anomalous: in representative democracies detention without trial is generally frowned upon and a case for it has to be made, for example under terrorist legislation.

Whatever viewpoint we hold on this matter, one thing is clear: risk management is not a level playing field in public policy. People smoke, drink heavily, and have unprotected sex. Mountain climbers, racing-car drivers, boxers, and rugby players are national heroes, not detainees of the state. Horse-riding and skiing are risky hobbies and maintain the high salaries of orthopaedic surgeons. Alcohol use, young age, and male sex all are good predictors of risk to self and others (see Box 6.2).

Given these various examples of unconstrained risk, we can all reflect critically on the euphemism of "mental health law". This exists primarily as a mechanism of social control in the interests of public order and third parties, other than identified patients. It is not designed to enhance mental health but to control *one* type of risky conduct. This scenario is a glaring example of the betrayal of citizenship by the general public, mental health professionals, and policymakers in the state. It is a complex topic, but coercive social control is coercive social control, whichever way we describe it and however we might justify its existence.

Managing risk in "mental health services"

When I was working in the NHS, my clinical work on some days was in outpatient work and on others with those on locked wards this point became obvious in practice. For example, I once asked a nurse heading a locked ward about why a particular patient, with a diagnosis of schizophrenia, was still being detained. His initial response was not persuasive ("because he is suffering from schizophrenia"). I pointed out that the day before in my outpatient clinic I had seen a patient who also had the same diagnosis but was living in the community despite this. The nurse replied that the patient still locked up might seem fine for now but when released he drinks alcohol with his friends and smokes cannabis. This could make him aggressive in a neighbourhood in which his unpredictable and scary reputation has surrounded him for years. So, I noted to the nurse that it was not acute schizophrenia that was the reason for the patient's current detention but instead fears about his disruptive conduct in a community setting. The nurse graciously agreed. We then weighed up options about how to negotiate with the patient about reducing his drug and alcohol use when discharged. The context of this case example is one of the assumed and actual risk posed by psychiatric patients to others (see Box 6.2).

> Box 6.2 Perceived and actual danger of psychiatric patients
>
> Because madness is frightening to those encountering it (especially for the first time) it is common to rush to judgement that all or most psychiatric patients *really are* more dangerous than the general population. Actually, some psychotic patients are dangerous, especially if their delusions entail hostile grudges about others (Appelbaum, Robbins, & Monahan, 2000). Also, some with command hallucinations that target people for attack can indeed increase the risk of actual violence (P. J. Taylor, 1985; Junginger, 1995). As with non-patients, substance misuse increases risk to others in psychotic patients (Soyka, 2000; Swartz, Swanson, Hiday, & Borum, 1998). However, *overall,* psychotic patients are *not* more dangerous than the general population. Indeed, they are more likely because of their alienated isolation and passivity (called "negative symptoms") to be victims of crimes (Silver, Mulvey, & Monahan, 1999; Steadman et al., 1998).
>
> A number of social or personal characteristics are very strong predictors of violence generally in society and "out-trump" psychiatric status. Men, especially young men, are the main perpetrators (and victims) of non-sexual violent assaults. They also predominate overwhelmingly as sexual offenders. The use of substances (alcohol being the commonest) that affect the frontal lobes of the brain, causing disinhibition, is a strong predictor of violence. Given this constellation of factors, young drunken males are the main perpetrators of violence (see my discussion in Box 6.1). Given that some of these are also psychiatric patients, then it is little surprising that violence appears in the latter group *as well as* in non-patient comparisons.
>
> The prison population containing those sentenced for violent crimes reveals another cross-cutting social variable that is predictive: poverty. The overlap, then, between populations in prisons and locked psychiatric facilities becomes obvious but they are not identical. First admissions are as likely to be female as male (counter to the penal population). However, men are detained for longer once admitted, reflecting concerns about risk from them as being more salient in professional decision-making. Another factor is sex roles in parenting responsibilities, with mothers being discharged quicker.

> A final consideration is race. As with prison populations, in post-colonial societies, black patients are over-represented in those coercively contained by the state. Young black men are treated more coercively at *all stages* in the process of psychiatric containment, from arrests by the police, right through to decisions to move inpatients into high levels of security.*
>
> ---
>
> *A discussion of competing explanations for the over-representation of black detained inpatients is provided in Rogers and Pilgrim (2021: Ch. 5). I note this picture as well in Chapter Five of this book.

In light of this example, and the discussion in Boxes 6.1 and 6.2, we can see that it is not the presence of mental disorder per se that determines decisions about risk but the way that those so labelled then conduct themselves, within an inconsistent set of norms about risk management. It is their *conduct*, not their strange perceptions and thought processes, which really determine whether citizenship is retained or denied. Once it is denied, then agents of the state have a very wide discretion about how they might deal with risk to self and others. If risk to others has been linked to criminal conduct, then segregation in conditions of higher security is then warranted in the interests of public order and the protection of others.

Warehousing psychiatric risk

That convergence of criminality and psychological abnormality led to the provision of a particular structure of containment in the nineteenth century: the criminal lunatic asylum. This then created a hybrid deviant of particular concern: the mentally abnormal offender. The first example in the UK was Broadmoor Hospital, set up in 1863, but we can also note that the wider Victorian asylum system represented the need to adapt the pre-existing structure for the social regulation of the unemployed and unemployable. The specialist criminal lunatic asylum began as well to absorb a particular type of psychological deviance, other than ordinary lunacy (i.e., unintelligible conduct where the person is deemed to have lost their reason).

"Moral insanity" referred to those who superficially were rational[3] but were without conscience and capable of extreme anti-social acts (such as murder, rape, and arson) with no remorse. Unlike the acquisitive criminal who warded off poverty by the craft of theft and deceit at the expense of others, moral insanity was primarily personal. Those admitted with this label simply used others for their own personal gratification, whether or not any material gain was achieved. Today we tend to call these people "psychopaths".[4] When they are not in prison, or a high-security psychiatric facility, they are found in leadership roles in society in business and politics (Babiek & Hare, 2007). Their self-seeking rationality (cf. the psychotic patient) allows them to survive, and often thrive at the expense of others in open society, provided that they do not break the criminal law or are discovered doing so.[5] Put differently, clever or lucky psychopaths stay this side of the law and flourish narcissistically.

Returning to the earlier and original undifferentiated institutional policy solution, the workhouse, established in the first part of the nineteenth century, soon spawned specialist versions. From the outset across the political spectrum many deemed the workhouse to be problematic because of the poor conditions, drudgery, and social exclusion of its inmates. Some of these, who were insane, simply were unable or unwilling to comply with the daily labour routines expected of them and so separate lunatic asylums to manage this challenge were set up. Analogously, institutions emerged for those far too simple to comply. The lunatic and the idiot[6] started to be differentiated, for social administrative purposes, from those who were deemed to be psychologically normal but simply paupers.

---

[3] The classic description of psychopathy was from Cleckley (1941), who called it the "mask of sanity". Whether ruthless evil social actors should be called "insane" remains a matter of debate; witness the discussions about the mental state of Donald Trump.

[4] This term is not used in formal diagnostic systems, where we find instead "dissocial personality disorder" in ICD and "antisocial personality disorder" in DSM. Until 2007, in England and Wales the term "psychopathic disorder" was used in its "Mental Health Act".

[5] A fictional example that describes the psychopath operating precariously as a success in society is *The Undoing*, the Netflix drama with Hugh Grant playing the case study.

[6] In the Victorian period, what today are called people with "intellectual" or "learning" "disabilities", were called "idiots", "imbeciles", and "morons".

Before these populations became medicalised (and "inmates" thereby became "inpatients") the matter of precarious citizenship was dealt with very directly as a moral challenge. Early administrators of the asylum system applied a form of re-education to bring lunatics back into the fold of rational society. This "moral treatment" involved both imposed routines and expected residents to be moral agents, capable of gradual compliance and insight, which would warrant their release into wider society (Castel, 1983).

Even when the medical profession increasingly took charge of asylums, elements of this moral treatment were retained, some of which was gentle and respectful but some involved authoritarian and cruel demands. Until the middle of the twentieth century, medicinal, electrical, and surgical interventions from biomedical enthusiasts were only in a secondary role to the main rationale of containment and routine. Some argued for the abolition of the institution, even if in the interim a few medical psychotherapists made a case for its therapeutic potential (e.g., Main, 1946). The evidence of the chronic constraints on citizenship of these "museums of madness" posed the challenge of turning a pig's ear into a silk purse (Scull, 1979).

With this scepticism in mind, the word "institutionalisation" began to be used in two senses. In the first, there was a description of a policy of containment for one subgroup of the poor. In other words, a confidence in the utility and efficiency of the *system* of institutions continued from the mid-Victorian period for a century. The second sense was increasingly used after the Second World War to describe the deleterious *personal* impact of long-term institutional containment, when it was also dubbed "institutionalism" or "institutional neurosis".

Sociologists and social psychiatrists began to document its character (Goffman, 1961; Wing, 1962). One of these, Russell Barton, was a young medical student directly witnessing the opening of the Nazi concentration camps. Post-war, he noticed stereotypical behaviour in survivors common to that he subsequently was to witness in the asylum system (and, of course, caged animals in zoos), such as agitated pacing up and down (Barton, 1959). This attack on the old asylums from social psychiatrists was to continue within campaigns for their closure (Basaglia, 1964). Their social and cultural isolation ensured afforded a systemic risk of abuse to residents (Martin, 1985).

As with the poor house and the prison, residents of asylums typically left in a pauper's coffin. Before that, the limits of their world were shrunk, in what Goffman called the "total institution", which defined their lives day after day interminably.[7] In the meantime, those who were taking their chances in the open system of society may still have been poor, but they were at least free, to move around, associate with kith and kin, have sexual relationships, and vote (if their sex and age permitted). The lunatic, like the prisoner, could do none of these things. Even today we go mad at our peril if we lose, albeit now more typically in a limited and episodic rather than chronic way, our civil liberties. So simply closing the asylums did not necessarily equate to the restoration of citizenship for all, a point now considered.

Deinstitutionalisation and its consequences

The NSM that we now associate with one part of identity politics (the psychiatric survivors' movement[8]) has a range of demands but most of them come back to this core question of citizenship and its problematic status in modern societies governed by industrial rationality. Not surprisingly, objections to infringements of liberty and social exclusion more generally are a focus of campaigns. Psychiatric patients (note *not* that broad community-based population who are diagnosed with common mental disorders and treated in primary care or at the hands of privately paid therapists) are failed or impaired citizens, excluded and stigmatised by their sane peers.

The explanation for that failure to be respected even today is open to dispute. To the medical paternalist and many in the population agreeing with their view, citizenship fails because of the primary deviance of the patient. That is, they are *unable* to function as citizens because they are suffering from a mental disorder and this warrants care from others, if needs be imposed involuntarily. It suggests their impairment comes

---

[7] The lockdown under COVID-19 might have given those with no experience of institutional living a flavour of the existential challenges posed by a closed repetitive daily world. A sense of "Groundhog Day" was always known very well to the asylum patient, the monk, the nun, and the prisoner.

[8] Psychiatric patients have survived coercive treatment and iatrogenic treatment, social rejection, and often childhood adversity. Thus, the identity of "survivor" seems to be a highly warranted description.

from within the individual and that psychological pathology has social consequences. The counterview is that citizenship is denied to those incurring a psychiatric diagnosis for a range of social reasons, including intolerance and distrust. These processes include stigmatisation, disadvantage in the labour market, and discrimination in legal policy. The last of these refers to my earlier point about psychiatric patients being treated pointedly in relation to risk. Why do we have special legal provision for this group and not others?

This contention and tension between explanations about the need or otherwise to socially control mental abnormality was at the centre of the movement to close the Victorian asylum system. However, not only did constrained citizenship motivate those campaigning for that closure, some also warned that such closure might trigger a mixture of neglect and short-term coercive control in smaller units (Scull, 1977). The latter, environmentally, might be *more* oppressive than the old asylums, which typically had grand high-ceilinged rooms in green spacious grounds. These institutions, by and large, were built in the greenbelt, lying outside of city boundaries, whereas modern low-ceilinged psychiatric units are typically in bustling general hospitals in urban localities.

The social character of madness

At this point we can take stock of the social features of psychiatric patients as a manifestation of inequality (Rogers & Pilgrim, 2003). First, they are predominantly poor. Whilst people of any social class may act in an unintelligible or incorrigible way to disrupt social order and frighten those sane by common consent, pauper lunacy has been the main social administrative challenge in modernity (Rothman, 1971; Scull, 1977). Once a subpopulation of those in the workhouse were identified as being resistant to immediate daily discipline because of their withdrawn irrationality, it became evident that "mental health policy" was, by and large, part of a wider policy to regulate the poor under conditions of an emerging capitalist economy.

Second, this impetus for social control was diffuse in the population, not just a top-down desire for order from the new capitalist state. The state formalised laws to ensure public order but the desire for it was popular. It is noteworthy that the asylum system and sewers emerged at the same time as popular policy measures at considerable cost to the state:

both were means to remove offensive waste in Victorian society. At the time of first-wave feminism and the calls for an inclusive form of universal suffrage, there were no mass campaigns to release lunatics from the asylums (indeed their numbers swelled). However, the public imagination was haunted by the prospect of "unfair detention" (Bean, 1980). That fear prompted a variety of legal mechanisms, still in place today, to ensure that only those "deserving" the fate of psychiatric detention received it.

These checks and balances were weak compared to those applied to people deemed to be sane and dealt with in the criminal justice system, but they were there. An important aspect of this fear of unfair detention was that it signalled something that most people knew (hence the fear). Being locked up without trial, stripped of your right to free association and movement, regulated in an environment that is not of your choosing, and having your body interfered with against your consent is not a desirable scenario. It will not fill most of our hearts with desire or predict our enjoyment or flourishing. It will not offer us enhanced mental health; hence why this term is so often an ironical or preposterous euphemism, when tagged with "services" or "legislation" or "law". If people are scared of madness, which they are, they are also scared of the way in which the mad are treated, and for good reason. A resolution to that angst is to accept the benefits, not just the costs, of mental health law, so called. Detained patients are the ones paying the price for ensured social order and reassured sane citizens.

Biomedical technology to install the internal straitjacket of "antipsychotic" medication is part of the same piece. These drugs are used primarily to tranquillise patients (the are called "major tranquilisers" for good reason) and so reduce their social threat. They offered a practical solution after the Second World War to mad patients living in community settings and were claimed as the prime condition of the possibility for deinstitutionalisation. User critics have described this chemical "long-leash", imposed on medicated community patients, as a sort of "tranquil prison" (Fabris, 2011), with leverage by professionals to ensure compliance in notionally voluntary patients (Quirk, Chaplin, Lelliott, & Seale, 2011). However, pharmacological **reductionism** to explain the decline of the Victorian asylum system has been challenged sociologically (see Box 6.3).[9]

---

[9] A chapter-length account of these competing explanations can be found in Rogers and Pilgrim (2021).

Box 6.3 Why did the lunatic asylum system decline?

In the UK, between 1950 and 1990, the number of beds in the old asylum system was cut by two thirds. A "pharmacological revolution" explanation preferred by biomedical psychiatry is summarised here: "The introduction of chlorpromazine in 1952 made it easier to manage disturbed behaviour, and therefore easier to open wards that had been locked, to engage patients in social activities, and to discharge some of them into the community" (Gelder, Mayou, & Cowen, 2001: 769). The problem with this explanation is that the deinstitutionalisation of other populations, who were not psychotic, such as those with learning disabilities, also took place during the same period. Also, for a while in the 1950s in some countries bed numbers actually *rose*, despite the widespread availability of the drugs. This prompted social and economic explanations to augment or challenge this bio-reductionist account. Scull (1977) argued that this was a fiscal matter: the long-term warehousing of unproductive state-dependent patients, inviting coercive social control, was costly, and so cheaper solutions were required.

After the Second World War, unpaid labour from patients was scorned more and more on ethical grounds and the medical profession gained more confidence (rightly or wrongly) in its therapeutic, rather than custodial, role. Cost inflation also arose from unionisation of labour, so that psychiatric nurses increased their aspirations beyond the manhandling of patients in the older asylum regime.* Shorter working days and holiday entitlement doubled labour costs rapidly. Scull argued contra those favouring deinstitutionalisation that it had been a policy disaster and had led to neglect in the community. A problem with Scull's account is that it is more applicable to the 1980s than the 1960s as an explanatory candidate. That later decade kickstarted **neoliberalism** and the state was being "hollowed out". Although Scull's time frame was faulty, fiscal considerations have certainly been important in accounting for asylum run down.

An alternative multi-factorial explanation is that fiscal factors and easy-to-administer tranquillisation emerged in a context of the expansion of mental health work to the whole population. Now an organisational range of mental health services was promoted by various interest groups, including liberal policymakers, the drug companies, community-orientated social psychiatrists, general practitioners, clinical psychologists, psychotherapists, and service-user groups angry at institutional psychiatry. This then encouraged a shift in thinking about a neat boundary between inpatient and outpatient work. It also generated patient subpopulations, including stable ex-patients living at home to come back to hospital episodically, specialised secure units and locked wards for the very risky, and that wide range of never-to-be-hospitalised groups diagnosed with "common mental health problems".** If community care was a scandal of neglect for Scull, for these groups it was a worthy aspiration, because it aimed for expanded citizenship for those put away, out of sight and out of mind, as well as those fearing that unwanted scenario.

---

* Unlike general nursing, with its feminine caring role led by Florence Nightingale, the Victorian asylum was populated largely by low-paid male attendants employed as physical enforcers: patients were manhandled. This created a divergence of trajectories between the unionisation/professionalisation of nursing, with a separate "mental" branch (Carpenter, 1980).
** Some psychiatrists describe this group as the "worried well", thereby rendering mainstream psychiatric services as mainly "psychosis services", which is a reasonable empirical description of what they are, for the most part.

The debates about the desirability and achievability of community care remain today and are unresolved because of the fiscal challenges about the social control of psychological deviance noted by Scull in Box 6.3. In addition, there has been a lack of imagination in mainstream state services. There are several aspects to this lack of resolution but three stand out. First, what should *any* society do with people who are mad? Second, is madness irredeemable? Third, are mad people controlled in a particularly oppressive manner, compared to others who might act in a risky manner?

I dealt with the last of these in Box 6.1 but it has relevance to the first two questions as well. For example, the original ideal of moral treatment explicitly acknowledged that madness is a moral matter. We are an interdependent species and that means as language users we have codified the rules of our relationships with one another. This means that although norms might vary across time and place, normativity is ubiquitous. A consistent meta-rule is that we should account for ourselves when we transgress culturally shared and contingent rules, especially when they cause social disruption or offend others. Whereas the criminal knowingly breaks rules for personal gain and then covers and lies about their transgression to evade detection and accountability, this is not the case in madness.

Those who are mad inhabit a subjective world which is oblivious, or is indifferent, to expectations of social accountability. Typically, we call this subjective state one that is "lacking insight". They do not dissimulate like the criminal (with some exceptions) but simply speak from, and act upon, their idiosyncratic world. In particular it is their *actions* that matter (the practice of madness I noted earlier). Those working with mad patients know that a sort of dual group membership often occurs. For example, the hallucinating patient responding audibly to their voices can interrupt their inner conversation and listen to the views of others or readily obey instructions for a rational task they wish to cooperate about.[10]

By contrast, those with "common mental health problems" are not only distressed, they are fully aware that they are breaking "emotion rules" (Thoits, 1985). This places them in a different socio-ethical space to those who are mad because their awareness, indeed their heightened self-consciousness, of their deviance is marked. Consequently, the expressed need for moral rectification, to return to previous expectations of their role success as ordinary citizens, is anxiously sought and gratefully received. They will take their anti-depressants (the currently preferred panacea in primary care) or they will turn up dutifully for their psychological therapy, typically the alternative panacea of cognitive-behavioural therapy (Healy, 1997; Herzberg, 2009). But throughout this process, even for those in long-term contact, who are, say, chronically on anti-depressant medication, their citizenship is not curtailed by the application of "mental health law". Miserable, maybe, but they are free nonetheless.

By contrast, those who at times have had their citizenship impaired by agents of the state may well, quite understandably, have strong views about staying out of acute locked wards to avoid the pain of the past. However, within this group, ambivalence has been evident. In particular, this relates to what has been called the "recovery movement". This has

---

[10] This dual membership was noted by the "anti-psychiatrist" and psychoanalyst R. D. Laing, when he suggested that claiming that a psychotic patient is not capable of a rational conversation is rather like saying that a tightrope walker is incapable of walking on the ground (Laing, 1967). Mad patients are very rarely mad all of the time about everything.

been the prosaic aspiration of Dylan Thomas' poetic lines, "though they go mad they shall be sane, thought they sink through the seas they shall rise again".

Recovery and its reception

If moral treatment and its later iteration, the therapeutic community movement, remind us from the past about bringing madness back into the moral fold, then another version in the 1990s can be considered: "recovery". Citizenship is central to it but so too has been a contrarian current in some circles of the right to be mad and the right to be "unrecovered". Here I summarise relevant points from these debates.

The policy push at the turn of this century is put well here as a "guiding vision" for mental health services:

> Recovery is a deeply personal, unique process of changing one's attitudes, values, feelings, goals, skills, and/or roles. It is a way of living a satisfying, hopeful, and contributing life even with limitations caused by illness. Recovery involves the development of new meaning and purpose in one's life as one grows beyond the catastrophic effects of mental illness. (Anthony, 1993: 527)

Pilgrim and McCranie (2013) picked up this starting point to note four discursive trends. These are a personal journey, critique of services, therapeutic optimism, and a social model of disability. The first one being benign and individualistic is readily agreed upon and is the focus of user researchers (e.g., Faulkner & Layzell, 2000; Wallcraft, Read, & Sweeney, 2003). However, some user critics are very wary of the concept of recovery because it means those who do not change are then subjected to new forms of stigmatisation and oppression. Thus, even the personal journey account of recovery is contested within the survivors' movement (see https://recoveryinthebin.org).

The critique of the services approach to recovery poses a different question: should we abandon coercive biomedical psychiatry and ensure instead voluntary person-centred care (Deegan, 1996)? This was a central concern of the survivors' movement beginning in the 1970s.

Sedgwick (1982) argued that psychiatry realistically was not going to be abolished but we should ask whether services are capable of being both "kindly and efficacious", a concern still debated today (Pilgrim, 2018b; Coffey et al., 2019).

The discussion of recovery recently also revisits the matter of therapeutic optimism or nihilism. In the nineteenth century, that tension was between those advocating moral treatment, typified by the lay administrator William Tuke at the York Retreat, and the eugenicists, typified in the leadership of the psychiatrist Emil Kraepelin (Kraepelin, 1883; cf. Manning, 1989). The eugenic view prevailed for the first half of the twentieth century, hence the acceptance of the long-term warehousing of madness. At times, the social and fiscal burden of this warehousing was augmented by psychiatric eugenicists with a policy strategy of mass murder (Meyer, 1988).[11]

However, optimism reasserted itself in the 1960s with a range of initiatives from social psychiatrists and the "anti-psychiatrists". The legacy of that period can be found now, for example, in the Soteria Project (Spandler & Calton, 2009). These alternatives valorise recovery as a positive prospect, but it requires person-centredness and an abolition or minimisation of coercion. In particular it requires the abolition of the conceptual constraints of diagnostic systems like DSM and ICD, in favour of a non-judgemental and exploratory approach to the meaning of psychotic symptoms for individual patients and the coping options in their lives. That appeal for sophisticated tolerance and the abandonment of diagnosis, in favour of patient phenomenology, can be found in the Hearing Voices Network (Romme, Honig, Noorthoorn, & Escher, 1992). It is also there in the Power Threat Meaning Framework emerging from the British Psychological Society (Johnstone & Boyle, 2018). Both give credibility to the patient rather than seeing them as objects of the clinical gaze and targets for biomedical interventions.

In the social science literature on recovery, the social disability model of recovery has not always been persuasive to some groups. It was developed originally in relation to *physical* disability and its associated NSM, which emerged separately from that in mental health. Some physically

---

[11] The Nazi example of medical killings stands out, but the same policy option was rehearsed in the 1940s by some American psychiatrists (Pilgrim, 2008).

disabled groups reject the legitimate presence of psychiatric patients and vice versa (Mulvany, 2000; Pilgrim & Tomasini, 2012). The model has, as its starting point, a critical scrutiny of how society and its norms would need to change (note, not the identified patient).

If we apply that stricture to madness (and the incorrigibility that is medically codified as "personality disorder") then what would this mean? These widespread social changes would be both discursive and practical on a range of fronts (Weller, 2013). The general health impact of common poverty in this patient population is amplified by the iatrogenic impact of drugs and poor primary care. Basically, psychiatric patients tend to have shortened lives because of this pathogenic mix (Saxena, 2018). Poverty reduction then is implied, and the toxicity of psychiatric drugs recognised. The negative images of psychiatric patients in the mass media would need to be abandoned in favour of positive ones (Philo et al., 1996; Rose, 1998; Wahl, 1995). Psychological difference would simply be tolerated or ignored by those sane by common consent (or its positive value appreciated).[12] In other words, de-stigmatisation campaigns would not only be launched and sustained but they would also need to *succeed* in practice. To date this has not occurred (Pescosolido, Medina, Martin, & Long, 2013).

Certainly, mental health law would have to be abolished but, from the World Health Organization down, such legislation is considered to be a positive boon, not a threat, to mental health. With or without such laws, to lose one's reason, in conditions of modern rationality, impairs citizenship.[13] We certainly know that having a psychiatric record disadvantages people in the housing and labour markets and this is one key driver of anti-stigma campaigns. This suggests that if legalism is to be helpful it should focus not on loss of liberty (and protections against unfair detention) with its necessary coercive interference with resistant bodies but on positive rights of care and support for patients.

---

[12] The positive valorisation of madness is rarely considered. We can note though that arguably, Jesus, the Buddha, and the Prophet Mohammed might through their grandiose claims, hallucinations, and wandering outside of society be diagnosed retrospectively as being psychotic. Their views have a mass adoring following but the average psychiatric patient is held in suspicion and offered little or no personal credibility.

[13] As one user activist Peter Campbell noted in the 1990s, "having a diagnosis of schizophrenia has not exactly helped me on the dance floors of life".

These are difficult considerations with strong and competing arguments from interested parties. The contestation is not a mere by-product of modern rationality and the expectations from above and below about public order. Madness has *always* been socially challenging. After all, its recurring hallmark has been a lack of social intelligibility and accountability, which is the requirement of adults in any society, when and if rules are transgressed.[14] In antiquity, madness was associated with aimless wandering, unpredictable aggression, and violence, hence the two connotations of the term "to be mad" (Rosen, 1979). Consequently, there has always been a micro-political stand-off between the sane and the insane.

Madness from a social perspective is a form of personal obdurate defiance and hence the need to make special provision for lunatics in the poor houses, who would not engage in the daily routines of labour expected of them (Porter, 1987). The sane concur with one another about when and how to codify insanity and what to do about it in context, so their options are not on tramlines. The mad can be put in chains or the internal straight jacket of major tranquillisers (see earlier). They can put them in cages, as happened until recently in Eastern Europe. They can be left to roam free, maybe provided that they go mad discreetly and do not scare others.

Whatever we do in terms of public policy, madness is a challenge to social order and therefore this has implications for citizenship for sane and insane alike. These imply an exercise in deliberative democracy to weigh up what should happen next about legalism and effective de-stigmatisation. I return to the challenge of deliberative democracy in the final chapter. However, the treatment of madness is not debated, by and large, because most of us have been content for mental health professionals to get on with their state-devolved role of social control.

---

[14] Although psychiatrists may offer their special skills in diagnosing psychotic states, madness is an ordinary attribution: we all learn when socialised in our culture to spot when a person is acting in an unintelligible manner and is transgressing rules without good reason. Psychiatric labelling is merely a medical redescription of social judgements made in the lay arena (Coulter, 1973). This is why complaining about the (undoubted) problems of psychiatric diagnosis, without reference to ordinary language descriptions, misses the point about the "bottom-up" complexity of describing and responding to madness.

We are happy to believe that with the existence of due process under "mental health legislation", ethical matters are assuredly resolved. Clearly this is not the case. Moreover, agents of the state are just that; I played a small part in that role, at times, in my own clinical career.

Mad Studies

A final variant of patient activism can be noted in relation to the responses described earlier to the recent policy ethos favouring recovery. This has come from "Mad Studies", which are those activists who have come together to articulate a theorisation of their collective position today. Apart from discussing the promise and limits of recovery, and the previously rehearsed inadequacies of coercive biomedical psychiatry, they also develop an alternative notion of the "good life". They favour counter-cultural communities, which aim for social justice and demand human rights in the mental health system (Adame & Knudson, 2008). There is an emphasis on documenting the lessons of their own collective history, such as on the Survivors History website, which encourages both archiving and discussion of its implications (Lindow, 1994; Campbell, 1996; Russo & Sweeney, 2016; Castrodale, 2015).

This activism has a wider intention reflecting the common poverty in patients. It campaigns to deliver appropriate and desirable welfare and other assistance, as well as to encourage social respect and recognition. For example, the group "Recovery in the Bin", noted earlier, state on their website: "We want a robust 'Social Model of Madness, Distress & Confusion', placing mental health within the context of social justice and the wider class struggle."

This wider aspiration includes as a central aim that of reclaiming madness as an oppressed political identity, raising the prospect of it being a *life-long identity*.[15] The latter resists the oppressive call for recovery and signals a permanent existential state of victimhood. This victim identity may well be warranted if **the actual** victimisation, demonstrably suffered in the past, has created a position of nihilism or stoicism; that which cannot be cured must be endured. The allusion to class struggle signals the position of madness in modern times, as part of the

---

[15] Being a user-researcher may also encourage this fixity of identity.

lumpenproletariat, well documented by social historians of the Victorian asylum and its personal legacy today. Being "unrecovered" concedes a long-term social ontological presence in this part of society. Apart from victimhood, the identity can also claim special insights about an alienated society (a theme since the 1960s in both "anti-psychiatry" and the survivors' movement). These insights are denied to conformists who do not enter the role of being a psychiatric patient.

This brings us back to a central challenge for this form of identity politics. How far will those who are sane by common consent concede demands for improved citizenship from those who are unintelligible, socially disruptive, and frightening? Those personal characteristics of irrationality at the level of the individually identified patient are transformed into reasonable collective demands from user activists in their NSM and in groups of patients committed to this recent project of mad studies. How persuasive they can be remains an open question for now.

Conclusion

This chapter has examined mental disorder and its implications for identity politics. It is not a comprehensive account of all the sociological aspects of the topic, but the following points can be made in conclusion to place the NSM of angry and disaffected psychiatric patients and their legitimate claims to civil rights into context.

First, psychiatric patients (not those with a diagnosis of a "common mental disorder", who do not encounter specialist services or ever become an inpatient) are treated differently from other social groups. They are detained without trial and their bodies are interfered with without permission. Most countries have a whole legal apparatus for this to occur so that agents of the state are not accused of assault and false imprisonment and this is seen as wholly socially progressive as a public policy. Few have queried this highly questionable assumption, within policy-making circles.

Second, an NSM emerged to protest against the offence this scenario poses routinely in civil society to those affected. What happens to them is life diminishing and sometimes even life threatening. In other words, there are reasonable empirical and ethical grounds for challenging the political orthodoxy of "mental health legislation". The harm this has done renders the term an oxymoron.

Third, the assessment and management of their risk to self and others are governed by different criteria to others. Many non-patients are demonstrably risky in their conduct at times, but they remain free citizens. Psychiatric patients thus suffer multiple forms of discrimination. They are treated coercively, even though the great majority of them have committed no criminal offence. They are stigmatised, distrusted, and socially rejected and suffer as a consequence in the labour market, rendering the majority of them unemployed and unemployable.

The response to this oppressive scenario has been varied, with some arguing for a recovery-based approach, some demanding structural changes to encourage social acceptance, and some defying the demand that patients should recover and be brought back into the moral fold of society. What all of this has in common is a focus on citizenship. Accordingly, it is not surprising that psychiatric patients have organised themselves to protest about its constraint or negation, and that mental health professionals have been ambivalent about what constitutes social progress in this regard.

Underneath or beyond these discussions, the wider public, who are sane by common consent, by and large leave them to the debate provided that no one is thought to be at risk of "unfair detention". For this reason, the legitimacy of the demands from disaffected patient groups and their professional allies is less clear cut than, for example, demands from the anti-racist movement or from feminism. I return to this point in the final chapter.

CHAPTER SEVEN

Religious identities

Introduction

An important aspect of identity formation is the finitude of our lives and the recognition of the eventual disappearance of our conscious egos. An existential position is adopted by us all about this fact, even if it entails the denial of death or its implications for our ultimate irrelevance. Most cultures have negotiated an organised form of sense-making and hence the ubiquity of religions, theistic or non-theistic. A religious commitment helps us to counter the absurdity of our existence and keep the wolf of our personal irrelevance from our door. To avoid despair, we may opt for a leap in faith but at times in a sense of irritation about the brevity of our position in eternity. As Eifion Wyn put it: "Oh, Lord, why did you make Cwm Pennant so beautiful/And the life of the old shepherd so short?"

That individual existential challenge for us all leads to many of us joining some form of organised "faith group". Once that happens, or it is simply a continuation of primary socialisation from childhood, this moves from the ubiquitous biographical challenge of sense making in conditions of finitude (Plane 4 in the **four planar social being**) to Planes 2 and 3 as well. Religious observance brings with it social capital and a group sense of belonging. When religions become enmeshed with the state or seek control over its functioning, they are then political organisations. When they accumulate wealth, they then become financial players in warfare and civil existence in peacetime. Fighting with God on your side is politically important for powerbrokers and ordinary combatants alike. The tentacles of organised religion reach far and wide in both our inner lives and our social actions.

Equality and diversity training today includes the topic of religion. However, its relationship to oppression is, to say the least, ambiguous. An irony is that in liberal democracies it is the non-religious (humanists and secularists) who tend to defend religious freedom vigorously in principle. There are certainly ecumenical campaigns to defend religious freedoms across the world for Christians, as well as interfaith movements for the same purpose locally and internationally. However, this lobbying is based on the evidence that religious intolerance can come from *any* authoritarian or repressive regime, whether secularist or theocratic.

This aspect of religious politics is important: religion can both capture the state and be a focus of its persecution. That campaigning for tolerance from religious groups themselves is based predominantly on the assumption that the religious are only ever victims and not victimisers. In fact, this is a two-way street. When theocratic capture occurs, then the state itself becomes persecutory. Few faith groups seem to be exempt from this trend.

Look for example at Islamic theocratic power in Iran today, which has tortured dissidents, or the strong control of Buddhism on politics in Myanmar, with its persecution of Muslims on its Western border. Another example to cite on this point is theocratic power in India. As Hansen (2021) demonstrates in his book, *The Law of Force: The Violent Heart of Indian Politics*, there has been a recent norm of Hindu nationalists terrorising Muslims and those of lower castes. The author notes the direct parallels between this conduct and that of Nazi Brownshirts in Germany in the early 1930s.

Moreover, persecutor–victim dynamics can even include denominational or sectarian features; they are not necessarily about one religion pitched against another but can be about factionalism *within* a faith group. Examples of this have included power struggles within Islamic factions in the Middle East and the sectarian violence in the north of Ireland between Catholics and Protestants. In the first of these (for example in Syria), sectarianism is linked to tribal loyalties. In the second, Christian denominations became proxy descriptions for political loyalties (to the United Kingdom centred on Great Britain or to a postcolonial united Ireland), during "the Troubles" in the six counties of the North in the 1970s.

Objections that sectarian violence in Ireland was *not* about religion are only partially plausible. Its roots were indeed historically within British colonialism, but its cultural maintenance was expressed through religious allegiance. Between the Irish Free State being formed in 1922 and its formal designation as a republic in 1948, its leader Eamonn de Valera consulted extensively with the Catholic hierarchy about the health and welfare infrastructure of the new nation. The predominantly Protestant north was governed by the broader polity of Great Britain just over the water.

Thus, when we think about religion, as an aspect of identity politics, we find that this is a complex and contradictory field. This chapter unpacks those contradictions and thereby problematises religion within identity politics. A starting point is to separate a generic human trend to value the *spiritual* aspects of being alive, from a commitment to a *religious* belief system. The generic tendency has encouraged the latter but cannot be conflated with it. Religions are variants of spirituality, not its totality (see Box 7.2 later).

Our sense of awe and uncertainty about our small temporary individual position in a larger, mysterious, and eternal cosmos is ubiquitous in all societies across time and space. It is the way that spirituality has been co-opted by particular elite groups first on their own behalf (in cults and schisms) and then in relation to the governmental arrangements of states that distinguishes religion from spirituality.

And when religion has been weaponised in this way for political ends, even the notion of "nation" (as political entities) has then been challenged. I noted the tension still unresolved about the United Kingdom and a united Ireland (and pick this point up again in Chapter Eight). We can also note the separatist "Nation of Islam" movement in the USA and the aspirations of a universal caliphate by ISIS. Different nations in recent history have dealt with this tension in a range of ways. For example, secularism has been an emphasis in French political culture. However, in the USA conservative Christianity has constantly shaped policy formation (the "religious right" as a source of support for constraints on the rights of women and gay people). There the separation of the state from religion in modern societies has been precarious (see Box 7.1).

> Box 7.1 Limits to secularisation in modern states
>
> Some states today are explicit theocracies. Examples here include the Islamic Republic of Iran and the Kingdom of Saudi Arabia. These examples indicate that theocratic power has been incorporated into both republican and monarchic forms of governance. The counter to that trend in the past 200 years has been secularism. The latter involves the claim to be governed by the "secularity principle": there should be no favouring of particular religious groups by the state and nor should individuals be discriminated against because of their religious beliefs. The principle emerged from the push from Enlightenment thinkers at the end of the eighteenth century to reject arbitrary religious authority, which had been enmeshed with regal power (C. Taylor, 2007). An example of the latter was the establishment of the Church of England by the serial wife murderer Henry VIII in opposition to the rule of the Vatican. Today it is still the established religion within the constitutional monarchy of the United Kingdom. Its bishops sit in the House of Lords and there has been no Catholic Prime Minister to date.* It is common for government leaders in Britain to define it as a "Christian country" and the Queen is the head of the Church of England.
>
> Expectations of secularisation in post-Enlightenment states were articulated in both the Constitution of the United States (1787) and in the French Declaration of the Rights of Man (1789). The extent to which today those states are fully secularised is debatable, given that legal principles do not always align with cultural powers to elect representatives. An example here is of the power of religious fundamentalist ideology in the voting public of the United States. This leads to a paradox whereby the legal protection to religious freedom might facilitate the power of theocratic aspirations (for example, the tolerance of radical Islamic teachings in European states). The relevance here is that the vehicle of diversity and inclusion principles (a reflection of identity politics) defends forms of teaching which are anti-secularist, anti-pluralist, and reflect a regression to feudal forms of ideology in the twenty-first century.
>
> Thus, paradoxically, identity politics defends these tendencies by valorising personal beliefs, even if they are anti-democratic in their aspirations.

For example, legitimate critiques of the theocratic and patriarchal character of some Islamic teachings in European countries will be deemed to be "Islamophobic" because they are primarily framed as an attack on individual belief rather than on the ideology underpinning it. The alignment between identity politics and religious fundamentalism is also reflected in the authoritarianism of both, especially in the tendencies of black-and-white reasoning and moral pronouncements focusing on the inferiority of non-believers. The scorn of the religious for heathens and blasphemers is now replaced by contempt for those who refuse to be committed to the expectation of norms within identity politics and for saying the wrong things. I return to dogmatic thinking in the final chapter.

---

* The twice Conservative Prime Minister Benjamin Disraeli was born into a Jewish family, but his father baptised him as a child as Christian, reasonably anticipating anti-Semitic prejudices in public life. The New Labour Prime Minister Tony Blair waited until leaving office before converting to Catholicism (the faith of his wife).

Religion and politics in recent times

How might we understand the **emergence** of religious fundamentalism in recent times and the limited success of secularisation after the Enlightenment? The answer to this question resides in two broad antecedents. The first is universal and rooted in evolution, which is our capacity to use language and reflect on our position in time and space. Spirituality is the latter quest to make sense of our finite lives as part of the larger whole and its overwhelming mysteries. It may or may not be codified in beliefs and dogma but, in some form, it has been there at all times in our species. It reflects our relationship to nature in the first plane of our four planar social being. It also accords with the assumption in critical realism that most of reality is absent, not present (the latter being the preoccupation of positivism) and the implied need for constant **epistemic humility**. What do we know for certain about anything? This sense of mysterious absence about the world around us and the unknown future for us all create an emotional desire for security. Spirituality, and, within that, religion, is that emergent human response. It is that left-over feeling when we are surrounded by mystery, with the latter being plentiful in our lives.

Spirituality is, then, an emergent characteristic of our species, entailing the obligatory, or at least likely, struggle for reflection, afforded by our use of language. Religion offers us a pre-ordered or "oven-ready" resolution of that struggle, made available in most cultures with their particular faith groups, scriptures, dogmas, and moral strictures. It is little surprising that those with a committed faith are happier on average than atheists (Myers, 2000). Faith groups offer both belonging ("social capital"), as well as existential ordering, which give confidence and comfort to believers. Religion may, as it were, "colonise" spirituality, but it is responding to a universal human need for existential sense-making. The relationship between religion (contingent in time and place) and spirituality (ubiquitous across time and space in the human species) is represented in Box 7.2.

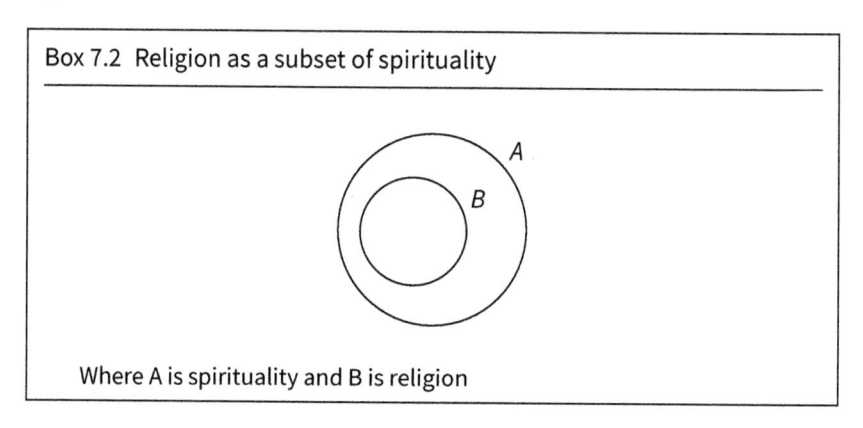

Box 7.2 Religion as a subset of spirituality

Where A is spirituality and B is religion

The second broad antecedent can be located in the third plane (social and economic structures). Religious leaders preceded modern political leaders, with their newly found secularist aspirations. During the medieval period, church and state were enmeshed in Europe and this was also the case analogously in India (the relationship with Hinduism) and in most of the Middle East in relation to Islam. So much of the history of feudal times entailed the imposition of particular religious beliefs on those conquered in imperialist military adventures. Battles for control over the peoples of the Middle East and the Mediterranean between Christian and Muslim crusaders exemplifies this trend.

If, experientially, religious beliefs fulfil the generic psychological need for sense-making about our short-lived egos in eternity (first point just noted) then such political conflicts elicited passionate martyrdom. For example, when the Turks invaded Italy in the fifteenth century, they slaughtered hundreds of Catholics who refused to obey the Muslim foe;

their bones are on show still today in an enormous glass structure at the side of the altar in Otranto Cathedral.

This point about martyrdom has also become apparent when authoritarian atheism, under Marxist-Leninist regimes, has attempted to suppress religious belief. The justification for this was the aphorism from Marx that religion was "the opium of the people". But more than that, the clerical power of the old regime had been bound up with aristocratic or monarchic power. That lockstep between the two remains today, for example, in the Wahabism of Saudi Arabia noted earlier. When Marxist-Leninism came to power, organised religion could be cast as an enemy of the working class and, more importantly, a threat to the vanguard party and its authority.

However, a problem it encountered was that the evolutionary human need for spiritual reflection was still acculturated and unremitting. Examples of this were the retention of beliefs in version of orthodox Christianity in the Soviet Union and its satellites (in the non-aligned Yugoslavia this included Catholic and Muslim faiths). In China, Marxist-Leninism never succeeded in eliminating Buddhism, Taoism, Confucianism, or Shintoism. Recently the Chinese state has turned its attention to Muslims in a process of suppression through re-education.

Thus, the post-Enlightenment consensus in North America and France to tolerate religious pluralism alongside atheism and agnosticism, which was played out with varying degrees of success in the secular West, was not respected in the communist East. However, that intolerance ultimately failed because we are "genetically wired" to be spiritual and often the latter is expressed via a commitment to religious belief. Later socialist writers such as Erich Fromm and Jurgen Habermas, within the post-Marxist tradition, returned to a defence of a co-presence of religion and humanism. Such a continued dialogue between the organised religions and modern forms of secular humanism was also advocated by liberal critical rationalists, such as Karl Popper in his book *The Open Society and Its Enemies*. That copresence between religion and humanism did not need to be invented, as it has always been there (see next section).

In Box 7.1, I summarised examples of theocratic religious power. However, the other side of the same coin is that the post-Enlightenment value of religious toleration for individuals and different minority groups has been precarious in all authoritarian states. In Box 7.3, that countervailing tendency is summarised.

> **Box 7.3 Global threats to religious freedom in recent times**
>
> The Pews Research Centre, which investigates religion in public life, reports annually on the global pattern of religious persecution. In 2018, the centre offered the following picture. In Myanmar, 14,500 Rohingya Muslims fled to Bangladesh to escape abuses. In Uzbekistan, around 1,500 Muslims were imprisoned for practising their form of religion. The most restrictive country reported was China, which bans religious groups, attacks places of worship, and detains and tortures religious practitioners. During that year, the Chinese government targeted Uighurs, ethnic Kazakhs, and other Muslims. In Xinjiang province, between 800,000 and 2 million Muslims were kept in detention facilities designed to re-educate faith practitioners. Other stand-out offenders included the Tajikistan government, which targets Muslims and Jehovah's Witnesses.
>
> In India, Hindu nationalism encouraged the suppression of other faiths. For example, in Uttar Pradesh, hundreds of Christians were arrested, accused of trying to convert people by drugging them and "spreading lies about Hinduism". Hindu domination saw the Shiv Sena Party, advocating the mandatory birth control of Muslims to limit their population growth. In the other direction, in the Middle East and North Africa, the majority of Islamic countries demonstrably persecuted other faiths or those from minority sects. For example, in Saudi Arabia, more than 300 Shiite Muslims remained in prison in its Eastern Province. There the Saudi government had arrested more than 1,000 Shiites since 2011, who had demonstrated in favour of their religious freedom.

Religion and humanism

The above very broad-brush strokes of the enmeshment, past and present, between religions and political power emphasised their dogmatic, brutal, and patriarchal character. At the same time, those in religious minorities have been subjected to persecution by both theocratic and secular states at times. Religion can be both the source and the target of oppressive forces in society.

Within these contradictory tendencies, all the organised religions have also contained some degree of respect for non-religious or cross-faith values, as well as containing rather than necessarily persecuting contrarians in their midst. Since antiquity, these opposing tendencies have included a commitment to science and to reasoned debate, as part of valued education. For example, modern science owes its origins to developments in the ancient religious traditions of a range of countries. At a personal level, religion may breed its many superstitions (the scorn of atheists) but when organised and disciplined, it has cultivated sophisticated learning, not just in science and engineering but also in art and architecture. Even atheists can be overawed by the grandeur of a city cathedral or the outstanding beauty of the Sistine Chapel, or they might appreciate the rich social history of a quaint Norman church in the English countryside.

Valued forms of doubt and learning took the horizontal relationship between people seriously alongside, and sometimes at odds with, the vertical relationship with God, the gods, or religious leaders. In the case of non-theistic religions, such as Buddhism, the role of wise monks was important. This copresence of horizontal and vertical authority was an inevitable outcome of our genetic tendency to be inquisitive language users. It confirmed Aristotle's mantra that "man is by nature curious". If we are curious and reflective then that will include an ongoing scepticism about what we are expected to believe by our teachers and leaders.[1] It will also prompt new leaps in faith about the mysteries of existence. This is reflected in all of the ancient regimes which contained their versions of religious orthodoxy, alongside sceptics and revisionists.

In polytheist ancient Greece, Socrates favoured self-discovery and critical thinking over obedience to the deities. Aristotle emphasised reason, science, and honest self-reflection, as sources of both wisdom and flourishing. He was opposed in particular to blind or dogmatic faith (in anything) and so encouraged deliberation about how we should conduct ourselves in the interests of humanity as a whole.

In polytheist India, containing the oldest organised religion Hinduism, there were strong currents that grounded humans in their daily life and material constraints. These included atheistic Buddhism and around the same time, there were the sceptical Charvakas, who rejected

---

[1] Even in the early cult surrounding Jesus, there was "doubting" Thomas, the apostle who refused to believe his peers about the resurrected Christ.

the supernatural realm and advocated a form of empiricism as a source of knowledge and wisdom. We might associate empiricism with the Enlightenment, but its advocates have been around for over 2,000 years.

The spread of Buddhism to China meant that it joined other non-theistic and anti-clerical currents like Confucianism. The thinker leading the latter bequeathed a focus on being kind and unselfish, as well as respecting education, so that we might act in a harmonious manner with one another and with nature. God was not required in these goals. If authority emerged about these religions, it was invested in its teachers and monks, not in a supernatural entity.

The latter, though, was central to the Abrahamic traditions of Judaism, Christianity, and Islam.[2] These created then a triple layer of vertical authority. Above it all was one all-seeing God but beneath were prophets and clerics, leaving ordinary believers in a constant state of sinful and anxious compliance. Their actual and potential moral failures entered the realm of mass psychology in societies governed by organised religion (theocracies). This was also true at times in secular societies respecting not just private beliefs but the moral and political expectations arising from religious dogma, prescriptions, and proscriptions; hence the quite limited gains of secularism I noted at the outset of this chapter.

Thus, when we come to appraise how religious identities have been added to the menu of diversity in modern secular societies, we can note some paradoxes. The postmodern expectation of unending perspectives to be tolerated and respected is out of sync with the dogmatic moral authority of organised religion. If that authority were to ever gain substantial power, then it would not offer the same tolerance in return to others. Take the example of homosexuality being a criminal offence in Iran punishable by death. Some gay men have survived that fate by seeking biomedical transitions (many members of the Iranian national women's soccer team are transsexuals). Reproductive rights are still curtailed by religious patriarchy, with Irish women, until 2020, having to take the short flight to England to obtain an abortion.

---

[2] The monotheism of the Abrahamic traditions was predated by the ancient Iranian prophet Zarathrustra. His followers, still active today in the religion of Zoroastrianism, introduced binary reasoning (heaven and hell, good and evil, angels and demons). I return to this type of black-and-white reasoning in relation to identity politics in the final chapter.

Such is the hostility of patriarchs in the Abrahamic traditions to women that a fundamental assumption in diversity and equality training today would be discarded by theocracies. For example, at the time of writing, the Taliban in Afghanistan have shot dead women simply for their senior position as government officials. In Bangladesh, women have been banned from officiating at marriages because they menstruate. Those championing the rights of girls to an equal education also have had their lives threatened. A notable example of this has been Malala Yousafzai, who with two other girls, was shot in an assassination attempt in Pakistan by a lone Taliban gunman on a school bus in 2012. She had been targeted for campaigning for educational rights in opposition to Taliban strictures about the subservient role of girls and women in Muslim society.

And if this scenario seems a distant prospect in current European countries, consider the role of Biraderi[3] in controlling local Labour Parties in the North and Midlands of England in the recent past, which even entailed efforts to set up male-only meetings. This reflected attempts on the part of Muslim patriarchal elites ("community leaders") to control the local political apparatus. This strategy had been imported to the UK in the 1960s by New Commonwealth immigrants from the Indian subcontinent and it remains evident today. This political role has allowed English fascists, like the British National Party, to disguise their original racism (now illegal under the *Race Relations Act*) by an attack on Islam, as code for an ethnic group[4] they despise.

Given the retention of the humanistic edge of the diverse religions noted earlier, provided that secularism keeps religion properly in check, a common humanitarian agenda across those of all faiths and none

---

[3] "Biraderi" (clan-based loyalty) from the Persian word for "brotherhood" is pragmatic and patriarchal, with a focus on the advantages to immediate networks. See Baston, L. (2103) *The Bradford Earthquake* London: Democratic Audit. (https://democraticaudituk.files.wordpress.com/2013/06/bradford-earthquake-full-report)

[4] Like "race", "ethnicity" has a working meaning as an aspect of **social ontology** but is not that definable by hard empirical criteria. It tends to connote religious, linguistic, and cultural resemblances within a human subgroup and may or may not also allude to skin colour or national origins; hence the ambiguous term "black and ethnic minority". For example, "the Irish" in Great Britain might be classed as an ethnic minority. Joe Biden described himself as being Irish as he became President of the USA, even though he was born and raised in Pennsylvania.

might still be achieved. I return to this common cause in deliberative democracy across these boundaries of faith in the final chapter.

Identity politics, transhumanism, and posthumanism

If we need to reflect on the tensions about religion and humanism in the theory and practice of identity politics, then we also need to reflect on the brave new world of transhumanism and posthumanism. If the compromises about religion and humanism reflect the past, then posthumanism reflects an imagined future. As with the past it contains ambiguity and dissent about its prospects for human survival and flourishing. It may offer us utopia or dystopia (or maybe elements of each). Its relevance to identity politics is most obvious in relation to the technological manipulation of our bodies.

This might include that already present, such as biomedical transitioning, discussed in Chapter Three. But it is more than this, as it includes body modifications so that we live longer or enjoy added experiences or conveniences in our lives. We might live longer, run faster, or simply turn our thoughts into speech or writing by becoming partly machines rather than just flesh and blood.

These technological possibilities place a question mark over whether being human is over-rated as it is readily modified by non-human machinery (of course, note, invented by human activity). Not only might we become more or less robotic androids or cyborgs, we might not be that distinguishable from other animals. These ambiguities give some confidence to the prospects of posthumanism, but the question is whether that scenario is desirable (a value question) and whether it would enhance or subvert our humanity. The latter word, like others such as "humane" and "humanitarianism", connote our uniqueness as a species. Can a machine be compassionate? What about feelings like guilt or inchoate sensibilities in human life, such as our sense of nostalgia or falling in love? Most of us experience these but would struggle to explain them to a computer.

Whilst the religious faiths designated us as being unique, because we contained souls whereas other species did not, non-believers still retained and even valorised that unique status. This put man, not God, at the centre. Accordingly, homo-centrism could then be attacked from both pre-modern religions *and* postmodern philosophers, who offered us "subjectivity without a subject" or "history without a subject". The consequence then was the "twilight of man" with the postmodern preoccupation with discourses and discourses about discourses (Lemert, 1980). Humanism is now being scorned from all sides; squeezed between the religious thoughts of antiquity and the florid imagination granted by postmodernism, where anything might be possible.

If transgenderism and transracialism have tested the patience of those discussing identity politics, then these prospects for ditching humanism exert even more pressure on our credulity and sense of wonder. Body manipulation might now start with cosmetic surgery, move through gender reassignment surgery and hormones, to arguments about changing our race or even becoming cyborgs and chimeras. Cryogenics might offer us eternal life without needing to commit ourselves to Jesus.

Being human has been the focus of several critical realist texts but what is clear is that postmodernism has created one possibility for abandoning that state in favour a bodily existence that rejects its old limitations and flaws. We might seek perfection and immortality and that is either a wonderful prospect or a terrifying promise, depending on our value system. The postmodernism that underpins so many of the assumptions of identity politics seemingly supports this shift towards transhumanism and its ultimate direction of being posthuman.

As one of the advocates of posthumanism has pointed out, "At a certain point, human beings will not be the most intelligent creatures on the planet" (Goertzel, 2013: 128). As Porpora (2017) notes when citing this view, this is the logical outcome of the aspirations of Nietzsche, the seminal leader of postmodernism, towards the "superhuman". Generally, these lovers of an imagined future, which would leave flawed humanity behind in the dustbin of evolution, tend to be both anti-humanist *and* anti-religious. This scenario leaves identity politics itself with an uncertain future. Will cyborgs, transracials, and chimeras become the new ruling class or just more oppressed groups, special-pleading from their own new "lived experience"? Maybe it could be a bit of both as class warfare of some form or other will continue.

Religion and identity politics: plus ça change, plus c'est la même chose?

A theme that runs throughout these discussions of contradictions about religious belief, in first a modern and now a postmodern world, is that some things have remained the same for the past 3,000 years. We still need to reflect on the links that exist between our private beliefs and the wider context we are thrown into, which shapes them. Living before Christ, the moral leader Confucius ipso facto could not be a Christian, so could he not have gone to heaven if Christ is the *only* vehicle for that prospect ("the way, the light, and the truth")? We might ask the same today of a peasant child in rural India, who lives and dies in their village as a Hindu: is he or she debarred from heaven? It is preposterous for us to link adherence to specific religious ways of thinking to personal salvation. Those ways of thinking might offer defensible collective wisdoms at times (such as compassion or peace, love, and understanding) but they can never deliver *individual* redemption simply by demanding and then acquiring fidelity, to this rather than that particular cause.

We can also still reflect on the vertical and the horizontal: do we live our lives according to the expectations of those above us or those by our sides? As the paradox of tolerating authoritarian forms of patriarchy, which assuredly would not make the offer in return if in power, points up the need to distinguish our compulsion to make sense of ourselves and the world from whether others can offer us solutions on a plate.

Then there is the matter of identity politics itself having more than a whiff of religiosity. So many of the secular political forms that have succeeded religion have retained its broad moral imperative. Those at the vanguard of identity politics ("social justice warriors" or the "wokery") tell us what we can say and what we can do, without receiving social censure or banishment. The hell that awaits us is personal invalidation, not subterranean scorching. To complement this, to be virtuous at all times in thought and deed ensures that we avoid both excommunication *and* we retain the bliss of being the righteous ones. Group belonging and inner peace are guaranteed in tandem by keeping the faith; a win–win scenario of sorts.

This is the sort of existential insurance policy known of old, when we were asked why we believed in God and replied that we would be a fool not to. So, too, today, why would we not keep parroting the right things and watching our "Ps" and "Qs"? And yet, our contrarian and critical curiosity will continue to chafe against the obvious survival value of conformity. Identity politics may garner popular support for a while, but like all forms of religiosity, they will fail for two reasons.

First, there will be factionalism and disputes about what being "right" means. The most striking example of this, evident already, is the stand-off between second-wave feminists and transgender activists. This is why we cannot, any longer in truth, speak of feminism but must concede that feminisms reflect our current political reality (Watkins, 2018). Second, the advantages of each variant of identity politics, just as with religious belonging, will bring with it satisfaction to those on the inside but always at the expense of those without. In-group and out-group, us and them, right and wrong will divide us against one another, in a never-ending failed zero-sum game of human improvement. Organised religion has been a good role model for identity politics and its educational imperative for diversity and inclusivity. But if the former came to a state of unconditional power, it would soon destroy identity politics more widely. What chance diversity training in a theocracy?

CHAPTER EIGHT

Class war, blood and soil

Introduction

Although the left, since the **emergence** of new social movements in the 1960s, is often the target of derision or scorn about being "woke", the right also places identity centre stage.[1] Religious conservatism and ethnocentric nationalists[2] appeal to versions of identity politics. Indeed, the term "**identitarianism**" is used sometimes as a neutral synonym for "identity politics" but it is also used to describe a pan-European white supremacist

---

[1] Recently in the UK, polling suggests a disconnect between activists in the Labour Party and regular Labour voters. Activists are significantly more "woke", with many ordinary people either being unaware of "culture wars" or, if they know about them, dismissing claims from critical social justice warriors. Within the polls, an age cohort effect is obvious, with younger voters being more "woke" (Walker, 2021).

[2] A contradiction of ultra-nationalism is that it at times celebrates international collaboration. This has been the case with pan-European fascist cooperation since the 1930s. Likewise in the USA, the White Power movement emphasises its cross-national loyalties with Aryans of all lands; it cannot be conflated narrowly with American nationalism. Indeed, white terrorism in the United States has attacked, not defended, the American state.

movement (Fekete, 2016; François & Godwin, 2008). In Britain, this has manifested itself in the appearance of the ultra-right group Generation Identity, which argues that British identity is genetically "wired in". This continues the tradition of British exceptionalism, feeding both its fascist and reformist right wing (Gottlieb & Linehan, 2003).

Class politics and cultural distinctions

When Marx and Engels hailed the beginnings of socialism, with the encouragement of "workers of the world unite!" they were indicating that the international proletariat were a diffuse, or what we now call a "virtual", social group connected proudly as oppressed citizens of the world. One imagined community (workers of the world) can be contrasted with other versions, based upon specified national identities (Anderson, 1983). Another imagined community, as a comparator, is the caliphate aspiration of ISIS, harking back to the Muslim rulers of the seventh century after the death of their Prophet; even then, it was more imagined than real.

As far as class politics is concerned, anyone on the left understands the cachet derived from identity, when claiming, with or without some artistic licence, that they are from a working-class background. In this sense Marxism was, from the outset, a sort of identity politics. It still has an outgroup (the rich and powerful) though the relationship between those working by hand or brain brought with it an ambiguity about the status of the educated middle class: were they part of the proletariat or part of the bourgeoisie (Carchedi, 1975)?

Turning to another ambiguity about identity, centrist consensus policies now are difficult to use as valid markers to differentiate Labour and the Conservatives in Britain, given the triumph of the Blair project and the failure of the Corbyn project. For example, after 1997, Tony Blair reformed the welfare state in neoliberal ways that were beyond the dreams of Margaret Thatcher. In another example, the current Prime Minister, Boris Johnson, is heading for a reform of the NHS and social care that seems be to the left of anything that the Labour Party have done in the past fifty years. Maybe the ruling class has spotted that an efficient and integrated health and welfare system serves the interests of capital. It might afford more benefits to the rich

CLASS WAR, BLOOD AND SOIL   167

and powerful than merely feeding the profits of their cronies in the private care sector,[3] which had been the trend in Tory politics after the Second World War.

However, despite this difficulty of no longer being able to readily discern left from right in British politics, we still hear regional working-class accents in one group of MPs more than the other. The boozy posh-boy[4] Bullingdon Club, at Oxford University in the 1980s, produced two Conservative British Prime Ministers, a Foreign Secretary, and a Chancellor of the Exchequer. Apart from those entering government, this elite social network also ensured a version of crony capitalism with its super-rich membership.

So, if class has survived in the ranks of each party, then this has been as much about *cultural* background, within the class structure, as it has been about wealth per se, or the ownership of the means of production and exchange. As Bourdieu (1984) noted, our structural class of origin (part of what he called "field") brings with it a wide range of shared subjective experiences and ways of communicating with "people like us" (part of "habitus"). This then distinguishes "us" from "them". That networked tribalism is central to identity politics and applies as much to the cultural capital peculiar to the rich as it does to the desire for ontological security from the parochial poor, with their optimistic but probably forlorn nationalist sentiments.

With these starting thoughts in mind, this chapter explores the chaos that still prevails about national identities and their intersection with class interests. Here I am returning to the original use of **intersectionality** to refer to objective features, which have causal powers. When

---

[3] From the outset, the NHS was never fully socialised but more importantly its fiscal challenges had to be dealt with by governments of any hue. At the same time, the welfare state stabilises the capitalist economy by containing and sometimes rehabilitating the sick, the old, and the disabled. As Claus Offe demonstrated, capitalism cannot live with the welfare state, but it also cannot live without it and so those in government always must manage this contradiction (Offe, 1984).

[4] Its focus was on elite ex-public-school boys drinking excessively. This vehicle of disinhibition enabled them to abuse women and animals and make the poor and homeless a butt of their humour. Their culture of excess reflected a complete contempt for many who were relied upon for electoral success thirty years later, when David Cameron, Boris Johnson, George Osborne, and Jeremy Hunt were to be in high office.

understood as a web of **generative mechanisms**, rather than merely an additive prism of interacting subjectivities, **intersectionality** remains a useful frame of analysis. In multicultural Britain today, with its sedimented layers of Celtic, Anglo-Saxon, Pict, Viking, Norman, Jewish, African, Caribbean, Chinese, South Asian, and, more recently, other European heritages, their cultural lineages will mix and flux together in a range of cross-cutting ways in mainstream politics.

Accordingly, even the (conservative) Conservative Party boasts parliamentarians from this mix, though its white, male, upper-class core still predominates. But it was a female white Tory leader, Theresa May, as a counter to Marxist internationalism, and an appeal to British pride, who told her Party Conference in 2016 (the year of Brexit) that, "If you believe you're a citizen of the world, you're a citizen of nowhere. You don't understand what the very word 'citizenship' means." This illustrates perfectly why nationalisms and identity politics fit hand in glove on the right and why the left is not isolated with its emotive contradictions.

Chaos in the British Isles about national identity

The British Empire slowly ceded autonomy to its overseas territories but at home today, old scores are still not settled. For those inside and outside the British Isles, it is easy to forget that Britain is *not* a nation, but it *has been* an imperial power, now exhausted. That empire was Anglocentric, and the other nations of the islands played their role, with more or less enthusiasm in its ascendency, as well as in its decline and fall.

The outcome of Brexit may have achieved what the Irish Republican Army (IRA) failed at in the 1970s (i.e., a realistic move to a united Ireland).[5] During the twentieth century, Great Britain[6] was unperturbed, by and large, by its native nationalisms, apart from the odd pipeline blown

---

[5] For now, this is unpredictable. The young in Northern Ireland are less enthusiastic than their nationalist parents about Irish unification, though they tend, as elsewhere in Europe, to be pro-EU. However, many political pundits, including the conservative historian Max Hastings, are predicting a united Ireland within a generation.
[6] Great Britain is the largest island in the British Isles, constituted by the nations of Scotland, Wales, and England, as three of those forming the United Kingdom. For now, across the Irish Sea, Northern Ireland is the fourth nation.

up or second home torched by the Free Wales Army. Scotland slowly developed a more substantive autonomous movement and again the Brexit outcome galvanised more optimism in the Scottish National Party (SNP). The latter now cultivates an image of a Scandinavian-style social democratic party, but ideologically it has had a range of activists, including those with a "blood and soil"[7] hatred of the English.

Scotland, like the rest of the Celtic fringe, had been ultimately subservient to the English monarchy and aristocracy and then the priorities of English capitalism. The material relationships (political, economic, and geographical) within the British Isles shaped both the prospect and the end of Empire as a world power with its attendant ideology of pride and confidence.

In light of this necessary juxtaposition of **ontological realism** (the objective conditions) and **epistemological relativism** (imperialist ideology), we can see how the British Empire both relied upon the Celtic fringe in a mixture of incorporation and exploitation. This, of necessity, spawned resistance, which is still being enacted today. But it also flushed out the need for the English to reflect falteringly on their own sense of national identity. As the dominant nation, the English took themselves for granted for so long that, like dinosaurs slowly recognising that they were dying, they began to thrash around. Narratives were found to give comfort. Since the Second World War, and especially in relation to Brexit, these have tended to shorten the historical gaze, so that London defined itself against Berlin in the 1940s, rather than Delhi, Dublin, Johannesburg, or Kingston, Jamaica, in the nineteenth century.

By the turn of this century, the English far right had recreated its forms of fascist party, which were sullied by Oswald Mosely's failed British Union of Fascists in the 1930s. As with other post-colonial European countries, England contained fascist elements reacting to loss of empire but other less coherent forms of ethnocentricity and casual racism predominated culturally in the twentieth century.

---

[7] The term "blood and soil" is used in the parlance of ultra-right nationalists today in order to celebrate an assumed gene pool of race and territory to be defended and imperialistically expanded. Its use in Nazi ideology (Blut und Boden) also connoted the rural idyl of ancient agricultural territory. A dreamy mystique of the bucolic past is sentimentally favoured by a range of ultra-nationalists.

The relationship between British fascism and a wider appeal to ethnocentric populism in the general population is summarised in Box 8.1.

By comparing the columns in Box 8.1, we can see then that in a postcolonial context of the decline of English power in the world, ethnocentric consciousness *includes* fascism on its margins, but it predominantly resonates with a wider conservative populism. The latter was a target of appeal for the Conservative right as well as UKIP in the runup to the vote on Brexit. During that time, the soon-to-be-friend of Donald Trump, Nigel Farage, with his UKIP obsession with the EU and immigration, merely said what much of the Conservative right already believed.

Box 8.1 Comparing English fascism with English ethnocentrism

Features of English fascism
- An organised ideology, with the following motifs: anti-democratic, proudly racist, palingenetic* ultra-nationalism (emphasises national rebirth), anti-Semitic, focus on current fraternal values of white Britons, charismatic leaders who are "men of destiny", nostalgic mystique, violent masculinity, positive view of militarism.
- Tries to use democratic process as a goal to a one-party state (e.g., British Union of Fascists, National Front, British Movement, British National Party, National Action).
- Jewish conspiracy aimed at the genocide of white people and the imposition of immigration and "miscegenation". Can shift its focus beyond Jews to any ethnic and religious minority; hence both the "Protocols of the Elders of Zion" *and* the "Great Replacement Theory".**

Features of English ethnocentrism
- Ethnocentric mass consciousness and a spectrum of racism (from covert to overt). Rejects fascism for being a threat to England, but retains a vague nostalgic mystique. Brexiteers invoke the isolation of Britain during the Second World War, thus now emotively blurring fascism with the intrusive interference of the EU, as a new invading threat.
- Retains commitment to multi-party liberal democracy (e.g., the "little Englanders" of UKIP and the Conservative Party right).
- General distrust of *all* foreigners, casual racism (open commentary about negative racial and ethnic characteristics of people in everyday life). Inchoate compared to fascist conspiracy claims.

- Focus on the white poor and disadvantaged working class ("British jobs for British people").

- Focus on "hard working British families" under threat from foreign labour; a position stated sporadically by both the Conservative right and the leadership of the Labour Party.***

---

* This word refers to the advocacy of the reproduction of national or cultural ancestry. For a discussion of its core defining position in fascism, see Griffin (1991). Other possible defining aspects of fascism, such as the role of racist ideology and its degree of autonomy from the capitalist class, are contested within writings on the topic. Parallels with Bonapartism have been drawn by some describing a theme in fascist theory and practice (Thalheimer, 1928/1979—https://bataillesocialiste.wordpress.com/english-pages/1928-on-fascism-thalheimer). Other Marxists emphasise it being a mass movement, not a top-down imposition (Vajda, 1976). Both of these writers were expelled by their respective Communist Parties for their thought deviations, confirming that George Orwell was correct about the replication of authoritarianism on the right and left (see Chapter Two).

** The Protocols of the Elders of Zion were fabricated by Russian anti-Semites in 1902 just before a spate of pogroms against Jews. The forgery sets out the case for world Jewish domination. The Great Replacement Theory is the work of the French white nationalist Renaud Camus. He argues that cultural elites in business and politics are actively promoting the replacement of white European populations with those from the Middle East and Africa. It draws upon the ideas of Enoch Powell.

*** This emphasis was evident in the statement of Gordon Brown when he was Labour Prime Minister. During the twentieth century, there was no evidence that Labour leaders were any more liberal about immigration than the Conservative ones. For electoral reasons, populist fears of immigrants always hovered influentially across the political spectrum.

The fear of brown faces invoked deliberately by Farage's spiritual forebear, Enoch Powell, in his "rivers of blood" speech in Birmingham 1968,[8] which had referred to New Commonwealth immigration, was now recast as a fear of Eastern Europeans and refugees from the Middle East. Farage lamented that it was possible to walk down the high street of any town and not hear English being spoken. This was a replay of the

---

[8] Powell deliberately staged a dour provocative speech in the presence of the press to warn about the risk of racial violence provoked by immigration and foreigners "swamping" white English culture. He dignified his call to violence by arcane literary allusions to antiquity, quoting the Aeneid: "As I look ahead, I am filled with foreboding. Like the Roman, I seem to see 'the River Tiber foaming with much blood'". He was of course aiming for a self-fulfilling prophecy. Powell was a hero of Margaret Thatcher and remains on the Roll of Honour of the Tory right today.

older contrived fear of "miscegenation",[9] the eugenic concern of genetically mixing the races.

However, now the white skin of the devout Catholic Pole had to be worked around, in order to create a new version of English prejudice about "Johnny Foreigner". The answer was that they did not speak English in a local accent. This created a contradiction, in relation to second-generation New Commonwealth communities supporting Brexit from self-interest. This came home forcibly to me a few months ago, walking at the side of a busy road. An angry motorist in a spat about a near collision got out of his car and shouted at a lorry driver: "Fuck off back to your own fucking country—we got Brexit now!"

The bemused lorry driver was white, and his truck had Polish plates. The verbal abuser was a British South Asian in a smart suit and collar and tie, with a brand-new GB-plated Mercedes saloon. He knew his rights as a British citizen in 2020 and he was now going to tell the world proudly in a perfect local accent. He was blithely indifferent to the obvious racism in his rant, and I could not tell if he would have passed "Tebbit's cricket test".[10] I was not in a position to ask him, if I had dared, before he sped off in fury. The electrifying spat, over in a few seconds, was telling, though.

Implications of the end of Empire for identity politics

The messy cost-benefit analysis of the complexity of British Empire, with its impact abroad and its multi-ethnic legacy at home, now invites historical commentaries from left, right, and centre (Dalrymple, 2019; Sanghera, 2021). Both celebratory and critical histories of Britain's

---

[9] This term was used in the middle of the nineteenth century in the USA by whites opposing the alleged dire consequences of mixed-race marriages.
[10] Norman (later "Lord") Tebbit was a right-wing Conservative who complained in 1990 that there were children of New Commonwealth migrants who did not support the English cricket team but opted for the teams of their parents or grandparents. This is another example, like that of Farage and speaking English, of defining true humanity by the features of a white English identity. The dominant group's assertions about their inherent superiority expects others to play catch-up about linguistic and cultural loyalties.

colonial past have to settle on some basic points. There *was* mass violence, there *was* slavery, and there *was* economic exploitation, whether this list is condemned or in some way justified for its benefits to colonisers or the colonised. As Amartya Sen[11] has pointed out in relation to India, we cannot assume that the start of British imperialism there in the late eighteenth century meant that a pause button on socio-economic development was simply taken off in 1947. We simply do not know how the country might have developed in the absence of British interference. However, here I want to focus on the current legacy of that imperialism for versions of identity politics in contemporary Britain.

If the twentieth century witnessed the disintegration of British imperialism abroad, back at home the old ambiguity of the precise meaning of "Albion" was reanimated with the build-up to Brexit.[12] John Gaunt, in his lament of the threat to English greatness in his "sceptred isle" speech from Shakespeare's *Richard II*, evokes a mixed but clearly celebratory picture. It contains regal domination and the obligatory need for military violence in order to defend the nearest we have to heaven on earth:

>This royal throne of kings, this sceptred isle,
>This earth of majesty, this seat of Mars,
>This other Eden, demi-paradise.

However, this speech was made not just as a celebration but was already looking back to better times. Gaunt is alluding to King Richard's political and fiscal adjustments at the time, suggesting an English idyll that was *already* slipping away.

This sort of grandiose and sentimental mysticism is favoured not only by English nationalism but can be found in other forms. For example, Irish nationalism contains the same trope, which implies the spiritual exceptionalism of the ingroup in their case about "mystical Ireland" full

---

[11] Illusions of Empire, The Guardian 29 June 2021.
[12] It is relevant to note that as a self-assured graduate of Eton and the 1987 Bullingdon Club, Cameron seemed to treat being Prime Minister as a sort of hobby or pastime and so he misjudged the mood of his party. He thought that a vote on Brexit would favour "remain" and thereby silence the grumpy Little Englanders to the right on his own parliamentary benches. How wrong he was and what consequences there were.

of Celtic crosses, misty green pastures, expelled snakes, St Patrick, and leprechauns.[13] If Great Britain is "sceptred" then Ireland is "emerald", both offering us aesthetic caricatures of historical idylls longed for nostalgically, which might still tug at the heart strings of nationalists and bring a tear to their eye. In the Welsh version of longing for a lost sense of an unmatched wholesome homeland, there is the aching nostalgic feeling of *hiraeth*.

Nationhood is mythologised then by a particular and preferred version of history. As Renan (1882) pointed out (from the French): "Getting its history wrong is part of being a nation." In a similar vein, we find in Inge (1948: 127): "A nation is a society united by a delusion about its ancestry and by a common hatred of its neighbours." Never mind the facts, just feel the emotion.

After all, the very idea of nationhood only began in earnest, within human history, from the thirteenth century. European colonialism (from the sixteenth century to the mid-twentieth century) then increasingly defined the claimed superiority of one nation over another. Prior to this, only fluxing regionalisms and their linguistic and religious communities co-existed with some groups that migrated or were roaming with no sense of defined territory. National identity, of any sort, has only really made sense during the past 800 years of the history of *Homo sapiens*.

Once colonial powers were established, they could then also demand that that regional, ethnic, linguistic, and religious differences *within* their boundaries could be standardised or homogenised as a condition of the civil benefits of natal citizenship. This process of cultural subordination has been called "civil enculturation" by Schiffauer, Baumann, Kastoryano, and Vertovec (2004). Once that condition was met, then all natives of a nation could contrast themselves legitimately, whether or not proudly, with outsiders or newcomers (see my example earlier of the spat with the Polish lorry driver).

However, colonial powers could also problematise such an integration, when and if colonial subjects moved to the "mother country", leaving

---

[13] The political ambiguity of Irish nationalism was evident in the 1930s when different factions of the IRA went to the Spanish Civil War to fight on either side. Eire was of course neutral during the Second World War and both Britain and Germany had contingency plans for a timely invasion.

the dominant white British culture to be suffused with new versions of racism about ethnic minorities in its midst (Gingrich & Banks, 2006). White nationalism as a form of identity politics then came into being across Europe, made even more rabid in its sentiments about "Johnny Foreigner" by the objective decline in colonial power. The brown-faced driver shouting at the Polish lorry driver in plenty of other contexts in his life was likely to have been the target of casual white racism from his fellow "Brits".

Brexit: England and the Celtic colonies

So apart from different narratives of a (debatable) mystical past favoured from nation to nation, which are an epistemic and emotive matter, there is the ontological question of British history since the medieval period and **the actual** role (and grievances) of the non-English. Apart from the Welsh, both Scotland and Northern Ireland favoured staying in the EU, reflecting maybe a preference for a postcolonial start in Europe, rather than remaining under the traditional narrow yoke of Westminster. If the non-English under British imperialism had played second fiddle at best, or been starved to death at worst, then a loyalty to the union of the "UK"[14] was always going to be challenging for the English elites (the rich Brexiteers like Johnson and Rees-Mogg) and their working-class ethnocentric followers.

Much analysis followed the vote in 2016 narrowly in favour of the UK leaving the EU. The narrowness of the result (basically divided in half), itself reflect a disunited United Kingdom in more ways than one. Reductionist arguments that this was *only* about the ill-educated and white racist poor driving themselves into an absurd postcolonial corner did not fit the complexity of the voting. This point is highlighted by Sobolewska and Ford (2020) in their book *Brexitland*. I summarise their main findings in Box 8.2.

---

[14] The concept of "the UK" is rarely used in the vernacular by its citizens but is like an international administrative badge. Typically, people say that they are from a particular country or describe themselves vaguely as "British".

Box 8.2 A sketch of Brexitland

The focus of Sobolewska and Ford, using a range of survey measures and a description of cultural flux in the modern history of the UK, was on a multifactorial picture to explain the Brexit outcome. One cultural tendency emerged from university expansionism and increased ethnic diversity, at the turn of this century. This led to an "us and them" separation between the early school leavers, who tended to become "identity conservatives", and those going on to become university graduates, who tended to become "identity liberals". The latter adhere to anti-racism as a central social value but that is not the case with the former. During the 1960s, Powellite resistance to New Commonwealth immigration reflected the beginnings of identity splits in the UK population (see earlier). This identity division was then amplified by the next immigration wave from the EU, encouraged under New Labour, which also pushed for the expansion in higher education noted earlier. Older predictable loyalties to the major political parties were then altered. It was no longer a given that working-class areas would vote Labour, and Labour MPs relied in some areas on leave majorities and in others on those favouring remaining in the EU. Moreover, in England and Wales, "them and us" were defined by many as the ingroup of *indigenous* fellow citizens nearby and the outgroup as the EU. Migrant workers from the latter were the embodied evidence of this split. By contrast, in Scotland, "them" was not the EU but Westminster and it was in Scotland that the British social democratic tendency was rapidly being lost to Labour in favour of the SNP. The Labour split was mirrored, though less dramatically, in Conservative ranks. Both MPs and voters were more prone to be Brexiteers, but this trend was moderated by pro-European sentiments as well. Small businesses reliant on the export trade advantages of the EU were particularly fearful of a "leave" outcome; today those fears seem to have been well-founded. Sobolewski and Ford (2020: 325) summarise the Brexit scenario as this: "Whilst both traditional governing parties have been shaken internally by the mobilisation of identity politics conflicts, other parties have sought to capitalise on the new divisions. UKIP and its rebranded successor the Brexit Party both caused turmoil by mobilising ethnocentric voters with an extreme 'us and them' message focused on assertive nationalism and opposition to the threats from Europe and immigration." Those ethnocentric voters were by no means only the white, ill-educated working class or *lumpenproletariat*.

But it did mean that often the traditional red vote for Labour morphed into the new purple vote for UKIP, or the leave campaign led by Boris Johnson. Also, in many areas the vote tilted in favour of Brexit because of the nostalgic loyalties of older middle-class (i.e., well-educated) people. Older people are more likely to vote than young adults and they are more likely to be partisan. Nostalgia for a real or imagined past also comes more and more with age (see later).

Ireland and Europe

Ireland has been in a particularly interesting position in relation to Europe. The six counties of the north in the past had been ethnically engineered, to include Scottish non-conformist (thus anti-Catholic) migrants. This deliberate strategy, at the beginning of the seventeenth century had taken place under the direction of James VI of Scotland (and I of England), thereby displacing the old Gaelic nobility.[15] This encouraged a flow of further Scottish migration. The political and economic favouritism then extended to that group of Scots Irish in Ulster and was systematised. It sowed the seeds of grievance from Irish nationalists, with long-term consequences. And those six counties (then) were the lucrative rump of the British involvement in the island of Ireland after the incomplete bid for legitimacy by the IRA, to secure a united Ireland at the beginning of the twentieth century.

The fact that this was a serious armed guerrilla struggle against English colonialism, rather than the weaker and ambivalent response from the Welsh and Scots on the "mainland" of Great Britain, reflected two material points. First, the separate island status of Ireland made it always more difficult to control politically and culturally. The Irish Sea is a small stretch of water—but so is the English Channel from Dover to Calais, making the point that sea boundaries shape nationhood as a place of identity formation. Also, the Western seaboard of Ireland afforded aspirations of escape from starvation to America, which in turn

---

[15] Most of these had fled to England after losing a nine-year war. James was strategically giving a sop to the Scottish part of his kingdom by using the colonisation of Ulster and favouring the Presbyterian Scots over the Catholic Irish. The latter were to be "pacified" and "civilised" with a good dose of "proper" Christianity. This scenario was pregnant with the sectarian violence and distrust we have witnessed in the six counties for so long.

created political allegiances for the Irish diaspora and the generations they spawned. By the turn of this century, over 33 million people in the USA claimed Irish ancestry (about seven times those actually today living in Ireland).[16] This size of diaspora does not include those in Great Britain and Australasia.

Second, the degree of persecution by the English of the Celtic colonies was at its worse in Ireland. For example, the Welsh language and Scottish Gaelic were both discouraged, in order to ensure cultural compliance by the English and swathes of rural land owned by the local aristocracy marginalised and pauperised many throughout.[17] However, the physical consequences for the Irish of this common English ruling-class strategy were more brutal. In Ireland, where most of the land was owned by a few rich Anglo-Irish families (often residing in England), rents were collected from peasant farmers and much of the agricultural products were then sent to England (Coogan, 2012).

When the Europe-wide potato blight struck in the 1840s, this pauperising economy was amplified. Three factors came together in a perfect storm that led to a million dying and twice that number emigrating. First, for climatic reasons, potatoes were the main food source for the poor. Second, the absent landlords continued to demand their rents. Third, laissez-faire capitalism was being encouraged by the British government. This mass starvation, which was felt disproportionately in the south and west, where Irish Gaelic not English was spoken, left its mark politically and it immediately galvanised resistance to British rule. In 1848, the Irish Republican Brotherhood was formed, which seeded the

---

[16] One musical expression of this is *Long Journey Home*, the soundtrack for the 1998 PBS/Disney documentary about the collective experience of the Irish in the USA. The final track is written and performed by the Anglo-Irish singer Elvis Costello, who spent his time as a young artist attacking Thatcherism and the absurdities of the clapped-out British Empire (Pilgrim and Ormrod, 2012).

[17] Given that Scottish Gaelic came from Irish speakers invading in the fifth century CE, it was conversationally indistinguishable from Irish Gaelic until the Middle Ages. Later nationalist movements in Scotland did not embrace it as a symbol of cultural separation and preferred instead to write and speak their own version of Scottish English. The Anglo-Norman spread from the south ensured the latter prevailed culturally in those both accepting and rejecting the political integration with England.

formation of the IRA. Its first insurrection in that year was snuffed out by the British and the military dynamic was triggered.

The identity of "being Irish" then was created in the modern period, linked in the main with the political aim of a united Ireland and culturally with an amalgam of language, sport (Gaelic football and hurling),[18] and religion (overwhelmingly Catholic). The IRA's Easter uprising of 1916 was suppressed by the British but guerrilla activity ensued until 1921, when the Anglo-Irish treaty was signed. Partition of the six northern counties in the north, retained in the UK, left the rest (the Irish Free State) relatively independent, though having to accept an oath of loyalty to the British crown.

This divided the IRA, with a faction resisting that demand and a brief civil war ensued. The victors led by Eamon de Valera then took charge of the Free State, ensuring gradual political separation from British influence. At first it was ceded "dominion" status before achieving its own constitution in 1937. Thus, the Irish Republic emerged very recently, historically speaking, which is relevant to today's sensitivities about national identity in the British Isles. The twenty-six counties in the south did not become a full republic until 1949, joining the United Nations in 1955 and the European Community in 1973.

To summarise, Irish identity emerged from conditions of strategic colonisation in the north, absent landlordism in the south, and starvation of the already poor Catholic majority. This triggered a form of nationalist militancy that was militarised with eventual political success, barring the ongoing stalemate over "the north". This extreme scenario was less marked on the mainland but independence movements for both Wales and Scotland ensued (today represented by Plaid Cymru and the SNP).

---

[18] Anomalies in the British Isles are the all-Ireland bodies of the Irish Cricket Union, the Irish Rugby Football Union (IRFU), and the Gaelic Athletics Association (GAA). The IRFU was formed in 1879 and survived first the Irish Free State and then the Irish Republic as did the GAA formed in 1884. Thus, the island of Ireland today in sporting terms has a dual reality—one combined and the other separated from the UK (e.g., Northern Ireland has its own national association football team and it combines with Great Britain in international athletic events).

Understanding British identities

The discussion of the meaning of nationalisms in the British Isles is illustrated by the work of New Left writers from England (Anderson, 2002) and Scotland (Nairn, 1973). Perry Anderson has been pro-Europe but critical of the EU. That distinction is important because on the right, being anti-EU and being ethnocentric blur into one another (as in the ideology of UKIP) but on the left there were "Lexiteers", whose agenda was anti-EU but still internationalist.[19] Tom Nairn has explored the role of post-colonial independence for Scotland as a vehicle for liberation on the left, with his critics accusing him of favouring nationalism over internationalism (Davidson, 1999).

The universalism of Marxism, which I cited from Sivanandan and Hobsbawm in the introduction to the book, has been dealt recurring blows from nationalisms, and this is no more evident than in the case of Britain. The fluxing formation of identities in the British Isles discussed earlier implicated each and every part of the British Empire, which morphed slowly, with more and more independence movements, into the Commonwealth.[20] I have focused mainly on colonialism close to home deliberately, in order to highlight how the indigenous British, who are a melting-pot genetic legacy of many invasions and a range of settling migrants, have spawned a complex picture about identity formation. That complexity can be understood by attending to aspects of our **four planar social being**.

For example, on the first plane the climate of Ireland created the condition of possibility for a restricted subsistence crop. On the second, the interpersonal aspects of belonging to a group bound by language, religion, and cultural traditions of music, dancing, and sport afforded an ingroup sense of what it was to be Irish, Scottish, English, or Welsh. On the third, the emergence of feudal authority based in the different countries led to wars of attrition for dominance throughout the British Isles,

---

[19] Democratic critiques of the EU from the left are well expressed in Mair (2013) and Guinan and Thomas (2017).
[20] The British Commonwealth originated in 1926 from the Balfour agreement about dominions of the United Kingdom and signalled the slow disintegration of the British Empire.

culminating eventually in the socio-economic dominance of London, both at home and abroad in the Empire. On the fourth plane rests all the individual subjective variants of what it means to be this or that national identity, which can allude to current residency, ancestry, or a combination. For example, data collected today by the UK government about these variants include the following.

1. White: English; Welsh; Scottish, Northern Irish or British Irish; Gypsy or Irish Traveller; any other White background.
2. Mixed or Multiple ethnic groups: White and Black Caribbean; White and Black African; White and Asian; any other Mixed or Multiple ethnic background.
3. Asian or Asian British: Indian, Pakistani, Bangladeshi, Chinese, any other Asian background.
4. Black, African, Caribbean or Black British: African; Caribbean; any other Black, African, or Caribbean background.
5. Other ethnic group: Arab; any other ethnic group.[21]

That long list reflects the range of identities emerging from the history of the British Empire, augmented by the free movement of some from Europe during EU membership. When we now come to understand the complexities of their co-existence today in the British Isles, epistemological and ontological considerations are both relevant. The epistemological aspects refer particularly to varying ideologies in citizens of the Isles, which include emotive not just cognitive aspects.

For, example, how do we make sense of the British Asian's ethnocentric rant against the Polish lorry driver I witnessed? Some of it might be about class, not race or ethnicity. The irate motorist with a brown face was in a smart suit and drove away in an expensive Mercedes saloon. (The fact he was driving a German car was noteworthy but not necessarily by him.) He was clearly glad Brexit had happened and was an embodied contradiction, being of immigrant heritage. Was this just a "pulling

---

[21] Probably the most ambiguous identity is that of being Jewish as it contains versions of religious observation as well as those who see themselves as secular Jews (non-practising or atheist). The arguments on the left in Britain about anti-Semitism was one contributory factor in relation to the failure of the Corbyn project.

up the drawbridge" or "I'm alright Jack" mentality of those who had lost a sense of their cultural past and its colonial roots? It was definitely not about being poor and white.[22]

Psychologically, this is complex stuff, as Darcus Howe discovered in 2000. He was an African-Caribbean journalist and antiracist campaigner, who left his home in Brixton with a Channel 4 film crew to find "the White Tribe" of England. What he found was a variegated cultural picture with the white English articulating a range of *parochially framed* identities. He certainly found racism and ethnocentricity, but it was *regional* differences that stood out in his travel, re-visiting the picture described by J. B. Priestley in his classic book *English Journey* (Priestley, 1934). Variegation is also the theme of the autodidact journalist Michael Collins, who defends his own culture of origin—the white English working class. He argues that they have been unfairly demonised by the left; they are not a homogenous culture and are not always ill-educated bigots (Collins, 2014).

The theme of English cultural variegation has continued, post-Brexit, with conservative commentators' special pleading for regionalism, reminding us that historians of nations tend to identify that precondition (see later). For example, writing in the conservative *Daily Telegraph* (7 August 2021), the Anglican Archbishop of York, Stephen Cottrell, attacked what he called the "metropolitan elite". He argued that the latter (wrongly) considered those in the English regions as being "backwardly xenophobic". He also made a plea for "an expansive vision of what it means to be English". He relished a vision of a country that could rediscover a sense of "national unity".

However, whether we consider this special pleading from the right, or Howe's (and Priestley's) search from the left, where precisely do we find what it is to be English? Apart from periods of jingoism in wartime, when does *any* country, but especially a politically dominant one, have a clear sense of "national unity"? Can it be "rediscovered" or, in the case of England, was it ever there in the first place? As the presumed benchmark

---

[22] That contradiction has been noted by the critics of Priti Patel, currently the Conservative Home Secretary, noted for her brutal policies on migration. Her paternal grandparents were from India and her parents were part of the Asian diaspora expelled from Uganda in the 1960s, settling in England.

of superiority, within proud British imperialism, being English did not usually necessitate considered reflection. It is only now that its power has been lost that England is looking restlessly for its own identity. Culturally it is in a collective state of ontological insecurity, which is a cue for the next section.

Ontological insecurity: our unquenchable thirst for belonging

In a different national context of exploring such contradictions, Arlie Hochschild explored the attitudes of white Trump supporters in her book *Strangers in Our Own Land: Anger and Mourning on the American Right* (Hochschild, 2016). What was striking about this study of white conservatism[23] in the southern states of the USA was that rationally many of them would have been protected much better by voting for environmental protections offered by the "big" federal government they despised. The Democratic Party, the *bête noire* of Trump and his supporters, as a perceived dangerous harbinger of socialism, would have actually protected their interests in the swamp areas polluted with petrochemicals and their pathogenic impact.

Many of these voters, then, rationally were supporting the wrong cause, if that was judged by a cool appraisal of their self-interest. This was overridden by a visceral reaction to the perception that their own status within the American dream, of being decent hard-working people waiting in line for their just desserts; others were queue-jumpers, such as the illegal Mexican immigrants and the poor black single mothers on welfare. There were relevant subgroups as well, such as conservative white[24] Christians, who since Reaganism had been looking forward to the "rapture",[25] as well as celebrating the free-market economy as a form of divine instruction to increase individual wealth as a virtuous lifestyle.

---

[23] A criticism of this study is that it did not include the views of black people in the locality investigated.

[24] Note non-white Christians in the US tend to be Democrat voters. The strong link between Republican voting and religious observance is racialised (white evangelicals, not Catholics). This was reflected in the pattern of voting for Donald Trump.

[25] This is a convenient belief, in some parts of American evangelical Christianity, that at the end of the world God will take true believers up into heaven, presumably leaving

This mixture began to constitute the "Make America Great Again" movement that both voted in Trump and continued to support him after his controversial term in office and his last gasp efforts at insurrection. Nelson (2019) traces how the Council for National Policy (CNP) mobilises funding from the white evangelicals (in particular) to promote the Republican right. It is a network of funders, media owners, and political strategists created for the cause. It started in the Reagan years and continued into recent times to promote Trumpism. During that time, the Southern Baptist Convention reacted against the civil rights period in the USA by pushing back against liberalisation and created the "Conservative Resurgence".[26] That has been central in challenging the sex-based rights demands about reproduction from second-wave feminism. It was then extended and systematised in its organisation when the CNP was formed.[27]

My discussion of ethnocentricity in the British context has some resonances then with similar trends in the USA. However, we can spot differences in the concrete singularity of that context compared to the ex-colonial powers of Europe in relation to national identities. In particular, wars during the twentieth century were important in both settings but in the case of the USA, they participated in one not shared with the UK: Vietnam.[28] This was a disaster by any measure but in particular it stimulated the emergence of a White Power movement in the USA, in the early 1980s, bringing together traditional elements of the Ku Klux Klan with Nazi skin heads (Belew, 2020). This culminated not just in opportunistic violence against black and ethnic minorities but

---

behind atheists, agnostics, those of other faiths or in the "wrong" Christian denomination. We are left to speculate whether heaven will be an all-white idyll.

[26] Diamond (1989) studying the growth of the white evangelical desire to control the state describes this as "dominionism".

[27] Though Trump initially was at odds with observant Christian sympathies, for a range of personal reasons (he was pro-choice about abortion and publicly lewd), in 2016 he agreed a deal with evangelicals to promote their political agenda in exchange for their network supporting his candidature. This is why the CPN has been politically powerful even in relation to the amoral Trump.

[28] There was a moment when the UK was nearly co-opted for the war in Vietnam but it passed because of stubborn objections from the then Labour Prime Minister, Harold Wilson, on pragmatic grounds of cost.

also against the US State itself. The latter was typified by the Oklahoma bombing in an example of "leaderless" white terror.[29]

Thus, ontological security at the individual level can be derived from, and even sacrificed for, group belonging. This draws attention to Plane 2, relationality, of our **four planar social being**. Its central salience in understanding identity politics, which I allude to repeatedly in this book, helps us to make sense of the need for solidarity and the high value we tend to place upon it. That social psychological process is as relevant in understanding, say, Women's Liberation as it is White Power. The comforts of belonging are highly motivating for human beings.[30] Belonging is an obvious source of both meaning and security in our lives. It is an important generative mechanism to appreciate when we are trying to make sense of what seem to be irrational acts.

So much of the content of this book indicates that the *psychological* function of identity politics (rather than its equally important historical conditions of emergence) needs to be taken seriously. This is why I argue in the final chapter that although identity politics is a form of psychological **reductionism**, there is a case for needing *more* psychology in order to understand its irrationalities.

In the case of British identities, a range of factors generate confusions driven by heart and gut feelings. For example, mirroring the point of the Trump supporters, just before the Brexit vote, in one of many examples of BBC-conducted vox pop interviews of the time, were three male white pensioners in a Cornish pub. They were keen and proud Brexiteers. One commented indignantly that Britain needed to leave the EU because "things could not get any worse". This statement was unequivocally stupid, if judged by the realities of life we are all aware of: of course,

---

[29] This was at the hands of the Gulf War veteran Timothy McVeigh in Oklahoma City in 1985. There were 168 fatalities and 680 injured. His White Power politics was directed at the federal government, continuing that trend in disaffected post-war veterans, since the US humiliation in Vietnam in 1975. He was executed for his crime in 2001.

[30] To avoid the reductionist excesses of this claim, we can of course note that some human beings seemingly prefer to be isolates. Whether their asocial existence is a source of happiness or alienation and distress will vary from person to person. They might be monks in their individual cells in silent orders or they might acquire diagnoses, such as "anxious-avoidant personality disorder", "schizoid personality disorder", or "autism". One person's pious devotion might be another's psychiatric diagnosis.

any situation for any of us, individually or collectively, can get worse in the future. The blatant contradiction in this case was that peripheral areas of Great Britain, such as Cornwall and Wales, which also voted in favour of leaving the EU, would lose being economically supported fulsomely by recent EU funding.[31]

But the interesting question psychologically is why did the interviewee not *realise* the stupidity of his statement, judged by rational criteria? The answer might lie in him not really being interested in rationally appraising the future at all, but instead being governed by a sense of warm nostalgia. Ethnocentrism and nostalgia go hand in glove for many older people and, as I note earlier, are felt in the heart and guts, not reasoned in the head, as advertisers interested in the "grey pound" know (Goulding, 1999).

Many Brexiteers were older votes, who believed that the past was good, the present was badly letting them down, and the future was threatening. The EU became a symbol of this existential appraisal and so those campaigning for a leave vote focused vaguely on "taking back control". Quite what that new form of control was going to mean in practice for the average citizen (rather than the rich ideologues remaining comfortably wealthy) was never clear. It is still not today, given the trading chaos it has created in Europe. But reality testing was never really the point: Brexit offered the *fantasy* of returning to a golden age of British culture, actual or perceived. Nostalgia is a non-rational driver of decision-making.

Another BBC interviewee from the same demographic, but female, when challenged by the interviewer that younger voters actually *liked* being attached to the EU, and they prioritised their European identity, said, "Yes but they can't remember what it used to be like in the past."

---

[31] A mitigating factor for those outside the Home Counties and the London metropolis is that some poorer post-industrial localities were expected to absorb immigrant populations in disproportionate numbers, placing local pressures on health and education facilities. This was one driver of the transfer of traditional Labour votes in the north of England to the Conservatives to support the leave outcome ("getting Brexit done"). Note, then, the link between the latter and the long-term anti-immigration sentiments in the wider English electorate. The "taking back control" mantra focused then on controlling immigration above all else.

This cosy preferred past, in living memory, inconveniently included police corruption, the Troubles in Northern Ireland, and casual sexism and racism at large in the workplace, at the fag-end of the British Empire. This harking back with a selective memory is a small resonance of the mystical appeal of nationalisms I noted earlier.

Since Brexit, identity politics from the left (such as the Black Lives Matter movement) have invited a similar logic of psychological reductionism from the right. In 2020 Keir Starmer, leader of the Labour Party, was wrong-footed by a very self-assured woman calling herself "Gemma" in a phone-in to LBC Radio. She asked him, "Should white people also start playing identity politics now before they become a minority themselves by 2066?" (We can only presume that this magical year was the 1,000-year anniversary of the Norman invasion, though its symbolism is ambiguous.)[32] "Gemma" explained proudly that her husband was a Millwall FC supporter, who had been amongst those who booed the players of both sides at a recent home game for "taking the knee" in support of Black Lives Matter. She went on, "because if anything, the racial inequality is now against the indigenous people of Britain".

This raises a wider point about the appeal of identity politics for good or bad, which valorises the psychological, especially emotional, aspects of power. If we narrow our understanding of power to personal identity and seek a sense of comfort and purpose in those political goals that provide us with a sense of ontological security, then many hares are set running. In this case the young are future orientated and open, optimistically, to their connections with an image of commonality in Europe. By contrast, their parents or grandparents maybe want their old world back and believe that it is being stolen from them by Europeans. Though diametrically opposed, both these forms of identity politics are centred on *experienced* ontological (in)security.

---

[32] Again, this reflects the absurdity of nationalists offering a romantic palingenetic account of Englishness: was it good or bad that the Normans came to displace Anglo-Saxon authority in 1066? "Gemma" and Starmer did not exchange views on this point in the LBC phone-in.

Final reflections on nationalisms

To return finally to the early point about the modern invention of nations, Hobsbawm (1991) suggested that the notion of "nation" represented "an attempt to fill the void left by the dismantling of earlier community and social structures". This implies, but does not spell out, the psychosocial matter of ontological security. One thing that Hobsbawm was clearly correct about is that nations are invented by humans and to offer them as natural kinds is a misleading reification. They are part of the **transitive** not **intransitive aspect of reality**.

Others have challenged Hobsbawm's version of linear sequencing and favoured a mixed picture of messy coexistence. For example, Weber, the historiographer of French regionalism, noted that, "France the political nation of the *Ancien Régime* functioned side by side with traditional community and social structures. The ideological nation of the Revolution had to come *with* these" (Weber, 1976: 113, emphasis added). Earlier I noted the matter of regionalism as a precursor to nationalism, when discussing it as a current regressive solution to a lack of a clear English identity.

Nationalisms, *all nationalisms*, have a provenance open to critical scrutiny for their mythologies about blood and soil. Their rhetorical preferences for a patriotic duty to humanly confected political entities, which are allegedly "one and indivisible", all invite scepticism. My view is that Hobsbawm was correct to adopt a "plague on all their houses" approach to nationalisms, as one version of identity politics. But to point out the profound irrationality of nationalism is not to underestimate its abiding political punch. Indeed, some commentators on the left have noted that today it may be undermining the apparently settled geopolitical regime of **neoliberalism**.

Therborn (2021) suggests that **neoliberalism** can be traced to the 1980s, with the alliance of Thatcher, Reagan, and the Chilean military junta, with its free-market reforms. With them, and their radical right ideological support from the likes of Ayn Rand, Milton Friedman, and Friedrich Hayek, global capitalism, consumerism, and selfish individualism came together in a temporary unifying ideology. Today that celebration on the right of a seeming permanent nirvana of free-market capitalism and self-centred thinking may be breaking up, ironically, because of new forms of reactionary nationalist populism, in a range of countries (including Chile, the USA,[33] and Britain). However, consumerism and individualism have remained intact, and they continue to sustain the presence and norms of identity politics.

Also, global capitalism is simply being reconfigured as nation states find new arrangements with trading partners to suit their parochial interests. With state capitalism in China continuing to have a strong global reach (including with an indebted USA), the subordination of democracy in any country to international economic forces is evident. Nationalisms, with their simplistic fantasised and nostalgic identities, offer one form of objection and proud resistance to this recent phase of late capitalism. A caution to this formulation is that their intersection with theocratic patriarchy is an additional twist to the story at times, which can drag societies back into feudal (i.e., pre-capitalist) forms of organisation and thought. Today the aspirations of both ISIS and Hindu nationalism reflect this tendency (see Chapter Seven).

Conclusion

To summarise, this consideration of the temporal and the spatial aspects of ontological (in)security is important because both are so contested across identity politics. For example, the future has offered the young European an identity and the revolutionary left the enduring hope of international socialism. In the other direction (and for now this seems to have more emotional power) the glories of days gone by offer comfort and solace to reactionaries of all creeds and colours, in a turbulent and uncertain world.

In its most extreme form this might entail a desire to return to feudal theocracies to counteract the neoliberal chaos of self-obsessed consumerism and sexual license. That corrective prospect, under the radical Islam I considered in Chapter Five, has an imagined identity based upon a group that transcends current national borders. And yet that has nothing in common with the open-ended appeal of Marx and

---

[33] Although Biden beat Trump in 2020, this was a marginal result. Forty per cent of the US population still seem to believe in the ethnocentric chant about American exceptionalism ("Make America Great Again").

Engels to the solidarity of the international proletariat. As for nationalisms, they can cut in so many dazzling directions; taking the fascist right back to past glories and into future new forms of domination; celebrating liberation struggles against colonialism on the left; and being a convenient vehicle for authoritarian leaders (Leninist or capitalist) in America, Vietnam, Russia,[34] or China. These imagined futures are so diverse, intuitively they seem like a zero-sum game. What they all have in common is the reductive logic of only two of our four planes of social being: the interpersonal and the biographical.

---

[34] At the time of this book going to press, Russia has just invaded Ukraine, with bold and opposing nationalistic claims being made on both sides.

CHAPTER NINE

Six lessons about identity politics

I will now flesh out my claim from the introduction to the book that identity politics can be described as a "curate's egg". In my view, the commonplace unconditional compliance of good people, especially the young, with support for all forms of identity politics now reflects a misguided turn on the left. Having said this, some of the time, some of these demands are based upon demonstrable sources of oppression affecting humanity today. I have sought to recognise those benefits or insights in the earlier chapters, when and if they are applicable. Indeed, without those traceable aspects of **ontological realism** (such as colonialism or patriarchy) there would be no plausible basis for identity politics on the left at all.

However, a credible starting rationale for an unreflective commitment to supporting diversity at all costs has now become authoritarian dogmatism, which is a regressive, not progressive cultural sign to consider. History has been a selective weapon in this oversimplification. "Decolonising history" is a limited project unless history is *also* called upon to explore both the legitimate legacy of the Enlightenment project and, more recently, the absurdities created by the postmodern turn.

In particular they have irrationally dignified ad hominem reasoning as an obligatory virtue. As George Santayana is often cited as saying, "Those who do not remember the past are condemned to repeat it." In this case, the past must be explored in its *entirety*, not simply used selectively to shore up a current marketing strategy.

For example, recently the University of Sheffield has issued a policy attacking Darwin for being a racist, for his eugenic position. This encourages the smug elision that science should not be trusted, and the personal views of the scientist should be our only guide when evaluating knowledge claims. Darwin was a slavery abolitionist and humanist. Moreover, eugenics was commonplace across the political spectrum of the educated class of his time.

This invites us to evaluate particular knowledge claims at the turn of the twentieth century in that context. However, these complex contextualising details are omitted in the cause of virtue signalling in Sheffield. In their short-term thirst for recognition by their students as consumers (remember higher education is now business, with highly paid Chief Executives, called "Vice Chancellors"), the university did not let the facts get in the way of marketing ideology.

In light of the above, I now summarise six key learning points from writing this book.

Lesson one: the spectrum of legitimacy

We can think of a spectrum of legitimacy in identity politics with clear anchor points. At one end are social movements that focus on eradicating global poverty and at the other are anti-social sexual identities, feudal theocrats, and white supremacists. The last of these reminds us of the caution that social movements are not intrinsically progressive or concerned with the basic needs of all humans. They can at times reflect a self-centred and very selective and convenient definition of human rights or expressed needs. At one end, then, is a focus on equality in defining social progress and at the other there is the fetish of diversity, no matter what the costs for others. The taken-for-granted yoking of equality and diversity is thus problematic.

I offer my view of the range of positions in different types of identity politics in Box 9.1., in light of the earlier chapters. The reader may or may not agree with the ranking of positions I suggest and with my commentary. However, what is not in doubt is that a range of *some sort* exists about legitimacy within types of identity politics. The amalgam claims about diversity, maybe nuanced with intersectionality, divert us from making such an appraisal. This is because differentiation may appear to excuse intolerance or exclude minority demands. However, this is not the case. For example, the defence of reproductive rights for women simply cannot be given the same moral equivalence as the demands of patriarchal theocrats. The antiracist and the white supremacist differ in the plausibility of their arguments. "Diversity" simply does not ensure moral equivalence, nor does it pre-empt fair-minded differentiations from those debating in good faith.

Whether my rankings are deemed to be fair comment or not (I fully accept that they are debateable), the commentaries in the right-hand column highlight some recurrent considerations for any of us. The first is that the more universal or widespread the claims apply in the population, then surely the more there are grounds for legitimacy. The second is that the consequences for others are relevant. For example, BDSM and paedophilia are about the domination of other human beings, putting their welfare at risk, despite the rhetorical denial that this is the case. The most egregious example of this is the incel movement, which is about pure angry entitlement and, with that, comes a blunderbuss attack upon humanity.

The third consideration is the extent to which subgroups within identity politics contradict one another in their explicit aims. For example, sex-based rights are threatened by transgender activism (and vice versa) and white supremacists would aim to eliminate anti-racism when and if they achieved power. This also is the case with theocracies, which would censure and criminalise homosexuality and abortion, as well as outlawing or persecuting other religions. In light of these three arguments, the vague sentiment of celebrating diversity at all times and in all circumstances creates as many problems as it solves.

Box 9.1 The range of legitimacy of identity politics

	Level of legitimacy	Commentary
Anti-poverty campaigns	Very high	Focuses on equality and refers to objective material criteria. Universalist goal.
Sex-based rights	High	Refers to half of the population. Respects biological reality linked to reproductive rights. Demonstrable pattern of oppressive patriarchy.
Anti-racism	High	Refers to large minorities in post-colonial context. Structural racism clearly demonstrable.
Homosexual rights	Medium	Universalist claims for citizenship of adults. Undermined by widespread religious conservativism.*
Psychiatric service-user rights	Medium	Universalist claims for citizenship. Rule transgressions undermine daily rationality so affects credibility of claims.
Transgender rights	Low	Anti-realist claims undermine sex-based rights. Subterfuge of a "no debate" strategy is anti-democratic.
BDSM rights	Low	Consensual emphasis is precarious in practice. Pain and domination are poorly compatible with human flourishing.
Incels	Very low	Both misogynistic and misanthropic. Little or no sympathy from out-group members.
Paedophile rights	Very low	Little or no sympathy from out-group members. In denial about harm caused to children. False moral panic claims.
White supremacists	Very low	No scientific or moral case for their claims. Contempt for out-group wrongly justifies violence.
Theocratic rights	Very low	Enmeshment with the state removes the rights of all non-believers and those from other creeds.

* Note I am rehearsing a point here about legitimacy, not agreeing with the moral basis for it being undermined.

As we go from top to bottom of this spread of identity politics, we see a shift from the whole of humanity to special pleading for minorities, with a decreasing popularity of out-group support for the latter. Within that shift, there is also a trend of moving from concern for others to one of narrow self-interest, about individuals or groups (i.e., from being other-orientated to being narcissistic).

Lesson two: the left has taken an understandable but wrong turn

If we neither reject identity politics wholesale nor obediently comply with all of their demands, then we need an exercise in **judgemental rationality**. This means spelling out my reasoning about why I consider that the left has taken a wrong turn by staying too closely to the position of slavish compliance.

First, identity politics, even at their best (the aspiration to eradicate global poverty), focus on the experience of the poor. This is still a version of epistemological privileging and special pleading from one subgroup of humanity. Beyond the spectrum I note in Box 9.1 is the risk to our species as a whole, not just one group within it (in this case the poor). Today we are still vulnerable to the scenario of collective self-elimination by nuclear warfare or ecocide. Maybe identity politics have diverted us from seeing this elephant in the room. This is why I noted in the introduction that identity politics strongly overlap with, but cannot be conflated, with new social movements. The latter are not *always* about subgroups in the population and the reported experiences therein.

Second, identity politics on the left (but not the right) rely on a spirit of an unending tolerance of diversity. However, paradoxically to enforce that prospect, intolerance must be ensured, via social censure, personal intimidation, or even legal measures (about "hate speech"). Throughout the book, I have highlighted that contradiction. The vague libertarianism underpinning leftish identity politics culminates often in crass forms of unreflective authoritarianism. Apart from the hurt and harm this can cause to individuals, the central casualty is freedom of expression. A time has now been reached when those on the left have to decide whether that liberal gain, once religious autocracy is left behind, should be a fundamental and inviolable principle in the pursuit of human flourishing. Many socialists today feel displaced from the left because that principle has been sacrificed at the altar of identity politics. There has been the loss of a focus on all people, rather than on one group (the point made forcefully in the introduction by Hobsbawm and others).

Third, and this follows from the previous point, the left would do well to revisit the project of the Enlightenment (see later). If reason and science were a sign of social progress to remove the arbitrary power of religious superstition and patriarchy, then identity politics appear to have reversed that gain. In their own way, to various degrees, they reject reason and science in favour of subjective and emotive criteria of worthiness. In the case of religious identities, and their defence and celebration within the rules of diversity training, they are regressing to forms of pre-Enlightenment norms. In the case of gender activism, biological science is held in contempt and biological ontology is denied. Identity politics today are a new version of religiosity.

Fourth, special pleading for and from subgroups ensures a separation of in-group and out-group members, dividing us in our common humanity. It also places us all in a state of anxious self-surveillance and even paranoia. A toxic emotional climate then ensues with its widespread rage and obligated self-righteous virtue signalling. People may have their careers jeopardised and risk social rejection if they say or do the wrong thing. Asserted notions of "privilege" then emerge, which are reifications maintained by confirmation bias in our decision making and the error of the **ontic fallacy**. What is then achieved by all this spiteful divisiveness is by no means clear.

Fifth, and this really is the nub of the problem about identity politics for academics and politicians, how much legitimacy should be afforded any longer to the postmodern turn? Without the lazy and implausible judgemental relativism flowing from this, there would be no Queer Theory or special pleading for paedophiles. More than that, the warranted scepticism about science I rehearsed in the previous point is at risk of being tipped into nihilism. This culminates in anti-realism and a lack of respect both for the natural world and our embedding and contingent social and economic structures. These false trails from unguarded judgemental relativism are important to understand if we are to have a comprehensive account of the way that power operates in open human systems.

If we have learned anything from the catastrophe of twentieth-century Leninism, not just fascism, it is that authoritarian politics fails, especially when it has been amalgamated deliberately with nationalist sentiments. The risk now is that identity politics are creating a different form of authoritarianism in their alignment with American exceptionalism and individualism. The philosophical roots of identity politics may be traceable to Europe, but the project emerged strongly, and was then nurtured within, the cultural context of the USA, including the attempt to render it more sophisticated and plausible by **intersectionality**.

Lesson three: we need psychological understanding but not psychological reductionism

What is clear, looking across the chapters, are the versions of psychological **reductionism** intrinsic to the rationale of identity politics. This might be because, as has just been noted, their context of nurturance was the American left and its pervasive background culture of individualism. The personal may well be political (and at times the political might be personal) but that is not the end of the story. Power operates beyond our personal experience of it: we make choices, adopt value positions, and pursue goals under conditions we cannot always control, and which are beyond our present and even potential awareness or understanding.

A sacralisation of the personal removes it from its full material context and reduces reality to our conscious beliefs and opinions. It ensures the production of one after another **epistemic fallacy** as we confuse reality with our conscious view of reality. The postmodern turn encouraged that tendency (already started by American humanism) and we are now all paying a price politically. Sometimes the price is very personal, when the gender-confused child is prescribed life-changing hormones in line with the contestable belief that any of us might be born in the wrong body or when a female prisoner is sexually assaulted by a transwoman. "Identifying" (as anything) is not the same as *being* anything; this form of magical thinking is the road to delusional solipsism, not a social justice.

If identity politics have a strong psychological character, then what do we know of the **generative mechanisms** operating experientially for people that maintain its limitations? I have complained that the two planar focus of identity politics has diverted us from a serious consideration of extra-discursive powers in the natural world and in social and economic structures. The utility of understanding our **four planar social being** is diminished when we only focus on the interpersonal and the biographical. However, I have not said much, until now, about the psychological reasons that sustain the blinkered outcome. Here are some ideas in this regard.

The psychological literature has frequently failed because it has flipped between searching for implausible positivist certainties, ignoring context, and succumbing to the postmodern turn, with its mantra that "everything is socially constructed".[1] With these cautions in mind, at times psychological research still provides genuine insights into the underpinnings of identity politics.

Bentall (2018) notes that beliefs are not freestanding inner checklists but emerge from socially negotiated activities. He argues then that *believing* as an activity is of more importance, psychologically speaking, than the content of *beliefs* in people's inner lives. His work has considered the problematic relationship between delusions and ordinary beliefs. At first sight this may be a simple distinction but it is not. It is true that delusions tend to be self-sealing and rigid ways of thinking but that tendency occurs to various degrees and from time to time in all people. Delusional beliefs are really only marked out because they are idiosyncratic to individuals.

When groups have *shared* rigid beliefs, then individuals within them are not considered to be mentally disordered but rational and loyal (hence religious and political commitments to common understandings and even devotions to particular football teams). Being in a *group* minority about believing warrants an oppressed status (hence the focus in diversity training on this), whereas being in a minority of *one* may warrant a psychiatric diagnosis. A stopping point between these is the existence of cults and their devoted members. For example, when it started, Christianity would have fitted that description.

Thus, the abnormality of a belief always has to be considered in the context of group activity. That being said, some people seem to be more prone to beliefs, which to others may be untenable or deserving of scepticism. It is here that we can think, then, of a more or less (analogue)

---

[1] I explore this point about critical realism, as an alternative in psychology to both positivism and radical social constructivism, elsewhere in more depth (Pilgrim, 2020).

approach to our judgements about beliefs rather than a digital distinction between the normal and abnormal. When exploring this "more or less" character of believing, Bentall (ibid.) notes a number of points, which have relevance for identity politics:

1. All animals have cognitive activity. However, elaborated language capacity has created a qualitative shift in human thought. With that comes the challenge of understanding how we come to believe some things and not others and why we might "change our minds". The totemic value of our beliefs means that we might "die on a hill" for them (and some of us do). As Bentall notes, your pet may wait in anticipation when you open a cupboard, as that might signal an imminent feed, but it will never become jihadist.
2. Human decision-making broadly entails rapid and intuitive choices on the one hand and, on the other, slower reflective versions of deliberative consideration. This is described by cognitive science as a "two process model" (Kahneman, 2011). Most of us are capable of both of these modes of thinking but some of us are more prone to one or the other. The first connects us within our evolutionary history to other animals and in some social contexts it is encouraged more than the second (see later).
3. Whereas our beliefs much of the time are mundane or non-contentious (e.g., it tends to be colder in the winter than the summer or there are probably no sheep living at the bottom of the ocean) we also have higher-level ways of thinking or "master interpretive systems". We all construe the world in certain ways, and these include overarching assumptions (e.g., God created the world in seven days, capitalism is exploitative but there is no alternative, socialism is desirable and achievable, global warming is occurring as a result of human activity, I can choose to be anything I want to be, etc.). These ideologies entail complex interdependent assumptions and require constant adjustment to be maintained. Freud (1935) explored these as "defence mechanisms" to protect the ego from anxiety. They are what Kelly (1955) called our "core" and "superordinate" constructs. They tend to be sustained for protracted periods of time (even without clear confirmatory evidence, hence religious beliefs). They might even survive evidence to the contrary, when we seek to reduce cognitive dissonance

or simply flatly deny reality (as in Donald Trump's reliance on the notions of "fake news" and "alternative facts"). We become defensive, confused, anxious, or angry when these are challenged by evidence or argument.
4. Whereas we are all governed by the points made above, some of us are more prone to beliefs at the "delusional" end of the analogue spectrum (i.e., we prefer rigid black-and-white certainties). Moreover, much that guides our beliefs is preverbal and not readily accessible to conscious reflection. For example, the constellation of conservative beliefs is linked to disgust as an emotion (an emotive turning away from offensive experiences). This would be apparent in, for example, hostility to homosexual practices in socially conservative groups.

This summary from Bentall about beliefs and believing is in tune with others exploring the fine grain of human thought. Believing as a social activity starts early and our attachment styles in childhood and cultural context shape what we believe (Ainsworth & Bowlby, 1991). For example, children are not born believing in God. They learn that assumption from their native cultural or family setting. God may or may not exist (an ontological matter) but the point here is what we are prone to *believe* (faith is an epistemic matter). Other animals cannot believe in God because they lack our enlarged cerebrum, bequeathed by evolution, which has afforded us language use, so we not only make statements but can make statements about them (meta-statements).

The tendency for human beings during their evolution as language users actively to categorise is now taken as a given by cognitive psychologists, tracing their case to Plato and Aristotle. Arguably their whole research enterprise is now about elaborating our understanding of that Platonic legacy. This is a mixed inheritance, as it offers us both strategies for survival but also gets us into tangles, as Dutton (2020) explains in his book *Black and White: The Burden of a Binary Brain in Complex World*. Dutton notes three overarching tendencies in our intra-specific cognitive character, which he calls "evolutionary super-categories" (fight/flight; us/them; right/wrong). These three foundational or primitive tendencies of thought are evident aplenty in identity politics. We must fight or be defeated (hence "social justice *warriors*"). It is us against them (in-group good *vs.* out-group bad). My belief is correct but yours is wrong.

Apart from these three super-categories noted by Dutton, we can add a fourth from the historical anthropologist René Girard with his notion of "imitative desire" (Girard, 1972). Throughout history[2] there has been evidence that we desire what others have, which leads to the restless experience of envy and the cathartic practice of rivalry, which is often unconscious. Laws and rules of restraint are then required in any society to keep the unruly consequences of covetousness and envy of the other in check (transgressed, of course, by the acquisitive criminal and apparent in the sibling rivalry of children). We see here then how identity politics is in part the politics of envy: citizenship is desired by those excluded from it, in part or whole, by those who in a range of ways might be in a state of "privilege", which they seek to protect. This power struggle throughout history (which Marx framed as one of class struggle) is emotionally driven, at least in part if Girard's generalisation is fair comment. For example, some on the left, if they are being really honest, may hate the rich more than they love the poor.

Together, these cognitive and affective aspects of our inner lives ensure that an aggressive virtue-signalling monologue soon emerges, when a group is in fighting mode, loyal to an in-group, hostile to outsiders, and is confident in their self-defined shield of truth. Of course, *all* forms of politics entail a degree of virtue signalling in their rhetoric, which is also the case with academic writing (this whole book is arguably a form of virtue signalling in part). However, what characterises identity politics is an *over-reliance* upon it, leaving other processes, such as the analysis of complexity, the tolerance of uncertainty, or the need to respect and negotiate with those we disagree with, withering away as skills and necessities in the background. Why negotiate when you can just "cancel"? Why examine nuance and contradictions, when you already know for certain the factual truth and the moral case in your absolute favour?

---

[2] More accurately, this means human history, once we moved from being hunter gatherers to settled farmers. In the first phase, as in other primates, restrictions of access to food might still trigger hostilities but they were infrequent and a function of space. (Compare the aboriginal cultures of Australia and New Zealand.) Once boundaries were erected about what land is mine and what is yours, then such hostilities were made more certain and routine.

Thus, virtue signalling borne of black-and-white reasoning can soon become the only game in town in identity politics. It favours what psychoanalysts call "paranoid certainty" over "schizoid doubting", but also over mature and open reflection. It ensures moral absolutism and authoritarian political practices. The moral philosopher Susan Neiman focuses on this question of black-and-white versus nuanced forms of reasoning and links it to degrees of psychological maturity (Neiman, 2011). She notes that when we grow up, psychologically rather than just physically, we have a capacity to deal with contradictions, uncertainties, and shades of grey. This links to the second mode of "two-process model" noted earlier. In the first mode, the tendency to make rapid and definitive decisions, on the immediate certainty that something is true, in the past had a survival function. When hunting in the forest, a sudden rustling of the undergrowth might signal the presence of prey (or maybe even predator). This encourages our fight or flight and "friend or foe" way of thinking and the action that quickly triggers.

This scenario is not absurd at all in principle, as it has served us well, but in a different context it might limit our capacity to reflect deliberatively about the complex reality we inhabit. When that technological context is the new digital age, we can see how these psychological processes can be inflected by forces outside of our control. A click (hence "clictivism") is a digital act (present/absent, right/wrong, agree/disagree, etc.), whereas inner deliberation and prolonged respectful debate are analogue processes (more or less degrees of certainty). Social media then encourage and sustain immature forms of believing, which are at odds with **epistemic humility**.

As well as our current social media, which afford clictivism and simplistic sloganising, the commitment to in-group beliefs set against those of enemies in a hostile world is important. Identity politics both drive and are built upon group loyalty, even if the group is a loose ensemble of "friends" we have never met and cartoon avatars with pseudonyms. This reinforces belief systems that are not open to challenge. If they are challenged, this confirms both the rightness and righteousness of the in-group position. Thus, social psychology has lessons for us about identity politics (and more broadly social movements). There is now a literature, for the reader to consult, which demonstrates the association between political beliefs and social networks (Sunstein, 2016) and how group processes shape and maintain individual values in political campaigns (van Zomeran, 2014).

A note on "the personal"

Before leaving the psychological aspects of identity politics, it is worth teasing out an important distinction about what we mean by "the personal". A potential inconsistency could be observed between rejecting ad hominem reasoning and confirming the importance of the biographical provenance of those involved in power struggles. The first of these used to be a taboo in academic reasoning (and in my view it should still be). An argument, theory, or evidential claim should be considered in its own right and weighed up in a process of judgemental rationality. We should go for the ball, not the player, is the usual sporting metaphor for this stricture. However, this is not the same as saying that academic researchers are value-free or that they do not embody vested interests in their **concrete singularity**.

For example, some leaders of disciplinary silos will amplify the legitimacy of their own work and that of their colleagues, ignoring the relevance of nearby disciplines.[3] Disciplinary imperialism relies on epistemological reductionism. Applied research brings this point about "interest work" out even more clearly. For example, clinical guidelines about best practice tend to be generated by those *already invested* in the current ways of working (I noted this in relation to transgender healthcare in Chapter Three).

Outside of the academy, in identity politics, this matter of cognitive interests can be seen in the ways in which evidence or theories are used to sustain particular forms of justificatory rhetoric. For example, second-wave feminism is the foundation ideology for recent gender-critical arguments, but third-wave feminism is a "go to" supportive ideology for transgender activism. Thus, to caution against ad hominem

---

[3] Academics often notice that in specialist journals it is quite rare to see work cited from other disciplines. Such silos not only close off the wider public from their knowledge but also from colleagues in other departments. Interdisciplinary knowledge is important but very difficult to achieve, given this norm of restrictively talking to and impressing your immediate peers with a common training.

logic does not imply that we do not all have interests, both financial and cognitive, that might shape our ways of reasoning in life. Clearly, they often do, and this is obvious when we examine the motivations of those leading and supporting particular versions of identity politics. For example, I noted in Chapter Six that academics who are sadomasochists or paedophiles have tended to become political authorities on these topics. Nonetheless, the arguments a sadomasochist like Gayle Rubin makes, or the paedophile Tom O'Carroll makes, can be weighed up in their own right, despite the personal convenience they might have for their advocates.

Lesson four: we need an alternative to both positivism and postmodernism

By the nineteenth century, the fruits of the Enlightenment project were evident and had taken a self-confident and arrogant turn, with the new authority of positivist science. The future seemingly looked bright with the prospect of the certainties of science offering a technical fix for every human woe or social problem. Eugenics represented an early example of this confidence, at the turn of the twentieth century.

However, a major problem was awaiting, which was positivism's asserted separation of facts from values. At the same time, this was also the period of the freethinkers, scepticism, and atheism, alongside the assertion of new forms of religious superstition, such as the popularity of spiritualism and the ongoing power of Romanticism in the arts, offering its own disdain for science and favouring instead the passions.

The reassertion of strong philosophical idealism in the work of Nietzsche was to signal a tension that was to arise in the twentieth century in politics, science, and the arts and humanities. This posed a central question: which comes first, reality or our view of reality? In the political realm outside of the academy, as the twentieth century began to unfold, chaotic violence ensued between, and within, the authoritarian left and right (Marxist-Leninism and fascism). This was the first part of what Eric Hobsbawm called a "century of blood" in an "age of extremes", which set the climate for all debates thereafter (Hobsbawm, 1994). Much of this blood was already spilt before the Cuban missile crisis, the Vietnam War, 9/11, and the unremitting forms of genocide and torture subsequent to the Second World War, with its hallmark holocaust.

This was the intellectual and political context for a return, over and over again, to the role of authority in public policy. For example, should religious leaders still be listened to (rather than merely *tolerated* in the spirit of the Enlightenment) or should it be scientists and secular politicians? Is the solution to complexity the simplicities of a vanguard party or a strong charismatic leader? The postmodern turn offered its own answer to these questions about authority in the final quarter of the twentieth century. Certainties and authority should now be discarded at a stroke. The underlying working out for this simple strategy was provided by deconstruction and an unending deluge of words about words, offered by French poststructuralism (Lemert, 1980).

Now individual lived experience, narratives, and perspectives were to be the starting path to human freedom. Leaving aside for a moment this being readily embraced by consumer capitalism ("because you are worth it"), for those pursuing social justice, this was the great opportunity that had been denied to the earlier collectivists on the left. With new technology alliances could emerge with complete strangers globally. This created a new set of conditions of possibility for our relationships. We could opt in and out of them on a whim. We could lie about who we were: anonymity and aliases became the norm.

Accordingly, the older rules of mutual accountability, when we could actually meet up with other human meetings in our shared and flawed ordinariness and speak to them face to face, could now be abandoned. All the pros and cons of deceitful power play were now evident. We could now punish people we did not know with anonymity allowing us to evade responsibility for our judgements and actions. We no longer cared about "keeping it real" (what is reality anyway?) and new technology aided and abetted this betrayal of the Enlightenment project.

Fictitious identities now are not only acceptable, they indignantly expect total respect from others. The cowardly tradition of the poison-pen letter is now replaced by the joys of unending anonymity in the puerile postmodern and evidence-free playground of Facebook and Twitter. Facebook pages of white virtue signallers (photoshopped picture kindly provided) are now blazoned with "Black Lives Matter" slogans and "cis" ("Queer") allies make it clear to a world thirsty for their opinion that "I will not respond to friend requests from transphobes".

The subtext of all of this narcissistic posturing is something like this: "I am a nice person but many of you lot out there clearly are not."

Preferences for pronouns now appear on websites and emails with no trace of irony or absurdity. (This is before we go into the ubiquity of gender in languages outside of English, making these preferences a culturally limited opportunity for these precious people.) Secularist social justice warriors are now upstaging traditional religious leaders in their preaching and berating. The Taliban's lash to the errant woman in public is now mirrored by a suffocating blanket of moralisations and earnest expectations online.

Looking back on this recent history, if opinion borne of experience was to define how we should live our lives, then what happens with the contradictions and huge differences this logic spawned, given the inevitable and obvious divisions of interests and opinions? Should reason and freedom of expression now simply be cherished, or should they be discarded? Are our limited lives now a prison for us as individuals and should small-scale personal breaks for liberation (what Cohen and Taylor (1992) called "escape attempts") now define human emancipation, rather than collective political campaigns? Should we now just make up reality as we go along? Can we be whoever we want to be by simple assertion? If no authority is to be trusted in the scientific academy, then will anybody's opinion or fantasy now do instead?

The postmodern turn offered answers to these questions and suddenly all bets were off about the survival of the gains of the Enlightenment. The authoritative claims of both religious dogma and learning in the academy could both be held in equal suspicion (even if this cynicism and nihilism was a version of epistemic authority in its own right). Perspectivism and epistemological privilege now guided both social scientific research and daily identity politics. A warm glow of self-satisfaction could now permeate the powerless and dispossessed, or at least those who chose to speak for them, to give comfort in their oppression.

Dominant forms of existing "privilege" (white, male, cis, heteronormative, ablest, or sanist, or whatever) were bled dry of their past-their-sell-by-date legitimacy. Because of their domains of power, they deserved now to be silenced without conscience (no question and definitely "no debate"). There was no need to wait for a long collective struggle to attain social justice, when this could occur simply by celebrating diversity and silencing anyone who raised doubts about this nearby instant success. The sinister underbelly of this seemingly liberal ultra-tolerance offered legitimacy for theocratic power, incels, and child molesters. And, of course, there was the conundrum of the intolerance of intolerance, defined by critical social justice warriors on their own terms.

For the left this entailed a flipping from its older authoritarian forms (the fetish for the vanguard party or for the Kafkaesque bureaucratic maze of social democracy, typified in the British Labour Party) to a new one based on a daily preoccupation with hating for those considered to be committing secularised forms of sin. In the case of religious identity politics, this meant a direct return to patriarchal rigidity (witness the Taliban in Afghanistan today). Objections to these trends were met with more moralisations; outrage was warranted in the face of their defiance. For example, simply noting the actions of the Taliban might warrant an accusation of Islamophobia or describing a man in a dress as a man would invoke wrath about "misgendering" and "transphobia".

After the postmodern turn, we no longer needed the rack to torture us. Now there was cyber-mob opinion, castigation, and banishment. Twitter can now ruin careers and ensure that, in the academy of all places, we find widespread censorship and self-censorship. Only moral re-education (the HR programmes of equality and diversity training) might rescue us from our social death, provided that we listen carefully to, and obey strictures about, our sinfulness. Some liberal commentators lamenting this sorry state of affairs blame it in part on ingrained faults on the left of authoritarianism and anti-positivism (Pluckrose & Lindsay, 2020). There is some merit in this sort of attack but it warrants a reply for their own version of partiality (mirroring the generic problem of identity politics). This is a cue to look at critical theory.

Lesson five: we need to revisit, not blame, critical theory

During the twentieth century, Marxists struggled internally on two fronts, prompting unending factionalism and in-fighting. On the first was the practical challenge of Leninism (strong, pragmatic, and well-organised but brutal in its response to actual and perceived enemies). On the theoretical front was the reconciliation of the early humanistic tendencies from Marx and his later more economistic writings. These challenges were exposed by the rise of fascism, which was to be both opposed from the left in practical struggle but also understood as a sociopolitical reality (Vajda, 1976). How could the left make sense of fascism as a mass movement, with "blood and soil" seemingly having more inspirational value for ordinary people than international solidarity?

The pragmatic answer for Leninists was to develop their own versions of socialism in one country. For example, apart from this Stalinist populist appeal to support Russian domination of the satellite "republics", the Vietcong were motivated as much by nationalism as by socialism. China and North Korea today still represent examples of the success and failure of this blend of vanguardism and nationalism. Leninism and state capitalism now fit hand in glove to enable Chinese global expansionism, whereas North Korean paranoia builds a nuclear arsenal while its people starve.

Before the Second World War, some Marxist intellectuals in Germany had already spotted the problem with authoritarian politics, with the shock of the rise of fascism but also the failures becoming apparent after the Russian revolution. Some of these turned to Freud for answers to the collective irrationality now apparent on the streets and within respectable German households. The Institute of Social Research had already been formed in the early 1920s in Frankfurt at the Goethe University and it attracted Marxists who were already hostile to Leninism. Inevitably a research focus, which this group returned to recurrently, was authoritarianism. In particular, Hitler's popularity prompted new reflections.

The left for a while took comfort from the assumption that the conditions of possibility for socialism might be deterministically bound up with the contradictions of capitalism. However, not only did it survive and adapt in various ways to potential challenges from the proletariat, the latter seemed to willingly and masochistically *embrace* strong leadership, to its own detriment. Given this paradox, for the Frankfurt School the question of psychic life and its interpersonal context needed to be understood within its wider social context. The term "critical theory" started to become a synonym for these thinkers, though today it remains ambiguous in the academy. Liberal critics of identity politics sometimes attribute their roots to critical theory, even if French post-structuralism is a stronger explanatory candidate.

Here I want to argue that the concerns of critical theory about the biographical and the interpersonal may well now give post hoc comfort to critical social justice warriors but the Frankfurt School is not "behind" what we are witnessing today. However, its history provides us with clues about the failure of representative democracies under capitalism to create social progress and ensure peaceable relationships between nations. Experienced injustice by ordinary people then prompts alternative solutions and these might be found in dogmatic certainties (offered by the right or the left). For the right this means religious conservativism, nationalism, and patriarchy. Within identity politics we see this in the rise of theocratic power and its mass following, as well as in a range of ethnocentric populist movements from Brexit and Indian nationalism to the white supremacist underpinnings of "making America great again" or the claims of Generation Identity in the UK.

Just as in the 1920s the left preferred one version of authoritarianism (Leninism) as a solution to the version on the right, today it seems to be repeating that tendency. However, now it is under new ideological conditions of American individualism and the technological alterations to mass communication. With the latter come new forms of solidarity, actual or rhetorical.

To make sense of this repetition we can look to a later Frankfurt School writer, Jurgen Habermas (1984). His writings help us to resolve the contradictions of identity politics and explain my assessment of it as "curate's egg". I will mention three relevant aspects of Habermasian reasoning. First, he has sought to retain the gains of the Enlightenment about science and freedom of expression (chafing somewhat against the strong anti-positivism of some earlier Frankfurt School writers). Second, he rejected theocratic authoritarianism but argues for the retention of religious sentiments provided that they are then translated into the common good in the secular world. Third, he focused on the relationship between good communication and true democracy.

On the first of these counts, identity politics, supported by postmodernism, seeks to suppress freedom of expression, rationalised by the protection of the vulnerable or oppressed. It is not primarily concerned with reasoned debate but instead with winning the battle. On the second count, we have the reminder that the Enlightenment challenged religious authority but crucially it also defended religious freedom, which is after all a variant of freedom of expression. Today identity politics have a strong religious character, with their leaps in faith, evangelism, and moral prescriptions and certainties. The question, following Habermas, is whether this new form of religiosity, with its witch-finding tendencies, does indeed translate into the common good; we all can come to our assessment of the answer to this question.

On the third question, Habermas distinguished between the social system we live in (say a market economy) and our daily life with others, which he called the "lifeworld". During modernity the latter was constituted by conversations between citizens (say in bars, cafes, and workplaces) as well as a range of voluntary interest groups in society, which met regularly. A free press both informed and responded to this lifeworld and its democratic potential relied upon a number of factors. These included the freedom of expression and respect for the view of others, honesty in public debate, and a respect for evidence and logic, as well as a wide or universal access to these forms of communication. To maximise this democratic potential, participants must be free from coercion or manipulation and hierarchies of participation must be as flat as possible. The rule of law should protect these communicative possibilities for us all.

At first sight, the internet, and within it social media as a central communicative vehicle for identity politics, seemed to offer the universalism proposed by Habermas. However, in practice it has become segmented into echo chambers and can be manipulated by a range of commercial and political interest groups. Moreover, the emergent cultural rules of identity politics did not defend the principles of free and democratic debate but centred instead on identifying and punishing fellow citizens who deviated from expectations of purity of thought and deed.

That spirit of *tolerant informed debate* from Habermas implied a civil right and a vehicle for democratic decision-making for the common good. In my view, identity politics have subverted, not defended, that vision, which is the alternative one of deliberative democracy. This cues my final learning point.

Lesson six: we need deliberative democracy, not identity politics

If the left is to avoid its authoritarianism from the past and its new version in the present, given its love affair with identity politics, then what is the alternative? One orientation to consider in order to retain the goals of humanistic socialism and the survival of the threats of nuclear warfare and ecocide is to focus on face-to-face co-operation guided by deliberative democracy. The ideas of Habermas, just noted, along with other Frankfurt School writers such as Erich Fromm and Claus Offe, as well as those on the libertarian left such as Noam Chomsky and David Graeber, would support that commitment.

The specific notion of deliberative democracy came from the work of a contemporary of the post-Second World War Frankfurt School: the political philosopher Hannah Arendt (2005). Its focus is a respect for the type-two mode of thinking noted earlier in my discussion of psychology, along with a retention of the gains of the Enlightenment, in relation to rationality, truth, and freedom of expression. It assumes that participatory democracy is more than voting every few years (representative democracy) but requires informed citizens speaking and acting together on a daily basis.

If Leninism led to its brutalities, then liberal capitalist democracies have not ensured Arendt's vision at all. For example, the rise of both Nazism and Donald Trump came *within* that model of representative democracy and even Conservative heroes, such as Winston Churchill, have damned it with faint praise. Once we handed over our trust to elected politicians then their own careers and the vested interests of extra-parliamentary groups shape their conduct and inflect their decision-making. As the anarchists note, "whichever way you vote the government always gets in".

Arendt envisioned direct participation, not this passive ceding of powers to our elected representatives. She also noted that the (inevitable) failure of our representatives to deliver on their pre-election rhetoric then created the conditions for impulsive mob rule (governed by the type one mode of thinking I noted earlier). In particular this recurrently turns against out-group members: hence the consistent theme of ethnocentricity and anti-immigration. Representative democracies may *claim* to moderate these barbaric impulses but they fail to do so in practice; indeed, conservative elements in the system actively promote them. Arendt did not live long enough to witness the cyber mob and its new form of rule via identity politics.

Although Arendt made the mistake of accepting the separation of technical-scientific knowledge from the citizens' discussion of values (she retained this positivist error), her practical suggestions are important. The operation of the early Soviets as well as of the Paris Commune are starting points for a discussion of their form, but the focus is on routine daily co-operation about our decision-making in relation to goals and their step-by-step achievement. Co-operatives and council democracy were the way forward for Arendt in order to avoid authoritarianism. This returns us to the active informed discussions in public spaces encouraged by Habermas.

Today we are miles from this vision of everyday living together and deciding together. Representative democracy has failed to ensure equality and has simply become enmeshed via crony capitalism with international crime (Kendzior, 2020). In the midst of this failure, we find then the false hope of identity politics, which seeks to create justice by ensuring that ordinary people distrust and turn against one another. It may have pleased the radical left in the USA because of its compatibility with individualism. However, whether it is a plausible global solution is a different matter. This means then that we must redouble our efforts to achieve the strategic aspirations of truly deliberative democracy. One first step is to take stock of the strengths and weaknesses of identity politics, which I have rehearsed in this book.

Glossary of terms

Axiology: The study of values or what is valuable in life. Critical realists consider that all activity, including in both natural and social scientific research, contains values which might be either implicit or explicit. Critical realists are thus concerned with not only how things are but how they ought to be. By contrast, positivism avoids this activity, when assuming, erroneously, that knowledge can and should be 'disinterested' and that facts and values can be readily separated from one another (when this is not tenable). Axiology contains an exploration of both ethical and aesthetic aspects of human existence, though the first of these tends to predominate in discussions about values in human science.

Concrete singularity: the particular and unique expression of concrete universal phenomena. Critical realism rejects abstract universals in favour of the latter. Take the example of the concept of "woman". Every woman will share some commonalities with other women but also be different from them in various ways. Women also come from different times and places, inflecting what it is to be a woman in this particular time and place and not another. Finally, a particular woman has unique features as a person, shared by no one else.

214   GLOSSARY OF TERMS

Covering laws: The erroneous assumption from positivism that there are permanent and fixed laws produced by science (both natural and social) that will apply in all contexts. (See empirical invariance.)

Emergence: A fundamental premise of critical realism is that events come and go in the world as a result of underlying generative mechanisms operating alone but, more typically, in interaction with one another creating a constant dynamic mixture of homeostasis and change. The complexity and flux of open systems affords the constant possibility of new events. Also because reality is laminated, new characteristics or capacities emerge at higher levels of systemic organisation than lower ones. For example, speech has arisen in humans, not other primates, because of our cerebral characteristics.

Empirical invariance: Refers to the misleading claim from positivism that there are lawful patterns in reality that occur across all times and places. This assumption can only be made about closed systems but human systems in the real world are open, not closed. Critical realism proposes that in open systems there is wide empirical variance, though some patterns may be more regular or probable than others (demi-regularities and tendencies). (See covering laws.)

Epistemic fallacy: This is when statements about the world are reduced to statements about knowledge. When this happens we confuse the map with the territory. This, and the closely related ontic fallacy, are common errors in research and its applications. (See ontic fallacy.)

Epistemic humility: A reminder that we need to be cautious at all times about our knowledge because it is fallible and partial. We do not understand, and may never understand, much of what is real. (See the empirical, the actual, and the real.)

Epistemological relativism: This refers to competing and shifting forms of understanding across time and place, within and across individuals. As language users we can make statements about the world and statements about statements (meta-statements). This intriguing complexity has often been a central preoccupation of Western intellectualism. However, this narrow focus on epistemology (the study of knowledge) can divert us from the importance of ontology (the study of being). For example, before chemists understood that graphite and diamonds were constituted by the same essence (carbon atoms), people would name and discuss them as being unrelated substances in their lives. The way we name and discuss aspects of our world may or may not correspond accurately to the character of the world itself. (See epistemic fallacy; and ontological realism.)

Explanatory critique: This is the exploration of how a theory came into being and is sustained, even if it is flawed. For example, we could explore the roots of creationism and the interests it serves today, even though it is an untenable theory.

Four planar social being is the assumption in critical realism that our experiences and decisions as moral agents, in particular social contexts (the constraints of social structures and their emergent processes), also take place in the natural world. This elaborated version of structure and agency then implicates four dimensions: (i) our material transactions with nature; (ii) our interactions with other people (relationality); (iii) social (including economic) structures particular to our world at a place and time; and (iv) the unique stratification of our particular embodied personalities. Any truly human science would need to keep all four dimensions in mind at all times, in order to avoid reductionism. (See structure and agency; laminated reality; and reductionism.)

Generative mechanisms: The focus of critical realism is on underlying mechanisms, which may or may not be actualised. When they are actualised, then they are the same as our common sense notion of causes but even if their causal powers are not actualised, they are still real. By contrast, naïve realism (the compound of empiricism and positivism) focuses on events primarily, not underlying mechanisms. Once events come into being, they may themselves trigger new ones so they can become part of a generative mechanism. Positivism has a narrow conception of the inference of causality, based upon the premise of "constant conjunctions", bequeathed to the philosophy of science by the empiricist philosopher David Hume. These constant conjunctions (sequences between two empirically measurable occurrences in time and proximal space) limit our understanding of causality and obscure its depth and complexity. (See structure and agency; covering laws; the actual; the empirical; and the real.)

Idealism is a term used in philosophy to indicate that ideas are primary; it is not the vernacular use that indicates utopianism or exaggerated optimism. The primacy of ideas may indicate their dominant causal powers (e.g., motives as inner cognitive states) as well as the constitution of reality by them. The latter then focuses on reality coming from ideas, with radical social constructivism being its ultimate expression. Extreme idealism then demotes or rejects the relevance of outer reality (ontology being separate from human experience). (See social ontology.)

Identitarianism is a term that is used sometimes interchangeably with "identity politics". It is also used at times to refer to a pan-European white supremacist movement.

Immanent critique involves taking a knowledge claim or theory seriously on its own terms, rather than merely rehearsing an immediate oppositional criticism of its premises or errors. This form of critique is called "immanent" because it entails going inside a claim and then working outwards to see if it then really works in practice. Does it do what it says it should do?

Interdisciplinarity refers to the intended advantages of collaboration between those in academic silos. Because critical realism emphasises complex ontology, it doubts the capability of single disciplines to accurately understand ourselves and the world in which we live. This problem is maintained by disciplinary silos and competition between them, which impedes the production of transdisciplinary knowledge. (See reductionism and laminated reality.)

Intersectionality may refer to the intersection of *generative mechanisms* to produce particular forms of oppression in their concrete singularity. It may also apply (sometimes only) to the *subjective experience* of those inhabiting overlapping membership of more than one social group.

Intransitive aspect of reality refers to the immutable aspects of the world that exist independent of our thoughts and actions. This reflects ontological realism but is not conceptually identical to it. Ontological realism refers to a premise about the *existence* of the natural world, which is separate from our existence as individuals and a species, whereas intransitivity refers to the many ways in which we are unable to *influence* that world, individually or collectively. Very occasionally our actions can modify it though, when we alter our natural environment and its properties, but generally features of the latter are not open to influence. For example we cannot alter the speed of light, the force of gravity, the fact of our eventual death, our chromosome count or the broad impact of evolution on a currently differentiated world of flora and fauna, with their characteristic genotypes and phenotypes. Note also that *ipso facto* historical aspects of reality are always intransitive because they cannot be changed. (See transitive aspect of reality, ontological realism and four planar social being.)

Judgemental rationality: The human capacity to weigh up what is likely to be true in a particular context. This can be contrasted with judgemental relativism: the proposal that truth cannot be established and that there only perspectives about the world. The latter error is a feature of postmodern philosophy. Human judgements are fallible and open to revision and so judgemental rationality does not necessarily imply a permanent verification of some aspect of reality (an aspiration of positivism). (See epistemic humility.)

Laminated reality: The assumption that reality is multi-layered and has depth both inside us and outside us. Lower levels of reality are required for higher ones to exist but the explanation of the character of the higher ones cannot be reduced to that of the lower ones. For example, cells in our bodies need to exist for our organs to function but, in explanatory terms, physiology cannot be reduced to cytology and histology. (See four planar social being; and reductionism.)

Neoliberalism: A political ideology espoused in the late twentieth century that emphasises free market principles, radical individualism, small government and the weak regulation of big business. It considers that economic freedom and personal freedom work hand in glove and is suspicious of state interference on both fronts.

New social movements (NSMs) refer to self-organising groups in civil society that campaign for social change in their own particular favour (hence the link with identity politics) but at other times they may be concerned with the survival of the human species or the rights of other species. They can be distinguished from the old labour movement, which focused on power differentials and oppression within work settings.

Omissive critique entails examining silences and absences. Why is question A being pursued in research but not question B? Why was the data interpreted in this way and not that way?

Ontic fallacy: A form of faulty reasoning in which we use a concept or notion to name an aspect of reality. We then deploy that named concrete aspect as *proof* of the concept or notion that we used in the naming at the outset. It is the opposite side of the same coin as the epistemic fallacy. For example, a flat earth enthusiast might use a spirit level to show that a sea promenade is completely flat in order to demonstrate a characteristic of the world they favour (that it is not round but flat). The ontic fallacy entails knowing in advance and with certainty what X is, and then seeking evidence of specific events to confirm the truth X to anyone in doubt. Sometimes critical realists use the compound concept of the "epistemic-ontic fallacy", as they are closely related in their (faulty) logic. (See epistemic fallacy.)

Ontological monovalence: This is the implication of empiricism; we limit our understanding of reality only to what is positively present and observable. This creates a misleadingly superficial and thin account of reality and its fixity. Reality is largely absent, not present and it changes, it does not remain the same. (See the empirical; the actual; and the real.)

Ontological realism: The premise that the world exists independent of our understanding of it. The world is simply there; it is not a product of human thought. This is part of the "holy trinity" of critical realist premises (along with epistemological relativism and judgemental rationality).

Reductionism: Events and processes at one level are explained by those at another in a fixed, non-dynamic manner. Typically this refers to higher levels of reality being reduced to lower ones but it can be applied in the other direction at times. The term may refer to ontology (e.g. "we are what we eat") or epistemology (e.g. "neurochemical theories will explain all mental processes and behavioural outcomes"). The term is also used when discussing simplistic explanations in a field of complexity (e.g. "fog caused the car crash") and in relation to narrow disciplinary arrogance or imperialism; hence "sociological reductionism" or "psychological reductionism". (See epistemic humility; laminated reality; and four planar social being.)

Retroduction: This is a form of inference that works back from what we currently observe to how it came into being. This can be contrasted with induction (inferring the general from a particular) and deduction (inferring a particular from the general). These two forms of inference are detached from context, whereas retroduction is always a contextualised form of reasoning. It deals with a recurring and fundamental question for critical realists: what would the world have had to be like, in order for us to observe what we observe now? The related term "retrodiction" reflects the summation of understanding across cases about the antecedent conditions, which are likely to have created current observable events, whereas retroduction refers to inference about a particular individual outcome or case (e.g. the epidemiology of influenza versus its aetiology in a particular patient).

Social ontology refers to the study of our social world and its features (e.g. social groups, neighbourhoods, cities, nations, economies). This can for analytical convenience be separated from studying the ontology of the natural world. However, in practice the human social world also is reliant on the latter (the first plane of our four planar social being). Methodologically, there can be less empirical detachment in social science (compared to natural science) because investigators are embedded in the object of their inquiry at all times. Realist versions of sociology focus on social ontology, whereas idealist versions are more concerned with social constructivist accounts. (See idealism.)

Structure and agency refer to the relationship between our variable capacity to be conscious reflective agents, who make choices, and our embedding structures, both natural and social, which enable or constrain that capacity. In social science more generally "structure" tends to allude to economic conditions and our normative context, i.e. what is expected of us by society in terms of rule conformity and role expectations learned during our primary socialisation as children. Thus social structures are enduring aspects of our embedding social system but they can and do change over time. They both constrain human action and can be altered by it; societal stasis and change coexist. This theorisation of the relationship between structure and agency entails some sort of concession that we are both determined and determining beings, i.e., it is not one or the other. (See four planar social being.)

The actual: That aspect of reality that actually occurs, whether or not it is observed. If we limit our understanding of reality to the actual ("actualism") then this does not exhaust our task of exploring reality. This is because underlying mechanisms exist and they may not be actualised. (See generative mechanisms.)

The empirical: That aspect of reality that is observed or processed through our other senses. If we limit our scientific understanding of reality to the empirical ("empiricism") then this does nor exhaust our task of exploring reality. Many actualised and non-actualised aspects of reality exist beyond what we experience and describe. Also we are not merely passive observers of reality, we are actively involved in its affirmation or alteration. (See agency and structure.)

The real: That aspect of reality beyond and beneath the empirical and the actual. It includes powers, tendencies and mechanisms, as well as events. It contains both presence and absence. For critical realists, the domain of the real then subsumes witnessed experiences of the world+ actual events in the world+ underlying generative mechanisms, bearing in mind that events may not be witnessed and mechanisms may not be actualised. (See all other entries in this glossary.)

Transitive aspect of reality is that created by human thought and its enactment. This is reflected in epistemological relativism and it includes perspectives, narratives, theories, ideologies, theologies, as well as forms of practice that may flow from them. Occasionally the intransitive can be altered by the transitive, for example when we use genetic engineering on crop production. The more politically dramatic example is the design and mass production of the internal combustion engine and its impact on the melting of the ice cap. Thus our thoughts can become generative mechanisms (they are "causally efficacious"). They may affect our world, when and if our motives and intentions are enacted. When this happens then it could alter the *status quo* or help to maintain it. The transitive aspect of reality may well disappear subsequent to "the Anthropocene": the period of geological time when the world was altered by human action and in turn this threatened the existence of the species (and many others), via the risks of climate change and nuclear annihilation. (See intransitive aspect of reality; and generative mechanisms.)

Woke refers to being aware of, or awake to, social injustice, especially racism. The term began in American black culture in the 1930s and has now generalised beyond the matter of race to any allusion to oppressed social groups or the legacy of their history. Whether it is a badge of pride, a slur, or a neutral description of personal sensitivity to injustice for now is ambiguous. It may or may not imply that those who are not woke are in some sense ethically or politically deficient. That ethical ambiguity also applies to the notion of critical social justice and those advocating it ("warriors").

References

Adame, A.L., & Knudson, R.M. (2008). Recovery and the good life: How psychiatric survivors are revisioning the healing process. *Journal of Humanistic Psychology*, 48, 2: 142–164.
Adams, A. (2020). *Iconoclasm, Identity Politics and the Erasure of History*. Exeter: Imprint Academic Ltd.
Ainsworth, M.D., & Bowlby, J. (1991). An ethological approach to personality development. *American Psychologist*, 46, 4: 333–341.
Alcoff, L.M. (2005). *Visible Identities: Race, Gender, and the Self*. Oxford: Oxford University Press.
Aldridge, D. (2014). *The Very Best of Noam Chomsky*. New York: Createspace.
Anderson, B. (1983). *Imagined Communities: Reflections on the Origin and Spread of Nationalism*. London: Version.
Anderson P. (2002). Land without prejudice. *London Review of Books*, 24, 6.
Andrews, P. (2021). This is hate, not debate. *Index on Censorship*, 50, 2: 73–75.
Anthony, W. (1993). Recovery from mental illness: The guiding vision of the mental health system in the 1990s. *Psychosocial Rehabilitation Journal*, 16, 4: 11–23.

Appelbaum, P.S., Robbins, P.C., & Monahan, J. (2000). Violence and delusions: data from the MacArthur Violence Risk Assessment Study. *American Journal of Psychiatry*, 157, 4: 566–572.

Arendt, H. (2005). *The Promise of Politics*. New York: Schocken.

Babiak, P., & Hare, R.D. (2007). *Snakes in Suits: When Psychopaths go to Work*. New York: HarperCollins.

Barton, W.R. (1959). *Institutional Neurosis*. Bristol: Wright and Sons.

Barber, B. (2007). *Consumed: How Markets Corrupt Children, Infantilize Adults and Swallow Citizens Whole*. New York: Norton.

Basaglia, F. (1964). The destruction of the mental hospital as a place of institutionalisation: Thoughts caused by personal experience with the open door system and part time service. London: First International Congress of Social Psychiatry.

Bean, P. (1980). *Compulsory Admissions to Mental Hospital*. Chichester: Wiley.

Belew, S. (2020). *Bringing the War Home: The White Power Movement and Paramilitary America*. Harvard: Harvard University Press.

Bell, D. (1973). *Race, Racism, and American Law*. New York: Little Brown.

Bentall, R.P. (2003). *Madness Explained: Psychosis and Human Nature*. London: Penguin.

Bentall, R.P. (2018). Delusions and other beliefs. In: L. Bortolotti (ed), *Delusions in Context*. Cham, Switzerland: Palgrave Macmillan.

Berger, P., & Luckmann, T. (1967). *The Social Construction of Reality: A Treatise in the Sociology of Knowledge*. New York: Random House.

Bermann, S. (2021). *Goodbye Britannia: Le Royaume-Uni au défi du Brexit*. Paris: Stock.

Bhaskar, R. (2016). *Enlightened Common Sense: The Philosophy of Critical Realism*. London: Routledge.

Bhaskar, R. (2008). *A Realist Theory of Science*. London: Verso.

Bhaskar, R. (1997). On the ontological status of ideas. *Journal for the Theory of Social Behaviour*, 27, 2/3: 135–137.

Bhaskar, R., Danermark, B., & Price, L. (2018). *Interdisciplinarity and Wellbeing: A Critical Realist General Theory of Interdisciplinarity*. London: Routledge.

Biggs, M. (2019). Tavistock's experiment with puberty blockers: an update. *Transgendertrend*. Retrieved on 5 August 2021 from https://www.transgendertrend.com/tavistock-experiment-puberty-blockers-update.

Bhopal, K. (2018). *White Privilege: The Myth of a Post-Racial Society*. Bristol: Policy Press.

Bloch, S., & Reddaway, P. (1977). *Russia's Political Hospitals: The Abuse of Psychiatry in the Soviet Union*. London: Victor Gollancz.

Bourdieu, P. (1984). *Distinction*. London: Routledge.

Brown, P., & Funk, S.C. (1986). Tardive dyskinesia: barriers to the professional recognition of iatrogenic disease. *Journal of Health and Social Behaviour, 27*: 116–132.

Brunskell-Evans, H. (2020). *Transgender Body Politics*. North Geelong, Australia: Spinifex.

Bury, M., & Gabe, J. (1990). Hooked? Media responses to tranquillizer dependence. In: P. Abbott & G. Payne (eds), *New Directions in the Sociology of Health*. London: Falmer Press.

Campbell, P. (1996). The history of the User Movement in the United Kingdom. In: T. Heller, J. Reynolds, R. Gomm, R. Muston, & S. Pattison (eds), *Mental Health Matters: A Reader*. Buckingham: Open University Press.

Carchedi, G. (1975). On the economic identification of the new middle class. *Economy and Society, 4*, 1: 1–85.

Carter, B. (2000). *Racism and Realism: Concepts of Race in Sociological Research*. London: Routledge.

Carpenter, M. (1980). Asylum nursing before 1914: A chapter in the history of nursing. In: C. Davies (Ed.), *Rewriting Nursing History*. London: Croom Helm.

Castrodale, M.A., (2015). Mad matters: A critical reader in Canadian mad studies. *Scandinavian Journal of Disability Research, 17*, 3: 284–246.

Castel, R. (1983). Moral treatment: Mental therapy and social control in the nineteenth century. In: S. Cohen & A. Scull (eds), *Social Control and the State*. Oxford: Basil Blackwell.

Catanzano, M., & Butler, G. (2018). Effect of pubertal blockade and cross-sex hormone treatment on the growth spurt in young transgender adolescents: A first report. *ESPE Abstracts, 89*: 1–11.

Charles, A."D". (2020). *Outraged: Why Everyone is Shouting and No One Is Talking*. London: Bloomsbury.

Children's Commissioner's Report (2016). Barnahus: Improving the response to child sex abuse in England. London: UK Children's Commissioner's Office.

Clapton, G., Cree, V.E., & Smith, M. (2012). Moral panics and social work: Towards a sceptical view of UK child protection. *Critical Social Policy, 33*, 2: 197–217.

Cleckley, H.M. (1941). *The Mask of Sanity*. St Louis, MS: C.V. Mosby.

Coffey, M., Hannigan, B., Barlow, S., Cartwright, M., Cohen, R., Faulkner, A., Jones, A., & Simpson, A. (2019). Recovery-focused mental health care planning and co-ordination in acute inpatient mental health settings: A cross national comparative mixed methods study. *BMC Psychiatry, 19*: 115.

Cohen, D. (1989). *Soviet Psychiatry*. London: Paladin.

Cohen, S. (2002). *Folk Devils and Moral Panics* (Third Edition). London: Routledge.

Cohen, S. (2001). *States of Denial: Knowing About Atrocities and Suffering*. Cambridge: Polity.

Cohen, S. (1972). *Folk Devils and Moral Panics* (First Edition). London: MacGibbon and Kee Ltd.

Cohen, S., & Taylor, L. (1992). *Escape Attempts: The Theory and Practice of Resistance in Everyday Life*. London: Routledge.

Collins, M. (2014). *People Like Us: A Biography of the White Working Class*. London: Granta.

Coogan, T.P. (2012). *The Famine Plot: England's Role in Ireland's Greatest Tragedy*. London: Palgrave.

Cooper, M., & Breunig, R. (2017). How Obama destroyed black wealth https://jacobinmag.com/2017/12/obama-foreclosure-crisis-wealth-inequality.

Coulter, J. (1973). *Approaches to Insanity*. New York: Wiley.

Council of Europe (2007). *Council of Europe Convention on the Protection of Children against Sexual Exploitation and Sexual Abuse* https://www.coe.int/en/web/conventions/-/council-of-europe-council-of-europe-convention-on-the-protection-of-children.

Crenshaw, K. (1989). Demarginalizing the intersection of race and sex: A Black feminist critique of antidiscrimination doctrine, feminist theory, and antiracist politics. *The University of Chicago Legal Forum, 140*: 139–167.

Crenshaw, K., Gotanda, N., Peller, G., & Thomas, K. (1995). *Critical Race Theory: The Key Writings that Formed the Movement*. New York: The New Press.

Cutajar, M.C, Mullen, P.E. Ogloff, J.R.P., Thomas, S.D., Wells, D.L., & Spartaro, J. (2010). Psychopathology in a large cohort of sexually abused children followed up to 43 years. *Child Abuse & Neglect, 34*, 11: 813–822.

Crossley, N. (2006). *Contesting Psychiatry: Social Movements in Mental Health*. London: Routledge.

Dalrymple, W. (2019). *The Anarchy: The East India Company, Corporate Violence and the Pillage of an Empire*. London: Bloomsbury.

Davidson, N. (1999). In perspective: Tom Nairn. *International Socialism*, 2: 82 (Spring).

de Vries, A., & Cohen-Kettenis, P. (2012). Clinical management of gender dysphoria in children and adolescents: The Dutch approach. *Journal of Homosexuality, 59,* 3: 301–320.

de Vries, A., Steensma, T.D., Doreleijers, T.A.H., & Cohen-Kettenis, P.T. (2011). Puberty suppression in adolescents with gender identity disorder: A prospective follow-up study. *Journal of Sexual Medicine, 8,* 8: 2276–2283.

Diamond, S. (1989). *Spiritual Warfare: The Politics of the Christian Right*. Brooklyn: South End Press.

DiAngelo, R. (2018). *White Fragility: Why It's So Hard for White People to Talk about Racism*. Boston, MA: Beacon Press.

Di Ceglie, D. (2018). The use of metaphors in understanding atypical gender identity development and its psychosocial impact. *Journal of Child Psychotherapy, 44,* 1: 5–28.

Discrimination in the European Union (2019). Perceptions of discrimination in the EU https://sokszinusegikarta.hu/wp-content/uploads/2019/11/ebs_493_ig_en.pdf.

Deegan, P. (1996). Recovery as a journey of the heart. *Psychiatric Rehabilitation Journal, 19,* 3: 91–97.

Dotson, K. (2011). Tracking epistemic violence, tracking practices of silencing. *Hypatia, 26,* 2: 236–257.

Dutton, K. (2020). *Black and White Thinking: The Burden of a Binary Brain in a Complex World*. London: Bantam.

Dyson, S.M., Atkin, K., Culley, L., & Dyson, S.E. (2014). Critical realism, agency and sickle cell: Case studies of young people with sickle cell disorder at school. *Ethnic and Racial Studies, 37,* 13: 2379–2398.

Eastman, N. (1994). Mental health law: Civil liberties and the principle of reciprocity. *British Medical Journal,* 308: 43.

Elder-Vass, D. (2012). *The Reality of Social Construction*. Cambridge: Cambridge University Press.

Everett, R. (2016). https://www.theguardian.com/film/2016/jun/19/rupert-everett-dangers-of-child-sex-change-operations-gender.

Fabris, E. (2011). *Tranquil Prisons: Chemical Incarceration Under Community Treatment Orders*. Toronto: University of Toronto Press.

Faulkner, A., & Layzell, S. (2000). *Strategies for Living*. London: Mental Health Foundation.

Fekete, L. (2016). Hungary: Power, punishment and the "Christian-national ideal". *Race and Class*, 57, 4: 39–53.
Finkelhor, D., Hammer, H., & Sedlak, A.J. (2008). *Sexually Assaulted Children: National Estimates and Characteristics*. Washington: US Department of Justice.
Fish, F. (1968). *Clinical Psychopathology*. Bristol: John Wright.
Fisher, M. (2013). Exiting the Vampires' Castle. https://web.archive.org/web/20180204081250/https://thenorthstar.info/2013/11/22/exiting-the-vampire-castle.
François, S., & Godwin, A. (2008). The Euro-Pagan scene: Between paganism and radical right. *Journal for the Study of Radicalism*, 1, 2: 35–54.
Freud, S. (1935). *The Ego and the Mechanisms of Defence*. London: Karnac.
Fromm, E. (1973). *The Anatomy of Human Destructiveness*. New York: Holt Rinehart.
Fromm, E. (1941). *Escape from Freedom* (in the UK published as *The Fear of Freedom*, 1973). New York: Farrar and Rhinehart.
Furedi, F. (2015). The moral crusade against paedophilia. In: V.E. Cree, G. Clapton & M. Smith (eds), *Moral Panics in Theory and Practice*. Bristol: Policy Press.
Fuller, S. (2018). *Post-Truth: Knowledge as a Power Game*. London: Anthem.
Gabe, J., & Lipshitsz-Phillips, S. (1982). Evil necessity? The meaning of benzodiazepine use for women patients from one general practice. *Sociology of Health & Illness*, 4, 2: 201–211.
Galtung, J. (1969). Violence, peace, and peace research. *Journal of Peace Research*, 6, 3: 67–91.
Gardner, L., & Tirthankar, R. (2021). *The Economic History of Colonialism*. Bristol: Policy Press.
Gay, R. (2020). Reach. In: R.O. Kwon & G. Greenwell (eds), *Kink*. New York: Simon & Schuster.
Gelder, M., Mayou, R., & Cowen, P. (2001). *Shorter Oxford Textbook of Psychiatry*. Oxford: Oxford University Press.
Gerbner, K. (2018). *Christian Slavery: Conversion and Race in the Protestant Atlantic World*. Philadelphia: University of Pennsylvania Press.
Geronimus, A.T. (1992). The weathering hypothesis and the health of African-American women and infants: Evidence and speculations. *Ethnic Disadvantage*, 2, 3: 207–221.
Gibbons, A. (2014). Shedding light on skin color. *Science*, 346, 6212: 934–946.

REFERENCES

Gibbons, A. (2015). https://www.sciencemag.org/news/2015/04/how-europeans-evolved-white-skin.

Gingrich, A., & M. Banks (eds) (2006). *Neo-Nationalism in Western Europe and Beyond: Perspectives from Social Anthropology.* London: Berghahn.

Gimson, S. (2021). The right to hold views not akin to Nazism or totalitarianism. *Index on Censorship,* 50, 2: 72.

Girard, R. (1972). *La Violence et le Sacré.* Paris: Grasset.

Goertzel, B. (2013). Artificial intelligence and the future of humanity. In: M. More & N. Vita-More (eds), *The Transhumanist Reader.* New York: Wiley-Blackwell, pp. 128–137.

Goffman, E. (1961). *Asylums.* New York: Anchor.

Goode, E., & Ben-Yehuda, N. (1994). *Moral Panics: The Social Construction of Deviance.* Oxford: Blackwell.

Gottlieb, J.V., & Linehan, T.P. (eds). (2003). *Culture of Fascism: Visions of the Far Right in Britain.* London: IB Tauris.

Goulding, C. (1999). Heritage, nostalgia, and the "grey" consumer. *Journal of Marketing Practice: Applied Marketing Science,* 5, 6: 177–199.

Griffin, R. (1991). *The Nature of Fascism.* London: St Martin's Press.

Guinan, J., & Thomas, H.M. (2017). Forbidden fruit: The neglected political economy of Lexit. *IPPR Review,* 24: 1.

Habermas, J. (1984). *Theory of Communicative Action* (trans. T.A. McCarthy). Boston, MA: Beacon Press.

Hansen, T.B. (2021). *The Law of Force: The Violent Heart of Indian Politics.* New Delhi: Aleph Books.

Healy, D. (1997). *The Anti-Depressant Era.* London: Harvard University Press.

Herzberg, D. (2009). *Happy Pills in America: From Miltown to Prozac.* Baltimore: Johns Hopkins University Press.

Hobsbawm, E. (1996). The Barry Amiel and Norman Melburn Trust Lecture. Institute of Education, London, 2 May.

Hobsbawm, E. (1991). *Nations and Nationalism Since 1780: Programme, Myth, Reality.* Cambridge: Cambridge University Press.

Hobsbawm, E. (1994). *The Age of Extremes: The Short Twentieth Century, 1914–1991.* London: Michael Joseph.

Hochschild, A.R. (2016). *Strangers in their Own Land: Anger and Mourning on the American Right.* New York: New Press.

Hoggart, R. (1957). *The Uses of Literacy.* London: Routledge.

Hunter, J.D. (1991). *Culture Wars: The Struggle to Define America.* New York: Basic Books.
Inge, W.R. (1948). *The End of an Age and Other Essays.* London: Religious Book Club.
Jay, A. (2014). *Independent Inquiry into Child Sexual Exploitation in Rotherham (1997–2013).* Rotherham: Rotherham Metropolitan Borough Council.
Jenkins, P. (2004). *Beyond Tolerance: Child Pornography on the Internet.* New York: New York University Press.
Johnson, M.P. (2011). Gender and types of intimate partner violence: A response to an anti-feminist literature review. *Aggression and Violent Behavior,* 16, 4: 289–296.
Johnstone, L., & Boyle, M. (2018). *The Power Threat Meaning Framework: Towards the Identification of Patterns in Emotional Distress, Unusual Experiences and Troubled or Troubling Behaviour.* Leicester: British Psychological Society.
Joyce, H. (2021). *Trans: When Ideology Meets Reality.* London: OneWorld.
Junginger, J. (1995). Command hallucinations and the predictions of dangerousness. *Psychiatric Services,* 46: 911–914.
Kahneman, D. (2011). *Thinking Fast and Slow.* New York: Macmillan.
Keith, L. (2016). The girls and the grasses. In: R. Barrett (ed), *Female Erasure: What You Need to Know About Gender Politics' War on Women, the Female Sex and Human Rights.* New York: Tidal Time Publishing, pp. 288–299.
Kellam, A.M.P. (1987). The neuroleptic syndrome, so called: A survey of the world literature. *British Journal of Psychiatry,* 150: 752–759.
Kelly, G. (1955). *The Psychology of Personal Constructs.* New York: Norton.
Kendi, I.X. (2019). *How To Be an Anti-Racist.* New York: Bodley Head.
Kendzior, S. (2020). *Hiding in Plain Sight.* New York: Flatiron/MacMillan.
Kraepelin, E. (1883). *Compendium der Psychiatrie.* Leipzig: Abel.
Laing, R.D. (1967). *The Politics of Experience and the Bird of Paradise.* Harmondsworth: Penguin.
Lane, C. (2008). *Shyness: How Normal Behavior Became a Sickness.* New Haven, CT: Yale University Press.
Lebow, R.N. (2012). *The Politics and Ethics of Identity: In Search of Ourselves.* Cambridge: Cambridge University Press.
Lemert, C.C. (1980). *Sociology and The Twilight of Man.* Carbondale: Southern Illinois University Press.

Levine, S.B. (2018). Informed consent for transgendered patients. *Journal of Sex & Marital Therapy, 45*, 3: 1–12.
Lindow, V. (1994). *Self-help Alternatives to Mental Health Services*. London: MIND Publications.
Lorde, A. (1988). *A Burst of Light*. New York: Firebrand Books.
Main, T. (1946). The hospital as a therapeutic institution. *Bulletin of the Menninger Clinic, 10*: 64–71.
Mair, P. (2013). *Ruling the Void: The Hollowing of Western Democracy*. London: Verso.
Malik, K. (2018). "White privilege" is a distraction, leaving racism and power untouched. *The Guardian*. https://www.theguardian.com/commentisfree/2020/jun/14/white-privilege-is-a-lazy-distraction-leaving-racism-and-power-un.
Manning, N. (1989). *The Therapeutic Community Movement: Charisma and Routinization*. London: Routledge.
Martin, J.P. (1985). *Hospitals in Trouble*. Oxford: Blackwell.
Martinerie L. et al. (2018). Impaired puberty, fertility, and final stature in 45,X/46,XY mixed gonadal dysgenetic patients raised as boys. *European Journal of Endocrinology, 166*, 4: 687–694.
McGrath, T. (2021). A Bonfire for Dr Seuss. *The Critic March, 45*: 694.
Mercier, H., & Sperber, D. (2011). Why do humans reason? Arguments for an argumentative theory. *Behavioral and Brain Sciences, 34*, 2: 57–74.
Meyer, J.E. (1988). The fate of the mentally ill in Germany during the Third Reich. *Psychological Medicine, 18*: 575–581.
Moalem, S. (2020). *The Better Half: On the Genetic Superiority of Women*. London: Allen Lane.
Mulvany, J. (2000). Disability, impairment or illness? The relevance of the social model of disability to the study of mental disorder. *Sociology of Health & Illness, 22*, 5: 582–601.
Myers, D.G. (2000). The funds, friends, and faith of happy people. *American Psychologist, 55*, 1: 56–67.
Nairn, T. (1973). *The Left against Europe*. Harmondsworth, UK: Penguin.
Neiman, S. (2011). *Moral Clarity: A Guide for Grown-Up Idealists*. London: Vintage.
Nelson, A. (2019). *Shadow Network: Media Money and the Secret Hub of the American Right*. New York: Bloomsbury.

Norton, H.L., Quillen, E.E., Bigham, A.W., Pearson, N.L., & Dunsworth. H. (2019). Human races are not like dog breeds: refuting a racist analogy. *Evolution Education Outreach*, *12*: 17.

Nossel, S. (2020). *Dare To Speak: Defending Free Speech for All*. New York: HarperCollins.

O'Carroll, T. (1980). *Paedophilia: The Radical Case*. London: Owen.

O'Neill, B. (2018). Consistency is key to freedom of speech. *Spiked* (spiked-online.com).

Offe, C. (1984). *Contradictions of the Welfare State*. London: Hutchinson.

Ogata, S.N., Silk, K.R., Goodrich S, Lohr, N.E., Westen, D., & Hill, E.M. (1990). Childhood sexual and physical abuse in adult patients with borderline personality disorder. *American Journal of Psychiatry*, *147*, 8:1008–1013.

Patel, N. (2021). Dismantling the scaffolding of institutional racism and institutionalising anti-racism. *Journal of Family Therapy*, first published online: 12 October 2021.

Pescosolido, B.A., Medina, T.R., Martin, J.K., & Long, J.S. (2013). The "backbone" of stigma: Identifying the global core of public prejudice associated with mental illness. *American Journal of Public Health*, *103*, 5: 853–860.

Philo, G., Secker, J., Platt, S. et al. (1996). Media images of mental distress. In: T. Heller et al. (eds), *Mental Health Matters: A Reader*. Basingstoke: Macmillan.

Pilgrim, D. (2008). The eugenic legacy in psychology and psychiatry. *International Journal of Social Psychiatry*, *54*, 3: 272–284.

Pilgrim, D. (2018a). *Child Sexual Abuse: Moral Panic or State of Denial?* London: Routledge.

Pilgrim, D. (2018b). Are kindly and efficacious mental health services possible? *Journal of Mental Health*, *27*, 4: 295–297.

Pilgrim, D. (2020). *Critical Realism for Psychologists*. London: Routledge.

Pilgrim, D., & Entwistle, K. (2020). GnRHa ("puberty blockers") and cross sex hormones for children and adolescents: Informed consent, personhood and freedom of expression. *The New Bioethics*, *26*, 3: 224–237.

Pilgrim, D., & McCranie, A. (2013). *Recovery and Mental Health: A Critical Sociological Account*. Basingstoke: Palgrave Macmillan.

Pilgrim, D., & Ormrod, R. (2012). *Elvis Costello and Thatcherism*. London: Ashgate.

Pilgrim, D., & Tomasini, F. (2012). On being unreasonable in modern society: Are mental health problems special? *Disability and Society*, *27*, 5: 631–646.

Pluckrose, H., & Lindsay, J. (2020). *Cynical Theories: How Activist Scholarship Made Everything About Race, Gender and Identity—and Why This Harms Everybody*. London: Swift Press.

Plummer, K. (1981). The paedophile's progress: A view from below. In: B. Taylor (ed), *Perspectives on Paedophilia*. London: Batsford, pp. 12–26.

Pols, J. (2001). Enforcing patients' rights or improving care: The interference of two modes of doing good in mental health care. *Sociology of Health & Illness*, 25, 4: 325–347.

Porpora, D. (2017). Dehumanization in theory: Anti-humanism, non-humanism, post-humanism, and trans-humanism. *Journal of Critical Realism*, 16, 4: 353–367.

Porter, R. (1987). *A Social History of Madness: Stories of the Insane*. London: Weidenfeld & Nicolson.

Priestley, J.B. (1934). *English Journey*. London: Victor Gollancz.

Pūrasis, D. (2017). *Report of the Special Rapporteur on the right of everyone to the enjoyment of the highest attainable standard of physical and mental health*. Geneva: UN Human Rights Council.

Quayle, E. (2016). Internet risk research and child sexual abuse: A misdirected moral panic? In: V.E. Cree, G. Clapton & M. Smith (eds), *Moral Panics in Theory and Practice*. Bristol: Policy Press.

Quirk, A., Chaplin, P., Lelliott, P., & Seale, C. (2011). How pressure is applied in shared decisions about antipsychotic medication: A conversation analytic study of psychiatric outpatient consultations. *Sociology of Health & Illness*, 34, 1: 95–113.

Radford, L., Corral, S., Bradley, C., Fisher, H., Collishaw, S., Bassett, C., & Howat, N. (2011). *Child abuse and neglect in the UK today*. London: NSPCC.

Read, J., Agar, K., Argyle, N., & Aderhold, V. (2003). Sexual and physical abuse during childhood and adulthood as predictors of hallucinations, delusions and thought disorder. *Psychology and Psychotherapy: Theory, Research and Practice*, 76: 1–22.

Reed, A. (2018). Antiracism: A neoliberal alternative to a left. *Dialectical Anthropology*, 42: 105–115.

Reed, A. (2020). Socialism and the argument against race reductionism. *New Labor Forum*, 29, 2: 36–43.

Renan, E. (1992). "Qu'est-ce qu'une nation?", conference faite en Sorbonne, le 11 Mars 1882.

Rogers, A., & Pilgrim, D. (1989). Citizenship and mental health. *Critical Social Policy, 26*: 25–32.

Rogers, A., & Pilgrim, D. (2003). *Mental Health and Inequality*. Basingstoke: Palgrave Macmillan.

Rogers, A., & Pilgrim, D. (2021). *A Sociology of Mental Health and Illness* (Sixth Edition). London: McGraw-Hill.

Romme, M.A., Honig, A., Noorthoorn, E.O., & Escher, S. (1992). Coping with hearing voices: An emancipatory approach. *British Journal of Psychiatry, 162*: 99–103.

Rose, D. (2009). Survivor produced knowledge. In: A. Sweeney, P. Beresford, A. Faulkner, M. Nettle & D. Rose (eds), *This is Survivor Research*. Ross-on-Wye: PPCS Books.

Rose, D. (1998). Television madness and community care. *Journal of Applied Community Social Psychology, 8*: 213–228.

Rosen, G. (1979). The evolution of scientific medicine. In: H. Freeman, S. Levine & L. Reeder (eds), *Handbook of Medical Sociology*. Englewood Cliffs, NJ: Prentice-Hall.

Rothman, D. (1971). *The Discovery of the Asylum: Social Order and Disorder in the New Republic*. Boston, MA: Little Brown.

Rubin, G. (1992). Thinking sex: Notes for a radical theory of the politics of sexuality. In: C.S. Vance (ed.), *Pleasure and Danger: Exploring Female Sexuality*. London: Pandora.

Russo, J., & Sweeney A. (eds) (2016). *Searching for a Rose Garden: Challenging Psychiatry, Fostering Mad Studies*. Monmouth: PCCS Books.

Rutherford, A. (2020). *How to Argue with a Racist: History, Science, Race and Reality*. London: Weidenfeld & Nicolson.

Saad, T.C., Blackshaw, B.P., & Rodger. D.J. (2019). Hormone replacement therapy: Informed consent without assessment. *Journal of Medical Ethics, 105*: 611.

Saied-Tessier, A. (2014). *Estimating the costs of child sexual abuse in the UK*. London: NSPCC.

Sanghera, S. (2021). *Empireland: How Imperialism Has Shaped Modern Britain*. London: Viking.

Saxena, S. (2018). Excess mortality among people with mental disorders: A public health priority. *The Lancet Public Health, 3*, 6: e264–e265.

Sayer, A. (2000). *Realism and Social Science*. London: Sage.

Sayer, A. (2011). *Why Things Matter to People: Social Science, Values and Ethical Life*. Cambridge: Cambridge University Press.

Schiffauer, W., Baumann, G., Kastoryano, R., & Vertovec, S. (eds) (2004). *Civil Enculturation: Nation-State, School and Ethnic Difference in Four European Countries*, Oxford: Berghahn.

Schlesinger, P. (1991). *Media, State and Nation: Political Violence and Collective Identities*. London: Sage.

Scull, A. (1979). *Museums of Madness*. Harmondsworth: Penguin.

Scull, A. (1977). *Decarceration*. Englewood Cliffs, NY: Prentice Hall.

Sen, A. (2006). *Identity and Violence: The Illusion of Destiny*. New York: Norton.

Sedgwick, P. (1982). *PsychoPolitics*. London: Pluto Press.

Shackel, N. (2005). The vacuity of postmodernist methodology. *Metaphilosophy*, 36, 3: 295–320.

Silver, E., Mulvey, E., & Monahan, J. (1999). Assessing violence risk among discharged psychiatric patients: An ecological approach. *Law and Human Behavior*, 23, 2: 23.

Sivanandan, A. (1990). All that melts into air is solid. https://libcom.org/library/all-melts-air-solid-sivanandan.

Smeeth, R. (2021). When the boot is on the other foot. *Index on Censorship*, 50, 2: 76–77.

Sohn, A. (2019). Chest binding helps smooth the way for transgender teens, but there may be risks https://www.nytimes.com/2019/05/31/well/transgender-teens-binders.html.

Sobolewska, M., & Ford, R. (2020). *Brexitland*. Cambridge: Cambridge University Press.

Soyka, M. (2000). Substance misuse, psychiatric disorder and violent and disturbed behaviour. *British Journal of Psychiatry*, 176: 345–350.

Spandler, H., & Calton, T. (2009). Psychosis and human rights: Conflicts in mental health policy and practice. *Social Policy and Society*, 8, 2: 245–256.

Spivak, G.C. (1988). *Can the Subaltern Speak?* London: Macmillan.

Stock, K. (2021). What is a woman? *Index on Censorship*, 50, 2: 70–72.

Straus, M.A. (2011). Gender symmetry and mutuality in perpetration of clinical-level partner violence: Empirical evidence and implications for prevention and treatment. *Aggression and Violent Behavior*, 16, 4: 279–288. 7–247.

Steadman, H.J., Mulvey, E.P., Monahan, J., Robbins, P.C., Appelbaum, P.S., Grisso, T., Roth, L.H., & Silver, E. (1998). Violence by people discharged from acute psychiatric inpatient facilities and by others in the same neighbourhoods. *Archives of General Psychiatry, 55*: 393–401.

Sunstein, C. (2016). *The Ethics of Influence: Government in the Age of Behavioral Science*. Cambridge: Cambridge University Press.

Sunstein, C. (2002). The law of group polarization. *Journal of Political Philosophy, 10*, 2: 175–195.

Sussman, R.W. (2019). *The Myth of Race: The Troubling Persistence of an Unscientific Idea*. Cambridge, MA: Harvard University Press.

Swartz, M.S., Swanson, J.W., Hiday, V.A., & Borum, R. (1998). Taking the wrong drugs: The role of substance use and medication non-compliance in violence among severely mentally ill individuals. *Social Psychiatry & Psychiatric Epidemiology, 33*: 75–80.

Szasz, T.S. (1963). *Law, Liberty, and Psychiatry*. New York: Macmillan.

Taylor, B. (Ed.) (1981). *Perspectives on Paedophilia* London: Batsford.

Taylor, B. (1976). Motives for guilt-free pederasty: Some literary considerations. *Sociological Review, 24*: 97–114.

Taylor, C. (2007). *A Secular Age*. New York: Harvard University Press.

Taylor, L. (2007). The other side of the street: An interview with Stan Cohen. In: D. Downe, P. Rock, Chinkin, C. & Gearty, C. (eds), *Crime, Social Control and Human Rights: From Moral Panics to States of Denial: Essays in Honour of Stanley Cohen* London: Willan.

Taylor, P.J. (1985). Motives for offending among violent psychotic men. *British Journal of Psychiatry, 147*: 491–498.

Thalheimer, A. (1928/1979). On fascism. *Telos 40* (Summer 1979). New York: Telos Press.

Therborn, G. (2021). Inequality and world political landscapes. *New Left Review, 129*: 6–26.

Tosi, J., & Warmke, B. (2020). *Grandstanding: The Use of Moral Talk*. Oxford: Oxford University Press.

Thoits, P.A. (1985). Self-labeling processes in mental illness: The role of emotional deviance. *American Journal of Sociology, 91*: 221–249.

Uwagba, O. (2020). *Whites on Race and Other Falsehoods*. London: HarperCollins.

Vajda, M. (1976). *Fascism as A Mass Movement*. London: Allison & Busby.

van Zomeren, M. (2014). Synthesizing individualistic and collectivistic perspectives on environmental and collective action through a relational perspective. *Theory & Psychology* 24, 6: 775–794.

von Heiseler, T.N. (2020). The social origin of the concept of truth: How statements are built on disagreements. *Frontiers in Psychology, 28*, 11: 733.
Wahl, O.F. (1995). *Media Madness: Public Images of Mental Illness*. New Brunswick, NJ: Rutgers University Press.
Walker, B. (2021). Exclusive polling: the Labour Party's base isn't as "woke" as you think. *New Statesman*, 1 July.
Wallcraft, J. with Read, J., & Sweeney, A. (2003). *On Our Own Terms*. London: Sainsbury Centre for Mental Health.
Waller, W.W. (1936). Social problems and the mores. *Sociological Review, 1,* 6: 922–933.
Watkins, S. (2018). Which feminisms? *New Left Review, 109*: 5–76.
Weber, E. (1976). *Peasants into Frenchmen: The Modernization of Rural France, 1870-1914*. Stanford: Stanford University Press.
Weeks, J. (1985). *Sexuality and its Discontents: Meanings, Myths and Modern Sexualities*. London: Routledge and Kegan Paul.
Weller, P. (2013). The social model of disability in the CRPD: From theory to practice. Presentation given at the 2013 International Conference on Mental Health Law: The United Nations Convention on the Rights of Persons with Disabilities (CRPD): What does it mean for mental health law and practice?
Westermeyer, J., & Kroll, J. (1978). Violence and mental illness in a peasant society: Characteristics of violent behaviours and "folk" use of restraints. *British Journal of Psychiatry, 133*: 529–541.
Williams, B. (2002). *Truth and Truthfulness*. Princeton, NJ: Princeton University Press.
Williams, J. (2021). *Rethinking Race: A Critique of Contemporary Anti-Racism Programmes*. London: Civitas.
Williams, R. (1980). *Culture and Materialism*. London: Verso.
Wing, J.K. (1962). Institutionalism in mental hospitals. *British Journal of Social and Clinical Psychology, 1*: 38–51.
Wolfensberger, W. (2002). *The New Genocide of Handicapped and Afflicted People*. Syracuse, NY: Syracuse University Training Institute for Human Service Planning, Leadership & Change Agentry.
Wykes, T., & Callard, F. (2010). Diagnosis, diagnosis, diagnosis: Towards DSM-5. *Journal of Mental Health, 19*, 4: 301–304.
Yuill, R.A. (2004). Male age-discrepant sexualities and relationships. Unpublished PhD thesis available online at http//theses.glas.ac.uk/theses@glasgow.ac.uk.

Index

Note: **Bold** indicates glossary references

actual, the, 2, 119, 145, 175, **220**
Adame, A. L., 145
Adams, A., 100
Ainsworth, M. D., 200
Alcoff, L. M., 91
Aldridge, D., 21
Anderson, B., 166
Anderson P., 180
Andrews, P., 27
Animal Farm, 19
Anthony, W., 141
anti-racism, 7, 111, 176, 193, 194
    and neoliberalism, 101–120
    vagaries of, 97–101
Arendt, H., xxv, 211
Article 10 of the European Convention
    on Human Rights, xviii
asylum system, 136, 138–139
attachment tendency, 39
authoritarianism, 19, 24, 25–26
autogynephilia, 49, 50
axiology, 45, **213**

Babiak, P., 133
Baldwin, J., 93
BAME *see* black and ethnic minorities
Banks, M., 175
Barton, W. R., 134
Basaglia, F., 134
Baston, L., 159
BDSM, 71–78, 81, 88–89, 193, 194
    Elaine O'Hara murder, 74–75
Bean, P., 124, 137
Belew, S., 184
Bell, D., 106
belonging, 185
Bentall, R. P., 126, 198–200
Ben-Yehuda, N., 83
Berger, P., 4, 44
Bermann, S., 42
Bhaskar, R., 2, 5, 53
Bhopal, K., 116
bias, 59, 88, 113, 117, 196
Biden, J., xii, 159, 189
Biggs, M., 55, 57
Bilek, J., 61
Biraderi, 159

239

INDEX

black and ethnic minorities, 7–8, 9–10, 92, 94–95, 96, 98, 99, 104–113, 116–119, 132, 159, 181, 183, 184
    Emmett Till murder, 99
    Rosa Parks, 99
Black Lives Matter, 25, 92–93, 102–103, 104, 187, 205
Bloch, S., 124
Bourdieu, P., 167
Bowlby, J., 39, 200
Boyle, M., 142
Breunig, R., 117
Brexit, 168–170, 172–173, 175–177, 185–187
British identity, 168–179, 180–189
    see also Brexit; class politics
    end of empire, 172–175
    England and, 182–183
    England and Celtic colonies, 175–177
    English fascism vs ethnocentrism, 170–171
    Ireland and, 177–179
    Scotland and, 169, 176, 178, 180
    UK, 175
    Wales and, 169, 176, 179, 186
British politics, 166–167 see also class politics
Brown, P., 128
Brunskell-Evans, H., 60, 61, 63
Bury, M., 127
Butler, G., 57

Callard, F., 126
Calton, T., 142
Cameron, D., 167, 173
Campbell, B., 61
Campbell, P., 143, 145
cancel culture, xvii–xx, 11 see also freedom of expression
capitalism, xii–xiii, 37, 47, 102, 108, 167, 188–189, 199, 205, 208–209, 212
Carchedi, G., 166
Carpenter, M., 139

Carter, B., 91
Castel, R., 134
Castrodale, M. A., 145
Catanzano, M., 57
Charles, A. D., 9, 12, 20
child sexual abuse (CSA), 79–85 see also moral panic theory
Chomsky, N., 21
Church of England, 152
Clapton, G., 86
class politics, 165, 166–168, 189–190, 201
Cleckley, H. M., 133
clictivism, 12, 15, 17, 37, 202
CNP see Council for National Policy
Coffey, M., 142
Cohen, D., 124
Cohen, S., 82, 85, 87, 206 see also moral panic theory
Collins, M., 182
concrete singularity, 16, 25, 73, 110, 113, 184, 203, **213**, 217
constructivism, 4
    social, 4–6, 14, 44, 79, 86
    radical social, 82, 198, 216
conversion therapy, 60
Coogan, T. P., 178
Cooper, M., 117
Coulter, J., 144
Council for National Policy (CNP), 184
covering laws, **214**
Cowen, P., 138
Cree, V. E., 86
Crenshaw, K., 8, 104
critical realism, 1, 3–6, 53
critical theory, 207–210
Crossley, N., 124
CSA see child sexual abuse
Cutajar, M. C, 85

Dalrymple, W., 172
Danermark, B., 5
Davidson, N., 180
Deegan, P., 141
deinstitutionalisation see institutionalisation
democracy, 36–39

deliberative, 40–41, 210–212
freedom of expression, 40–41
individualism and neoliberalism, 36–38
judgemental rationality, 44–45
Popper on, 43
populist politicians, 42
positivism, 42, 43
risks of direct, 38–40
de Vries, A., 55
Diagnostic and Statistical Manual of the American Psychiatric Association (DSM), 126, 133, 142
Diamond, S., 184
DiAngelo, R., 113
Di Ceglie, D., 55
diversity, xxv, 7, 8, 68, 193
Dotson, K., 108
Doyle, A. *see* McGrath, T.
DSM *see Diagnostic and Statistical Manual of the American Psychiatric Association*
Dutton, K., 200
Dyson, S. M., 97

Eastman, N., 123
Elder-Vass, D., 5, 98
Elias, N., xxiii
emergence, xxi, xxvi, 7, 9, 13, 34, 47, 52, 64, 81, 85, 98, 101, 102, 105, 106, 119, 123, 153, 165, 180, 184, 185, **214**
empirical invariance, 1–2, **214**
empirical, the, 2, 6, 23, 24, 28, 30, 65, 77, 84, 92–94, 95, 105, 106, 112, 113, 117, 118, 119, 121, 125, 146, 158, 159, **220**
Engels, F., 8, 34, 102, 166 *see also* class politics
Enlightenment, 30, 32, 204
Entwistle, K., 56
epistemic fallacy, 197, **214**
epistemic humility, 2, 6, 45, 118, 153, 202, **214**
epistemic violence, 58, 108

epistemological privilege, xxi, 8, 65, 115, 195, 206
epistemological relativism, 5, 41, 43, 93, 169, **214–215**, 218, 220
ethnicity, 107, 120, 159
ethnocentrism, 170–171, 184, 186
Everett, R., 57
explanatory critique, 44, 85, **215**

Fabris, E., 137
Fekete, L., 166
feminism, 25–26, 47, 73, 77
    second-wave, 51, 203
    third-wave, 203–204
Finkelhor, D., 84
Fish, F., 126
Fisher, M., xv–xvi
Ford, R., 175, 176
Forstater, M., 25–27 *see also* gender
four planar social being, 14–17, 28, 38, 52–53, 215, 93, 59, 94, 105, 109, 112, 113, 114, 119, 120, 149, 153, 180, 185, 198, **215**
Francois, S., 166
Frankfurt School writers, 209, 211
Fraser, M., 80
freedom of expression, xiii–xvii, xviii–xix, xxii, xxv, 19, 21, 24, 34, 209–210 *see also* Orwell, G.
    in academic life, 41–45
    crisis of free speech, 23–28
    and democracy, 36–41
    expectation of, 28–32
    Habermas and, 209–210
Freud, S., xxiii, 126, 199
Fromm, E., 74, 89
Fuller, S., 43, 44
Funk, S. C., 128
Furedi, F., 86

GAA *see* Gaelic Athletics Association
Gabe, J., 127
Gaelic Athletics Association (GAA), 179
Galtung, J., 108
Gardner, L., 96
Gaunt, J., 173

Gay, R., 77
Gelder, M., 138
gender *see also* transgender
　politics, 25–27, 47, 61, 63–64, 193, 196, 203
　dysphoria, 54, 55
　identity, 76
　in language, 206
　mis-, 49, 65, 207
　pay gap, 104
Gender Recognition Act 2004, 63
generative mechanisms, 2–3, 6, 78, 105, 113, 119, 126, 168, 185, 197, **215**
Gerbner, K., 92
Geronimus, A. T., 98
Gibbons, A., 94
Gimson, S., 26
Gingrich, A., 175
Girard, R., 201
Godwin, A., 166
Goertzel, B., 161
Goffman, E., 134
Goode, E., 83
Gotanda, N., 8
Gottlieb, J. V., 166
Goulding, C., 186
Griffin, R., 171
groups, xx–xxiii, xxiv, 7, 8–9, 12–13, 14, 34, 37, 39–40, 44–45, 76, 83, 108, 139, 140, 166–167, 195–196, 198, 200–202
　faith, 149, 150, 154, 155–156, 162
　pro-paedophile, 80–82, 84–85
　racial, 96–97, 106, 110, 117–118, 159
Guinan, J., 180

Habermas, J., 155, 209–210
Hammer, H., 84
Hansen, T. B., 150
Hare, R. D., 133
hate speech, xv, 22, 40, 49, 106
Healy, D., 140
Heath, A., xii–xiii
Henry VIII, 101, 152
Herzberg, D., 140

Hobsbawm, E., xvi, 188, 204
Hochschild, A. R., 183
Hoggart, R., 29
Hopkins, K., 9, 11
Howe, D., 182
humanism, 161
　American, 197
　post-, 160–161
　religion and, 155, 156–160
　trans, 161
Hunter, J. D., xxv

iatrogenic treatments, 54, 56, 64, 127, 135
ICD *see* International Classification of Diseases
idealism, 3–6, **216**
identitarianism, 165, **216**
ILGA *see* International Lesbian Gay Bisexual, Trans and Intersex Association
immanent critique, 44, 82, 85, **216**
incel movement, 69–71, 88, 193–194
individualism, 36–38, 68
Inge, W. R., 174
insanity, 125–128
institutionalisation, 134
　de-, 135–136, 137, 138
interdisciplinarity, **217**
International Classification of Diseases (ICD), 126, 133, 142
International Lesbian Gay Bisexual, Trans and Intersex Association (ILGA), 76, 80
intersectionality, xxi, 104–105, 113–115, 167–168, 197, **217**
intransitive aspect of reality, 53, 188, **217**
IRA *see* Irish Republican Army
IRFU *see* Irish Rugby Football Union
Irish Republican Army (IRA), 168, 174, 177, 179
Irish Rugby Football Union (IRFU), 179

Jay, A., 85
Jenkins, P., 84
Jim Crow laws, 100, 112
Johnson, B., 42, 116, 166, 167, 175, 177

Johnson, M. P., 77
Johnstone, L., 142
judgemental rationality, 5, 20, 27, 44, 65, 73, 87, 88, 93, 115, 195, 203, **217**
Junginger, J., 131

Kahneman, D., 199
Keith, L., 73
Kellam, A. M. P., 127
Kelly, G., 4, 199
Kendi, I. X., 113, 114, 116
Kendzior, S., 212
King, M. L., 100, 120
Knudson, R. M., 145
Kraepelin, E., 142
Kroll, J., 124

Laing, R. D., 140
laminated reality, 117, **217**
Lane, C., 126
Layzell, S., 141
Lebow, R. N., 17
legitimacy, 107, 192–195
Lemert, C. C., 4, 161, 205
Leninism, 32, 207, 208, 209, 211
Levine, S. B., 55
LGB Alliance, 7, 48, 60, 76
LGBT, 48, 62, 76
Lindow, V., 145
Lindsay, J., 43, 207
Linehan, T. P., 166
Lipshitsz-Phillips, S., 127
literacy, 29
Long Journey Home, 178
Lorde, A., 73
Luckmann, T., 4, 44
lumpenproletariat, 102–103, 146
lunatic asylum system, 138–139

madness, 144–146
Main, T., 134
Mair, P., 180
Malik, K., 110
Malik, N., 23
Manning, N., 142

MAPS *see* minor attracted persons
Martinerie L., 57
Martin, J. P., 134
Marx, K., 166
Marxism, 31–33, 155, 166, 180, 207
  see also class politics
material reality, 3–4
Maya Forstater case *see* Forstater, M.
Mayou, R., 138
McCranie, A., 141
McGrath, T., xiv, xv
Mercier, H., 73, 28
Meyer, J. E., 142
minor attracted persons (MAPS), 78–82, 89
  hebephilia, 79, 80
misogyny, 60, 62, 69–70 *see also* incel movement
Moalem, S., 97
moral absolutism, 25
moral imperatives, 68–69
moral panic theory, 86–87, 194 *see also* child sexual abuse; paedophilia
Morgan, P., 9, 11
Mr Robot, 75
Mulvany, J., 143
Myers, D. G., 154

Nairn, T., 180
NAMBLA (North American Man/Boy Love Association), 75–76, 80
nationalism, 106, 156, 165, 168, 170, 173–174, 175, 180, 188–189, 208
Neiman, S., 202
Nelson, A., 184
neoliberalism, xiii, 19, 36–38, 69, 77, 112, 114, 117, 121, 138, 166, 188, **217**
  anti-racism and, 101–106
new social movements (NSMs), xxi, 7, 34, 39, 48, 51, **217–218**
1984, 3, 19
Norton, H. L., 94
Nossel, S., xv

nostalgia, 186
NSMs *see* new social movements

Obama, B., 93
O'Carroll, T., 81
Offe, C., 167
Ogata, S. N., 85
omissive critique, 12, 44, **218**
O'Neill, B., 24
ontic fallacy, 88, 116, 196, 214, **218**
    and gender, 58–59
    of white privilege, 109–115
ontological insecurity, 183–187, 189
ontological monovalence, **218**
ontological realism, 32, 53, 93, 169, 191, 215, 216, **218**
ontology
    of sex, 52–54
    social, 9, 21, 219
Operation Spanner, 72
oppression, 8–9
Ormrod, R., 178
Orwell, G., 3, 19, 171
outrage, 9–10

Paedophile Information Exchange (PIE), 80–81 *see also* minor attracted persons
paedophilia, 67, 76, 78, 84–88, 193, 194, 196, 204 *see also* child sexual abuse; minor attracted persons; moral panic theory
Patel, N., 116
Patel, Pragna, xvii
Patel, Priti, 182
Peller, G., 8
personal, the, 203–204
    in contemporary politics, 17–19
Perspectives on Paedophilia, 80–81
perspectivism, xxiv, 5, 31, 32, 42
Pescosolido, B. A., 143
Pews Research Centre, 156
phenotypical variation, 51, 93–95, 109
Philo, G., 143
PIE *see* Paedophile Information Exchange

Pilgrim, D., 56, 79, 91, 103, 124, 132, 136, 137, 141, 142, 143, 178, 198
Platt, S., 143
Pluckrose, H., 43, 207
Plummer, K., 80, 81
Pols, J., 123
polytheism, 157–158
Popper, K., 43, 108, 155
populism, 24, 170, 189, 209
Porpora, D., 191
Porter, R., 144
positivism, 1, 3–6, 42, 43
    alternative to, 204–207
postmodernism, 43, 53, 69, 102, 107, 110, 161
    academy, 35–36
    alternative to, 204–207
Powell, E., 171
Price, L., 5
Priestley, J. B., 182
privilege, 105–106, 196, 210, 206
    epistemological, 8, 31, 45, 65
    white, 109–115, 117, 118
psychiatry, 103, 123–126, 138–139, 141–144, 194
    Mad Studies, 145–146
    patients, 127–129, 131–132, 135–137, 143, 146–147
psychopathy, 133
Pūrasis, D., 124

Quayle, E., 87
Queer Theory, 53, 54, 59, 70, 75, 76, 77, 80, 196
Quirk, A., 137

race, 91, 92–95, 97, 103, 110, 119–120, 132, 159
    critical theory, 106–107, 109
    reductionism, 111–112, 116, 118
Race Relations Act 1976, 91
racism, 91–93, 96–97, 107–108, 159, 170, 157 *see also* anti-racism
    structural, 98, 109–110, 113, 115–120
Radford, L., 84
rationalisation, 88

Read, J., 85, 141
real, the, 2, **220**
Realist Theory of Science, A, 53
real, the, 2, **220**
Reddaway, P., 124
reductionism, 15, 61, 70, 97, 103, 106, 111, 112, 113, 116, 117, 118, 137, 185, 197, 203, **218–219**
Reed, A., 110, 111
religion, 149–152
    and humanism, 156–160
    and identity politics, 162–163
    and politics, 153–156
    religious right, 151–152
Renan, E., 174
retroduction, 6, **219**
Revolutionary Communist Party, xix
Righton, P., 80
Rogers, A., 103, 124, 136, 137
Romme, M. A., 142
Rose, D., 143
Rosen, G., 144
Rothman, D., 136
Rubin, G., 75
Russo, J., 145
Rutherford, A., 91

Saad, T. C., 57
sadomasochism, 72–75, 204
Saied-Tessier, A., 85
Sanghera, S., 172
Santayana, G., 192
Saxena, S., 143
Sayer, A., 5, 45
Schiffauer, W., 174
Schlesinger, P., 6
Scottish National Party (SNP), 169
Scull, A., 134, 136, 138
SCUM (Society for Cutting Up Men), 26
secessionism, 106–107
Secker, J., 143
Sedgwick, P., 142
Sedlak, A. J., 84
Sen, A., 40–41, 92
Sexualities and Their Discontents, 81

sexual orientations, gender identities, gender expressions and sex characteristics (SOGIESC), 76
Shackel, N., 110
Silver, E., 131, 180
Sivanandan, A., xvi–xvii
slavery, 92, 95–96, 98–99, 100, 108, 112, 120
Smeeth, R., 27
Smith, M., 86
SNP *see* Scottish National Party
Sobolewska, M., 175, 176
social ontology, 9, 17, 21, 36, 92, 93, 94, 109, 119, 159, **219**
SOGIESC *see* sexual orientations, gender identities, gender expressions and sex characteristics
Sohn, A., 57
Southall Black Sisters, xvii
Soyka, M., 131
Spandler, H., 142
Sperber, D., 28
Spivak, G. C., 108
Stalinism, xviii, xxiii, 19, 33, 208
statue toppling, 97–101
Steadman, H. J., 131
Stock, K., 27
Stonewall, 7, 48, 59–60, 62, 76
Stop Funding Hate campaign, 12
Straus, M. A., 77
structure and agency, **219–220**
Sunstein, C., 202
Sussman, R. W., 91
Swartz, M. S., 131
Sweeney, A., 141, 145
Szasz, T. S., 123

Taylor, B., 80, 86
Taylor, C., 152
Taylor, L., 88, 206
Taylor, P. J., 131
Tebbit, N., 172
Thalheimer, A., 171
Therborn, G., 188
Thoits, P. A., 140
Thomas, H. M., 180

Thomas, K., 8
Tirthankar, R., 96
Tomasini, F., 143
Tosi, J., 11
transitive aspect of reality, 188, **220–221**
trans-capture, 60–61, 63–64
transgender(ism), 49, 50–52, 161, 194
    activism, 48, 51
    autogynephilia, 49
    biomedical transition, 60
    detransitioning, 56
    gender reassignment, 56–58
    ideology, 50, 52, 54, 64
    paediatric transition, 55
    as policy phenomenon, 52
    social movement, 61
    transman, 54, 77
    transwoman, 13, 20, 22, 27, 34, 48, 54, 61, 65, 76, 197
transitive aspect of reality, **220–221**
transsexualism, 51
two process model, 199, 202

UK, the *see* British identity
Uwagba, O., 113

Vajda, M., 19, 208
vandalism, 100–101
vanguardism, 18, 32–35, 208
van Zomeren, M., 203
violence, 25–26, 27, 41, 64, 72, 77, 107–108, 131

virtue signalling, 97–101, 119, 201–202
von Heiseler, T. N., 28

Wahl, O. F., 143
Walker, B., 165
Wallcraft, J., 141
Waller, W. W., 82
Warmke, B., 11
Watkins, S., 163
Weber, E., 188
Weeks, J., 81
Weller, P., 143
Westermeyer, J., 124
white privilege *see* privilege
Williams, B., 29
Williams, J., 112
Williams, R., 4
Windrush scandal, 92
Wing, J. K., 134
woke, xii, xiv–xv, 23, 35, 165, **221**
Wolfensberger, W., 40
Wollstonecraft, M., 47
Women's Equality Party, 64
Wykes, T., 126

Yogyakarta Principles, 59, 60
Yuill, R. A., 80

Zoroastrianism, 158